The Kodály Method

Second Edition

The Kodály Method

Comprehensive Music Education from Infant to Adult

LOIS CHOKSY
The University of Calgary

PRENTICE HALL, Englewood Cliffs, New Jersey 07632

Library of Congress Cataloging-in-Publication Data

CHOKSY, LOIS.
    The Kodály method: comprehensive music education from infant to adult / Lois Choksy. —2nd ed.
    p.   cm.
    Includes index.
    ISBN 0-13-516899-6: $27.95.   ISBN 0-13-516873-2 (pbk.): $19.95
    1. School music—Instruction and study.   2. Kodály, Zoltán.
1882–1967.   I. Title.
MT1.C537 1987
372.8'73—dc19   87-15629
                                    CIP
                                    MN

Editorial/production supervision and interior design:
  Ben Greensfelder and Arthur Maisel
Cover design: George Cornell
Manufacturing buyer: Ray Keating

 © 1988, 1974 by Prentice-Hall, Inc.
A Paramount Communications Company
Englewood Cliffs, New Jersey 07632

Printed in the United States of America

10

ISBN   0-13-516873-2   01   {PAPER}
ISBN   0-13-516899-6   01   {CASE}

Prentice-Hall International (UK) Limited, *London*
Prentice-Hall of Australia Pty. Limited, *Sydney*
Prentice-Hall Canada Inc., *Toronto*
Prentice-Hall Hispanoamericana, S.A., *Mexico*
Prentice-Hall of India Private Limited, *New Delhi*
Prentice-Hall of Japan, Inc., *Tokyo*
Prentice-Hall of Southeast Asia Pte. Ltd., *Singapore*
Editora Prentice-Hall do Brasil, Ltda., *Rio de Janeiro*

To the memory of Zoltán Kodály

Contents

Foreword

In many parts of the world great numbers of music teachers are attempting to apply the pedagogical principles of the late Professor Zoltán Kodály in their own cultural environments. It is no exaggeration to state that people come to Hungary today from every corner of the globe to study the model in its place of origin. In this era of the superjet, geographical distances have disappeared, and with this disappearance the only distances that still remain are the kind between people! In an age when one may travel without difficulty from one side of the earth to the other, people travel for a variety of reasons: some for tourism, others for entertainment or out of curiosity, still others simply because they have nothing better to do. In a completely different category are those travelers who undertake a journey to learn, to gain knowledge, to learn to teach.

Teaching today is not an easy job, and in the field of education even more difficult is the task of the music teacher who wishes to sow the seed of humanistic culture in future generations; to pass on the method of the Greek muse Musiké. Will they listen? Will they pay attention to the message? Can the teacher exert an influence on the growing generation? All these are burning questions to the dedicated music teacher wherever he or she may live in the world. They must be dealt with, because the teacher feels a bit responsible for changing the face of the world.

This responsibility is felt by the author of this book, my dear friend and colleague, Lois Choksy. She has transplanted her Hungarian observations into American soil, observations made first from a distance, then by close association, made first in theory, and later with much practical work. Her book gives valuable guidance to all who wish to be guided. It is an able and gifted adoption which encourages the reader to further accomplishments, polishing, and discovery.

The structure of the book is very clear, logical, and well organized, but it is not intended to replace any teacher's own personal work. The recipes are here, but a good cook is always needed to prepare a delicious meal. The Kodály Method is not an "instant" method, however simple it may seem if one examines it only superficially. Good method, devoted teacher, and responsive children . . . given the first two, can one doubt that the third component is easiest to get?

Warmest greetings to the reader from the other side of the ocean! Let us join hands. Perhaps we can still save the world. In any case, if we try to realize the guiding principle of Zoltán Kodály's life, to help people "let music belong to everyone," we will have done what we could, and the after ages cannot call us to account for our negligence.

Erzsébet Szönyi
*Dean of the Faculty for Music
Education at the Franz Liszt
Academy of Music, Budapest*

*Vice President of the International
Society for Music Education (ISME)*

Preface to
the Second Edition

The Kodály Method is not a static process, but a continually evolving one. The 14 years since the first appearance of *The Kodály Method* have seen a number of changes, some quite substantial, in the pedagogy of the Method, although, of course, Kodály's principles remain immutable.

The many innovations, tried and tested by the author and others, have resulted in some alterations in the sequence of teaching skills and concepts in grades one to six. In addition, much has been discovered on starting with the Method in the preschool years.

Therefore, this second edition represents a greatly revised and augmented version of the first. Among the additional material is a detailed section on the preschool years. A specific curriculum is outlined, pedagogical procedures are given, and songs are suggested for the nursery school and kindergarten.

Two problems frequently expressed by teachers attempting to follow Kodály's principles are that they have difficulty with long-range planning, scheduling the work of a year in advance, and that they cannot find a sufficient number of songs through which to prepare, present, and reinforce new learnings.

For this reason sample yearly plans have been included for each grade level, and a specific core of songs has been suggested for each new learning within each grade.

The teaching repertory given at the end of the book now contains 172 songs, 80 of which were not in the first edition. Listening themes have been notated for singing and suggestions for specific listening lessons also are given for each grade.

Creative activities have been similarly sequenced, and there is discussion as to how best to encourage improvisation and composition in classes.

In grades four, five, and six there is new material on the teaching of harmony and theory, and on part singing.

I resisted for some years the idea of revising *The Kodály Method*. Revision was finally made imperative when I realized that in my own university teacher-training classes I was having to give far too much through lectures simply because it was not ''in the book.'' While the companion text, *The Kodály Context,* is helpful, it does not give grade-by-grade guidance.

I have tried in the following pages to retain the clarity and simplicity of the original text, while adding all those aspects that my experience has shown me to be necessary to a comprehensive Kodály program.

Lois Choksy
Professor of Music
The University of Calgary

Introduction

Some years ago I was teaching a lesson about the violin to a first grade class. I had taken a violin into the classroom with me for demonstration purposes. I held it up and said, "Can anyone tell me what this is?" A youngster in the front row said, "It's a fiddle." "Yes," I said, "Its nickname is fiddle, but its real name is 'violin'—just as your nickname is Billy, but your real name is William." "S'not either, it's Billy," came the reply. "Well," I said, "people call you Billy, but your real name is William." "Billy," he muttered. At this point the classroom teacher intervened and said in steely tones, "Your name is William!" Somewhat nonplussed I went ahead with the lesson, letting the children handle the instrument, pluck and bow the strings, then listen to an older child play it. At the end of the period, to review, I again held the instrument up and asked, "What is this instrument?" Came a voice from the back of the room—"It's a William."

I was young—I was confusing *naming* with *understanding: words* with *functions*. This book is not concerned with naming things, except occasionally, but it is concerned with basic skills and concepts—the functional side of music. This is what the Kodály concept is all about.

Shortly after the first appearance of the Kodály Method in this country, I began working with it in spite of the dearth of authentic information on it available in English. Then, it was my good fortune to meet Katinka Daniel, graduate of the Franz Liszt Academy of Music (Budapest) and pupil of Kodály, who became my friend and teacher and who guided me through the next two years of my work. When I felt that I had come to a point where I did not know what to do next, it was Mrs. Daniel who suggested that I go to Hungary and learn firsthand.

This I did in the summer of 1968. I attended the Danube Bend Summer University at Esztergom. At that summer course I saw and heard group after group of Hungarian school children—singing, reading, writing music. I saw music permeating the life of the Hungarian people, in villages and in cities. I saw enough in that three-week summer university course to know I had only scratched the surface. I *had* to return to study the Method in depth.

This I did during the academic year 1970–71 at the Franz Liszt Academy. I learned much in that year—and yet I still find myself wishing I could return to ask a question,

1

to observe again a procedure. The superficial simplicity of the Method is deceptive. There always seems to be something more to learn about it.

As of this writing I have been to Hungary three times and feel sure I shall be returning again, for the Kodály Method is an evolving method. It has changed greatly since its inception almost thirty years ago, and is sure to continue to change as better ways are found to instill in children love of music and knowledge about music.

For many beautifully-taught lessons and many helpful discussions about curriculum and methodology of music in Hungarian schools, I am greatly indebted to Mrs. Anna Hamvas, Mrs. Helga Szabó, Mrs. Emma Serényi, Mrs. Katalin Forrai, Mrs. Marta Nemesszeghy, Mrs. Eszter Mihályi, Miss Klára Nemes, and Mr. Miklos Csik.

To Laszlo Vikar, ethnomusicologist and member of the Hungarian Academy of Sciences, I owe my ability to analyze folk songs. The sessions with him on folk music research were invaluable.

A special debt of thanks must go to Mrs. Zoltán Kodály, who gave freely of her time to help me with the history of the Method, an aspect which has not previously been treated fully in English.

Great teachers are few—Erzsébet Szőnyi, Dean of the School of Music Education at the Franz Liszt Academy of Music in Budapest, is surely the most outstanding pedagogue with whom I have ever worked. I am grateful to her not only for the work she did in helping to arrange for my year in Hungary, but also for the many private interviews I had with her, and for the advice she has proffered at various stages during the writing of this book. I am deeply honored that she has chosen to write the foreword.

I am also indebted to Nicholas Geriak, Supervisor in Baltimore County (Maryland), for encouraging me to investigate something new and different in music education. Without the support, moral and financial, of an open-minded school system, the past years of experimentation and study would have been impossible.

In closing, I must thank the kind people who made Hungary a second home for me—György Czeller and his wife Sarolta—and also my husband, Lee, who encouraged me from the very beginning of this project, who read and discussed this book with me page by page as it was written. Neither the Czellers nor my husband is a musician, and yet without them this book surely would not have been written.

1
The Beginnings of the Method in Hungary and Its International Spread

Music seems to be part of the very fiber of Hungarian life. Hungary, a nation the size of Indiana, with a population of ten million people, has eight hundred adult concert choirs, fifty of the first rank and another one hundred of radio or public performance quality. There are four professional symphony orchestras in Budapest alone and five in country towns, as well as numerous amateur orchestras. A man without a musical education is considered illiterate. Almost all play instruments; almost all sing. Concert halls are full.

The situation was not always so. Early in the 1900s, Zoltán Kodály, the noted Hungarian composer and educator, was appalled at the level of musical literacy he found in students entering the Zeneakademia—the highest music school in Hungary. Not only were these students unable to read and write music fluently, but in addition, they were totally ignorant of their own musical heritage. Since they had grown up in the aftermath of the Austro-Hungarian Empire, a time when only German and Viennese music were considered "good" music by the elite, the only exposure these students had had to the vast wealth of Hungarian folk music was through the distorted and diluted versions played by gypsies in cafés.

Kodály felt deeply that it must be his mission to give back to the people of Hungary their own musical heritage and to raise the level of musical literacy, not only in academy students but also in the population as a whole.

As a first step in this direction he sought to improve teacher training. In his words:

> It is much more important who is the music teacher in Kisvárda than who is the director of the opera house in Budapest . . . for a poor director fails once, but a poor teacher keeps on failing for thirty years, killing the love of music in thirty batches of children.

Kodály was almost single-handedly responsible for causing the required music in teacher-training programs to be increased from one-half year to three years, to the present five-year teacher's diploma program at the Academy.

However, his interest in music education only began at the teacher-training level. His strong commitment to making music belong to everyone, not just to the educated upper classes, soon led him to become involved in the education of young children, and further, to involve all those around him. His fellow professors at the Academy, his colleagues in the area of folk music collection and analysis, even his more talented pupils, all became involved in his dream of a musically literate nation.

Kodály had been interested in the collection and analysis of Hungarian folk music since the turn of the century. With Béla Bartók he collected some one thousand children's songs which, when analyzed and classified according to mode, scale, and type by Dr. György Kerényi, eventually became the first volume of the massive *Corpus Musicae Popularis Hungaricae*. This work of collecting, analyzing, classifying, and publishing Hungarian folk music, started by Bartók and Kodály, continues today at the Academy of Sciences in Budapest. At present there are five volumes of the *Corpus Musicae,* covering the above-mentioned children's songs, holiday and festival songs, courting songs, wedding songs, and laments. Many further volumes are planned.

In view of his great knowledge of and love for the music of the peasants of Hungary, it is not surprising that Kodály chose this music as the vehicle through which to teach children. In doing this, however, he had reasons other than simply his love for it. He felt that as a child naturally learns his mother tongue before foreign languages, he should learn his musical mother tongue—i.e., the folk music of his own country—before other music. He likened the historical development of music from primitive folk song to art music to the development of the child from infant to adult. In addition, he considered the simple short forms, the basically pentatonic scale, and the simplicity of the language all characteristics which would contribute to good pedagogical use of such music with children.

But perhaps most important, he considered that folk music represented a living art. It was not contrived for pedagogical purposes. It already existed and fit well into a systematic scheme for teaching the concepts and skills of music to young children. Kodály insisted upon using only the purest of authentic folk music with children. This specification is still observed today. Although the textbooks used in the Singing Schools are written by master teachers, before publication they are given to ethnomusicologists at the Academy of Sciences for critical opinion. No spurious example is allowed to remain simply because it fulfills a teaching function. When a better variant of a particular folk song is known, changes in the books are made accordingly.

However, folk music was not to be the only material of the Method. If the step between folk music and art music was to be bridged, then it was necessary that there be good composed music suitable for children to sing. It was in 1923 that Kodály began composing works for children's choirs and studying musical education in the schools in depth.

The first book which might actually be considered as leading toward the Kodály Method as it is known today was a song book, *Énekes ABC,* compiled by György Kerényi and Benjámin Rajeczky, and published by Magyar Kórus, Budapest, in 1938. This was followed in 1940 by a companion text book *Éneklö Iskola* (A Singing School). This text, with its materials taken largely from the folk songs collected by Kodály and Bartók, was aimed not at young children but at the lycée or intermediate grade level. It was used in a number of schools in Hungary, and its pedagogy was tested by, among others, Kodály's friend Irma Bors, a Sister of Charity then teaching in the largest secondary school in Budapest, and also by György Gulyás, the present director of the Academy of Music at Debrécen, who was then teaching at a private resident school in the country, where music for the first time was taught daily as a core subject in the curriculum.

The next text in the Method, and the first attempt at a text for young children, was *Iskolai Énekegyüjtemény* (A School Collection of Songs) by Kerényi and Kodály, published in Budapest in 1943. This text contained one volume for ages six to ten and a second volume for ages eleven to fourteen. The material in them ranged from easy Hungarian children's songs to fairly difficult songs with evidence of foreign influence. It is to accompany these that Kodály composed his volume *333 Exercises.*

These books are of great interest to anyone studying the evolution of the Method, since they begin with a song built entirely on one pitch and then progress to songs built on the major second. It took very little time for teachers using these books to realize that a song built on a single tone was all but impossible for young children to sing in tune, and that even the major second as a starting point presented difficulties.

It was for this reason that when, at the urging of Kodály, Jenö Adám wrote his *Módszéres Énektanitás* (Systematic Singing Teaching), Turul, Budapest, 1944, he began melodic training with the minor third, the most natural interval for young children to sing in tune. Even in this Adám book, the speed with which the teacher was expected to move from one concept or skill to the next was found to be unrealistically fast, and is far removed from the slow systematic pace of the eight graded books, *Enek Zene,* by Márta Nemesszeghy (grades one–five) and Helga Szabó (grades six–eight) now used in the Hungarian Singing Schools.

It is unfortunate that many American adaptations of the Kodály Method have copied almost verbatim this early Adám text, and have not used the excellent Nemesszeghy ones as their guide.

The next volume of particular interest after the Adám book was one specifically aimed at *solfa* teaching as a preparation for instrumental study, *Introductory Course in Music,* by Vera Irsai, Cserépfalir, Budapest, 1947. In this the principles of deriving musical learning from folk song material were clearly defined.

Perhaps the most complete volumes to appear in the method are the *solfa* books of Kodály's pupil Erzsébet Szőnyi, who was at that time Professor of Music and Dean of Music Education at the Franz Liszt Academy of Music in Budapest and who is a composer of stature in her own right. These books, *A Zenei Írás-Olvasás Módzsertana,* Volumes I, II, and III (Methods of Sight-Reading and Notation), Zenemükiadó, Budapest, 1953, combine all the elements of what has come to be known as the Kodály Method: the tonic *solfa* system, the Curwen hand signs, the shifting *do* with key change, and the reliance on the best of folk and composed song material for teaching purposes. These books are used today in Hungary in the Special Music Preparatory Schools, the Conservatories, and the Academy of Music.

However, books alone do not make a system of education. It was in the schools and in the hands of the teachers that the Method truly evolved and is still evolving, for the Kodály Method is a living method, not a static one. As better ways are found, they are incorporated.

Together with his good friend Márta Nemesszeghy, Kodály persuaded the Ministry of Education to allow an experiment in music education in the town of his birth, Kecskemét. Starting with just one class, using the Kodály materials and method, and having music every day, Márta Nemesszeghy achieved such success that where there was one Singing Primary School in Hungary in 1950, there are now more than 160. More are planned as enough trained teachers become available.

One reason Kodály and Márta Nemesszeghy were able to convince the Ministry of Education to continue and even to expand the Singing Primary Schools was an unusual side effect of such music instruction on the learning in other subject areas. An unexpected result of daily music instruction via the Kodály Method was a marked improvement of achievement in other academic areas. This was particularly true of mathematics, seeming to bear out Thorndike's theory that disciplines having common elements are mutually affected by changes in either. The difference in achievement between the experimental music groups and the matching control groups was enough to be statistically significant, and has been reported by Gabor Friss in the book *Musical Education in Hungary,* Corvina Press, Budapest, 1966, as well as by psychologist Klara Kokas at the 1964 meeting of the International Society for Music Education (I.S.M.E.) in Budapest. Experimentation in this aspect of the Method is still continuing.

But it was not the transfer effect that attracted musicians and educators to Hungary. It was the quality of the music education itself. Music educators came to Hungary from all over the world to study the phenomenal results of the Singing Primary Schools.

The Kodály Method is being practiced today in schools of Eastern and Western Europe, Japan, Australia, New Zealand, North and South America, South Africa, and Iceland. Adaptations and expositions of the Method have been published in Estonian, Polish, Swedish, Japanese, French, German, Latvian, Spanish, Russian, and, of course, English.

International awareness of the Hungarian music education system perhaps began with the I.S.M.E. Conferences in Vienna in 1958 and in Tokyo in 1963, where reports on the Method were presented, and the 1964 Conference in Budapest, where Zoltán Kodály gave an address and was elected honorary president. It was the latter conference that seemed to cause the beginnings of widespread international interest, since those attending it could see the results of the system firsthand.

The first known export of the Method was to Estonia, U.S.S.R., in the capital city of Tallinn, where the Estonian educator Heino Kaljuste brought about the publication of the Hungarian singing school textbooks in Estonian. The Estonian language, like Hungarian, is of Finno-Ugrian origin, although the two languages have few words in common today. However, it was probably the commonality of ancient culture that made the Hungarian books and songs so appropriate to Estonia. When the work of the first experimental school became public knowledge, the Method spread rapidly and is practiced today in every Estonian school and in a number of schools in neighboring Latvia.

In Leningrad, Academician Pavel Filipovitch Weiss wrote a dissertation on the Method for his academic degree of candidature, referring to both the Estonian and the Hungarian examples. He later visited Hungary and addressed a conference on music education at Győr on the spread of the concept of Kodály in the Soviet Union.

The International Folk Music Council (I.F.M.C.), of which Kodály was president, met in Budapest in 1964. During this meeting Kodály arranged a visit for the participants to the singing primary school in Kecskemét. This visit resulted in the profound interest of two of the conference participants, Dr. Jacques Chailley of the Sorbonne University in France and Dr. Alexander Ringer of the University of Illinois. Dr. Chailley was instrumental in arranging for Jacquotte Ribière-Raverlat to spend the 1965–66 academic year in Hungary—a year which resulted in the first French language exposition of the Method: *L'Education Musicale dans Hongrie*. The results of Dr. Ringer's observations in Hungary were far-reaching. He returned to the United States convinced that the problems besieging American music education—problems of inadequate teacher training, insufficient time allotted to music teaching, lack of comprehensive curricula and worthwhile goals—would be in a large measure solved if the Hungarian system could somehow be brought to the United States. With support from the National Endowment for the Arts and, later, from the Ford Foundation, Dr. Ringer three times arranged for groups of young American teachers to travel to Hungary to receive training in the Kodály Method, and using the graduates of the first of these groups, he set up the first experimental American Kodály program at New Haven, Connecticut. There were many problems, not normally encountered in Hungary, involved in the establishment and continuation of this program, such as a highly transient population and bilingual schools; but in spite of these, the New Haven Project prospered and provided an excellent model for the nation of what Kodály-inspired education could accomplish in America.

The ideas of Kodály were first exposed in the United States through the writings of Mary Helen Richards, whose *Threshold to Music* books and charts, written after a brief visit to Hungary, if somewhat limited in scope and uncertain in sequence, nevertheless were responsible to a large extent for the early popularity of the Method in the United States. In 1966 Kodály and Erzsébet Szőnyi participated in the I.S.M.E. Conference at Interlochen, Michigan, and went on to Stanford University in August to attend a symposium on the Method. At this symposium Mrs. Richards gave demonstrations with children, and both Kodály and Erzsébet Szőnyi presented lectures. It was during the Stanford symposium that Denise Bacon became interested in the Method—an interest that led her to spend an academic year in Hungary, studying the Method firsthand in 1968–69. This culminated in the founding of the Kodály Musical Training Institute at Wellesley, Massachusetts, for the dissemination of accurate knowledge about the Method and for teacher training in the Method. The Institute is presently a part of the Hartt School of Music of the University of Hartford in Connecticut.

In 1969 Sr. Mary Alice Hein, Sr. Lorna Zemke, and this author separately traveled to Hungary for extensive study, and returned to North America eventually to establish teacher training programs in, respectively, Oakland, California, Manitowoc, Wisconsin, and Calgary, Alberta, Canada. At present there is hardly an American state or a Canadian province without some Kodály practice, and announcements of teacher training programs fill North American education journals.

In 1973 the first international symposium devoted to Kodály was held at Holy Names College in Oakland, California. At this conference the International Kodály Society was inaugurated and work was initiated that led to the founding of the Organization of American Kodály Educators.

The Kodály Method came early to Canada and was from the beginning widespread. Kaye Pottie, Supervisor of Music in Halifax, Nova Scotia, brought teachers from Hungary to train and work with the music teachers in that city's schools. The Kodály program in those schools continues to this day and is one of the finest in North America.

Two music educators from Western Canada, Alastair and Isobel Highet, went to Hungary for a year's study and returned to establish the first Kodály program in British Columbia at Nanaimo. In both the Halifax and Nanaimo programs music instruction was given daily in the schools.

Richard Johnston, then Professor of Music at the University of Toronto, was so impressed by the quality of the music education he observed in Hungary that he invited Zoltán Kodály to receive an honorary doctorate from the University of Toronto. Dr. Johnston, later Dean of Fine Arts at The University of Calgary and now Professor Emeritus there, has continued throughout his long career to promote Kodály's ideals in Canada.

The Method's spread to French-speaking Canada probably had its inception with the visit of Erzsébet Szőnyi in 1965 to Quebec where she presented a series of lectures on Hungarian music education. Work was furthered by the French Kodály authority Jacquotte Ribière-Raverlat who spent some years in Quebec and whose books for children were first tested there. Her work is being continued by Gabrielle Letourneau, Miklos Takacs, and others in Quebec.

Today Kodály training is a part of undergraduate music teacher training in most provinces in Canada, and there are certification programs and programs leading to advanced degrees with concentration in Kodály in several universities. Kodály-based textbooks and curricula exist in both English and French, and there is an active Kodály Society of Canada with headquarters in Toronto.

In South America, too, the ideas of Kodály are known. In Argentina, Ladislaus Domonkos worked with the Method, first using Hungarian song materials and later finding suitable Argentine folk songs for the skill and concept sequence. He reported on this work in the book *Metodo Kodály* in 1969. In 1970 Lasló Ördög, Supervisor of Music for the Budapest schools, spent a year teaching in Chile and reported that use of the Method was widespread in both Chile and Peru.

The existence of the Kodály Method in Japan is largely due to the efforts of one musician and teacher, Kyōko Hani, who spent some years studying in Hungary before returning to Tokyo to found the Japanese Kodály Institute. This institute has trained numerous teachers in the Method and has published books in the Method for the first four grades, using Japanese folk song materials. There proved to be a number of unexpected similarities in rhythms and scales between Hungarian and Japanese folk music, particularly early childhood music. Many Japanese teachers have since gone to Hungary for study. Japan is second only to Hungary in its membership in the International Kodály Society, and the president of that Society is Professor Kazuyuki Tanimoto, Professor of Ethnomusicology at the University of Sapporo.

The Method traveled to Czechoslovakia with Alois Slozil, director of the music school at Jesenik. Since his first contact with the Method at the Esztergom Summer University in 1967, Czech teachers have come to study at this Summer Kodály course in Esztergom each year.

The Summer University Course on Kodály at Esztergom has at this writing trained several thousand people from thirty-one countries. In 1975 Sarolta Kodály, widow of the composer, was instrumental in founding the Kodály Institute of Hungary at Kesckemét, Kodály's birthplace and the home of the first public singing school in Hungary. The primary purpose of this Institute is to train foreign teachers in the Hungarian method. While it is still possible for foreign students to arrange independent programs at the Liszt Academy in Budapest, as this author did, many students now opt for the more structured and directed work of the Institute.

As early as 1958 there was interest in the Kodály Method in Germany, fostered by Professor Egon Kraus, then the Secretary-General of I.S.M.E. By 1965 the Method was actively in use in a number of German schools, and in 1971 the third Kodály Institute was founded, this time in Germany.

The Method traveled to Belgium as a result of a cultural exchange program one of whose stated purposes was to incorporate the Hungarian method into Belgian schools. The extensive program in the schools through the Rijksmuziekacademie in Antwerp, under the direction of Professor Gilbert De Greeve, is one of the finest in Western Europe.

Large groups of teachers from Denmark, Iceland, Finland, and Switzerland have come to Hungary to visit the schools and to observe the Method. These visits have resulted in invitations to Hungarian teachers to present teacher-training courses in these countries. A Danish adaptation of the Method by Klara Fredborg is now in use in a number of schools, and the Finnish Kodály Society is achieving remarkable results in that small country.

England was one of the first countries to be aware of Kodály's pedagogical compositions. This happened through the translations of Percy Young, who wished to make them available to English choirs. Kodály, when he visited England, was deeply impressed with both the quality and quantity of choral training there. Much of his "method" grew from his English visits.

One might have expected that with so much tradition of choral singing using *solfa* and with its rich heritage of folk music England today would be a shining example of teaching via Kodály's principles. Unfortunately such is not the case. In the progressive educational movement of the 1950s and 1960s, the English choral tradition of centuries was almost totally lost. Today one would have to look far in England for a school in which musical literacy is emphasized and where only quality music is used for instruction.

There is a growing Kodály movement in Great Britain, led by Celia Vadja, Michael Stokes, Margaret Holden, and others; but so much of the tradition of good choral singing has been lost that many years will be needed to restore it to its previous level.

In Australia music instruction is usually handled by classroom teachers rather than by music specialists, so the depth with which Kodály's principles can be applied is limited. Nevertheless, largely through the work of Deanna Hoermann and her pilot project in the schools of New South Wales, Kodály practice is widespread in Australia. In Brisbane, where music is handled by specialists, and in a number of private schools there are exemplary Kodály programs.

In all these languages, in all these adaptations and approaches to the Method, one basic principle is clear: Kodály's conception of music as a basic academic subject equal in importance to language, mathematics, and the social sciences. Although he believed deeply in the emotional values of music, Kodály nevertheless felt it imperative that love of music be supported by knowledge about music. He felt that one could not exist intelligently without the other. In his own words:

Music is a manifestation of the human spirit, similar to language. Its greatest practitioners have conveyed to mankind things not possible to say in any other language. If we do not want these things to remain dead treasures, we must do our utmost to make the greatest possible number of people understand their idiom.

Preface
A Zenei Írás-Olvasás Módszertana
1953

It is unlikely that Kodály ever thought of what was taking place in the Singing Schools of Hungary as the "Kodály Method." He knew too well the numbers of musicians, teachers, and ethnomusicologists involved in its creation and ongoing development to take such credit for himself. It remained for foreigners visiting Hungary to give Kodály's name to what they saw. And yet he was the driving force behind what happened in the schools of Hungary. Almost until the day of his death he was visiting schools, talking with teachers, conferring on curriculum, and, in passing, jotting down a musical phrase to be sung at sight by a child here or there.

While the Method came from the joint efforts of many people, it was without doubt Kodály's vision that gave it breath. All who worked with him speak of him still as a continuing influence in their lives and work. The Kodály Method has become to Hungarians and to many others a living monument to the man who inspired it.

2
The Method: Its Sequence, Tools, and Materials

Zoltan Kodály wished to see a unified system of music education evolve in Hungary, capable of leading children toward love of and knowledge about music from earliest nursery school years to adulthood. To this end he devoted a significant part of his creative life. The method which emerged under his direction and which is the official music curriculum of schools in Hungary is based on singing, on the study of good musical material—folk and composed—and on the method of relative solmization. Its objectives are twofold: to aid in the well-balanced social and artistic development of the child, and to produce the musically literate adult—literate in the fullest sense of being able to look at a musical score and "think" sound, to read and write music as easily as words. Although interested in the training of professional musicians, Kodály's first concern was the musically literate amateur. He wished to see an education system that could produce a people to whom music was not a way to make a living but a way of life.

WHAT IS THE SEQUENCE OF THE METHOD?

The sequence which was developed in Hungary, after much experimentation, is a child-developmental one rather than one based on subject logic. In a subject-logic approach there is no relationship between the order of presentation and the order in which children learn easily. The subject matter is simply organized in a fashion that seems reasonable in terms of content.

Most music teachers are familiar with the subject-logic approach to music teaching. Rhythmically, it begins with the whole note and then proceeds to halves and quarters–a mathematically reasonable progression, but a very difficult one for the beginning student who has not yet been taught even to feel the basic beat. Melodically, the diatonic major scale is generally considered the subject-logic starting point for teaching music. Yet the average young child cannot accurately sing the diatonic major scale. According to research, most children are able to sing a range of only five or six tones and cannot produce half-steps in tune.[1,2] To use a subject-logic approach in teaching music to young children is to expect them to intellectualize about something that does not in reality exist in their own experience.

WHAT IS MEANT BY A "CHILD-DEVELOPMENTAL" APPROACH AS USED IN THE KODÁLY METHOD?

The child-developmental approach to sequence within a subject requires the arrangement of the subject matter into patterns that follow normal child abilities at various stages of growth.

In terms of rhythm, moving rhythms are more child-related than sustained ones. The quarter note may be related to children's walking pace, the eighth note, to their running. These are the rhythms of the child's day-to-day living. Singing games are largely made up of quarter- and eighth-note patterns in duple meter. They are a more reasonable starting place for teaching rhythm concepts to children than whole notes.

Melodically, the first recognizable tunes sung by most young children are made up primarily of minor thirds, major seconds, and perfect fourths; *so, mi,* and *la* in *solfa* terminology. They are the tones his mother uses to call him to dinner:

Tom - my!

They are the tones of many of his own sing-song chants:

I   am   big - ger   than   you   are

The common pattern in Hungarian children's chants is the *la* on a weak beat following *so:*

ha   én   ci - ca   vol - nék,
maj. 2nd

In most American three-note chants and songs the *la* is approached from *mi,* forming a rising fourth on a weak beat:

John - ny   is   a   sis - sy!
perfect 4th

[1]Orpha K. Duell and Richard C. Anderson,"'Pitch Discrimination Among Primary School Children," *Journal of Educational Psychology* 58, No. 6 (1957), pp. 315–18.
[2]Rosamund Shuter, *The Psychology of Musical Ability* (London: Methuen and Co., Ltd., 1968).

Interestingly enough, up to this point children seem to develop in the same musical pattern the world over. Young children's games and chants based on these two or three notes are found from the United States to Hungary to Japan. The order in which these notes occur may differ, but the major second, minor third, and perfect fourth appear to be part of a universal musical vocabulary for young children.

Obviously, then, a developmental approach to the teaching of vocal music would use duple-meter rhythms and these notes as its starting point.

There are other characteristics of the musical development of young children, which must play a part in determining any developmental sequence.

1. The range in which a young child can sing songs comfortably and correctly is limited—usually encompassing not more than five or six tones, and these of whole steps or larger intervals. Half steps are difficult for the young child to sing in tune.

2. Descending tones are easier for children to learn and reproduce accurately than ascending ones. This indicates that the initial lesson on new tonal patterns should be approached through songs in which the interval occurs in a descending melody line.

3. Small skips are easier for the young child to sing in tune than small steps: G E is easier than G to F♯. Wide skips, such as a sixth or an octave, are difficult.

4. In terms of range, one study has shown that left to his own devices the young child will most often pitch the upper note of the minor third around F♯. Thus the keys of D, E♭, and E would seem to be indicated for pitching teacher-initiated rote songs.

Most of these findings were made, curiously enough, almost simultaneously in Hungary by the people then working on the Kodály Method, in Switzerland where the Willems method, still in use at present, was being developed, and in the United States by a research team in California.[3] Even the Orff Institute in Austria, with its instrumental rather than vocal orientation, seems to have discovered these same basic developmental concepts.

Recognizing these principles as factors in the melodic development of children, Kodály felt that the pentaton—the five-tone scale—was the ideal vehicle for teaching children musical skills. The pentaton is one of the basic scales of folk music in Hungary and in most of the world, although the pentaton of Hungarian music tends to be minor in character, or *la*-centered, while the usual American pentatonic song is major, or *do*-centered.

The melodic sequence that gradually evolved in Hungary was

1. the minor third *(so-mi)*
2. *la* and its intervals with *so* and *mi*
3. *do,* the "home tone" in major modes, and the intervals it forms with *so, mi,* and *la*
4. *re,* the last remaining tone of the pentaton

After these five-tones, the octaves low *la,* low *so,* and high *do* are taught, and, last, the half steps *fa* and *ti,* to complete the diatonic major and minor scales.

[3]Gladys Moorhead and Donald Pond, *Music of Young Children,* Vols. 1–4 (Santa Barbara, Calif.: Pillsbury Foundation for Advanced Music Education, 1941–1951).

THE TOOLS OF THE METHOD

The first of the tools chosen for use in the Kodály Method was the movable-*do* system of solmization originated by Guido d'Arezzo in the eleventh century. In this system the home tone or tonal center of a song is *do* in the major and *la* in the minor modes, whatever the key may be. The advantages of this for teaching vocal sight-reading should be obvious. The basic tune of the minor third *so-mi* is the same in any key. Thus when a child knows only these two notes he can already read them in any placement on the staff. As his sight-singing vocabulary increases to the five tones of the pentaton, he can read far more than only three lines and two spaces.

Kodály first saw this system of "movable-*do*" *solfa* when he visited England and observed choral training there. The method he saw in use was essentially the one developed by Sarah Glover and later refined by John Curwen in the nineteenth century.

For teaching rhythm Kodály and the teachers working with him chose a syllable system similar to that use in French solfège—i.e., the quarter note is "ta" and the eighth note is "ti."

Example:

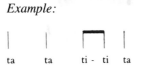

These syllables are not names but expressions of duration. They are voiced, never written as words. Their written representation is stem notation. With duration syllables it is possible for children to chant a pattern correctly in rhythm, which would be impossible if they used note value names. The words "quar-ter note" contain three separate sounds, although the quarter note has only one sound on one beat. A pattern read, "quarter note, quarter note, eighth note, eighth note, quarter note," if notated according to heard sounds of each syllable, would look like this:

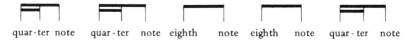

This is not to say that a child should not be able to identify and name quarter notes and eighth notes. Once he firmly understands their duration he should also learn their correct terms. However, for purposes of rhythm *reading* he needs rhythm syllables which express their *duration*.

Basically, the rhythm duration syllables used in the Method in Hungary are

Rests are taught as beats of silence.

Only the note stems are used initially for rhythm reading. That is, quarter notes are shown as | |, eighth notes as ⌐⌐ ⌐⌐. The body of the note is not necessary to rhythm reading except for half notes and whole notes ($\downarrow$). In all other cases the rhythm is determined by the note stems.

A third tool of the Method is hand signs, generally credited to John Curwen.[4] These signs, which had proved effective for many years in England, were incorporated by the Hungarian teachers, with only minor changes to reinforce intervalic feeling. They present a visualization in space of the high-low relationship among the notes being sung. For the pentaton the hand signs are

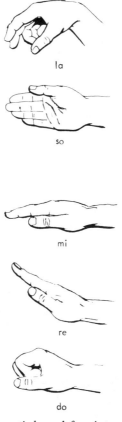

la

so

mi

re

do

The hand signs for the half steps *ti-do* and *fa-mi,* taught later, are *ti* which points up to *do*:

do

ti

[4]Hand signs as a kind of notation have been traced to the ancient Hebrews and to ancient Egypt.

fa which points down to *mi*:

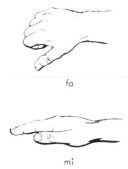

fa

mi

thus emphasizing the smallness of these half steps. The hand signs are shown here as the person making them with his right hand sees them. The child performing hand signs uses only one hand—the hand with which he or she writes.[5] The signs are made in front of the body, with the *do* sign occurring at about waist level, the *la* at about eye level. The distance between the hand signs should reflect, to some extent, the size of the interval being sung and shown. Thus, *so-mi*, a minor third, should be shown as a larger movement in space than *so-la* or *do-re*, major seconds. Octaves are shown by the same sign but in the correct high or low relationship to the rest of the scale. Notes above high *do* are shown in writing by a prime (or comma) above the syllable: *la'*; notes below low *do*, by a prime (or comma) below: *la,*.

In writing, only the first letter of the *solfa* scale step is used, not the whole word. Thus, *do* becomes *d*, *re* becomes *r*, etc. This, combined with stem notation, provides a sort of musical shorthand which makes writing music without staff paper both easy and fast.

Example:

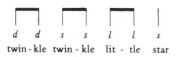

d   *d*   *s*   *s*   *l*   *l*   *s*
twin - kle twin - kle lit - tle star

Such notation can easily be converted to staff notation later from this shorthand.

THE MATERIALS OF THE METHOD

Nothing about this sequence or these tools is unique to the Kodály Method. Singly, each has been tried before, and even in combinations they may be found in some methods used many years ago in the United States and Europe.

[5]Research has shown that children who use hand signs identify intervals more quickly and correctly than children who do not. (Carolyn Steeves, "The Effect of Curwen-Kodály Hand Signs on Pitch and Interval Discrimination within a Kodály Curricular Framework," 1985 unpublished Masters Thesis, The University of Calgary.)

However, the one area in which the Kodály approach differs from its predecessors and achieves what none of the others has, is in the selection of materials. Kodály insisted that the materials used for teaching music to young children could come from only three sources:

1. Authentic children's games and nursery songs
2. Authentic folk music
3. Good composed music, i.e., music written by recognized composers

Kodály felt that the simple, expressive forms of nursery songs and folk music were more suitable for children because they were living music, not fabricated or contrived for pedagogical purposes. The language of folk music tends to be simple, drawn from speech patterns familiar to children even before they enter school.

In addition, Kodály felt there was a close relationship between the music of the people and the music of great composers. He believed that a love for the masterworks could be cultivated through a knowledge of and a love for one's own folk music.

To implement the use of good music in the schools, Kodály collected great numbers of children's songs and folk songs. Working with Kerenyi and Rajeczky, Kodály published six massive volumes of Hungarian folk music, the first of which contains more than one thousand children's songs.

Most of the teaching material in the school books of Hungary today is still chosen from the material collected by Kodály and his associates, of whom fellow composer Béla Bartók was one. Kodály's work of collection and analysis is still being carried on today by ethnomusicologists at the Academy of Science in Budapest.

To implement the third source of materials—good composed music—Kodály himself wrote much music for children: four volumes of pentatonic music, numerous volumes of two- and three-part exercises, the *Bicinia Hungarica* (two- and three-part compositions based on folk music), and many children's choruses. Bartók, too, wrote for children: the *Mikrokosmos* for piano students, and a number of songs for children's choruses. Among Kodály's composition pupils, Erzsébet Szőnyi has composed many works for children.

But the "good composed music" taught to Hungarian children is not all Kodály and Bartók. In the elementary years the children also sing works ranging from Monteverdi, Bach, and Handel, through Mozart and Haydn, to Beethoven, Brahms, and Schumann, and many other composers of the Baroque, Classical, and Romantic periods. In seventh and eighth grades the children also sing and study the works of twentieth-century foreign composers.

CONCLUSION

The Kodály Method is an approach to teaching the skills of music literacy to young children. Its sequence is a child-developmental one, based on the normal musical progression of children from the minor third, through the notes of the pentaton, to the full scales of the major and minor modes.

The tools used to implement this sequence are the movable-*do* system of solmization, rhythm-duration syllables, and hand signs.

The materials of the Method are authentic children's songs and folk song material, and the music of great composers.

It is probably this last—the insistence on authentic folk music and good composed music—that makes the Kodály Method unique. Music literacy is of little value if at the same time the child is not given the skills for musical discrimination. Without these he has no basis for selection. The child who has grown up in an environment of good music will perhaps be more likely to support and participate in musical organizations. Such has been the experience in Hungary, where the Method has produced musically literate amateurs—as is its aim—not just professionals. As an example, factory workers in Hungary form local symphony orchestras and concert choirs, rather than bowling teams, for their own recreation.

3
Kodály for North American Schools: Preschool and Grade One

The scope of the eight-year music program in Hungary includes a formidable amount of teaching material when thought of in terms of the typical North American school situation of music once or twice a week. However, the sequence of the Kodály Method is a valid one, and it is possible to accomplish much through it in the six or seven years of North American elementary school. That the basic skills of music literacy can be taught through the Kodály Method to North American children has been demonstrated in a number of schools from New England to California.

It is necessary to mention at the outset that the only way anything sequential can be taught to five- or six-year-olds in a once-a-week lesson is by having the full cooperation of the classroom teacher. He or she must attend all lessons and follow them with regular practice. There is too great a time gap from one week to the next to expect success from a sequential program with young children on a once-a-week basis. Twice a week makes the continuity of the sequence possible, and twice a week with reinforcement by the classroom teacher is even better.

The implications of this for scheduling are obvious. Two twenty minute periods with kindergarten or first grade are far more valuable than one forty minute period. The length of the period is not so important as the frequency. In the early years, where the whole foundation of musical knowledge is laid, it is important that the music specialist have at least two lessons a week with each class.

WHAT IS A FEASIBLE PROGRAM FOR EARLY CHILDHOOD CLASSES IN NORTH AMERICAN SCHOOLS?

A decade ago there could not be said to be any consistent program of early childhood education in most communities of North America. However, the ensuing years have brought with them such changes in family life and indeed in the structure of the family that today it is a rare school system that does not provide some form of preschool education for its children.

Nursery schools are flourishing, and for more and more children schooling begins by three or, at the latest, by five years of age. These are important years in a child's life, which can have enormous impact on all later acquisition of knowledge.

The program of music education for early childhood must be as carefully structured and prepared as it is for older children. Valid learning will take place only if the teacher is cognizant from the beginning stages of what can and should be taught and what should not be attempted.

Much is known today about how young children learn during the years referred to by Piaget as "pre-operational." It is a time when the child begins to use aural-verbal and visual symbols for objects and to acquire language facility. It is an optimum period for learning—a period critical for the acquisition of listening skills and important in the development of singing skills.

Musical Development of Children[1]

Age	0 1 2 3	4 5 6	7 8 9 10 11	12 13 14 15
Intellectual Development	Sensori-Motor	Pre-Operational	Concrete Operational	Formal Operational

Musical Development
Perception
  Dynamics — (ages 1–4)
  Timbre — (ages 1–5)
  Tempo — (ages 3–7)
  Duration — (ages 4–8)
  Pitch — (ages 4–9)
  Harmony — (ages 6–11)
Responses
  Listening — (ages 1–10)
  Moving — (ages 1–10)
  Singing — (ages 2–10)
  Creating — (ages 2–10)
  Manipulating — (ages 4–12)
Concepts
  Expression — (ages 4–9)
  Duration — (ages 5–10)
  Pitch — (ages 5–11)
  Form — (ages 5–12)
  Harmony — (ages 6–14)
  Style — (ages 7–15)

[1] Jean Sinor, "The Musical Development of Children and Its Application to the Kodály Pedagogy." Presented at the *Organization of American Kodály Educators Conference,* Oakland, California, April 5–8, 1979. (Used by permission.)

Sinor states that it is a time for "personal, active, physical, and concrete" musical experiences.

What then should a program of instruction in music for preschool age children include? First and foremost the program must have at its heart singing and moving. These are the most "personal, active, physical, and concrete" activities in which the young child can engage in music. Until a repertory of known and loved songs exists in the child's own experience, little meaningful learning *about* music can take place. As to what songs and which singing games, these should be carefully chosen so as to provide both a pleasant and happy immediate experience as well as suitable material for later, more specific, musical learning. Songs should be drawn from the heritage of North American children's songs and should lie within the comfortable singing range of the children. Old favorites such as "Ring Around the Rosy," "Here We Go Round the Mulberry Bush," and "London Bridge" should certainly be a part of the repertory, along with others perhaps less familiar: "Charlie Over the Ocean," "Sally Go Round the Sun," "Fox Went Out."

There should be songs for singing, songs for moving, songs for game playing, and songs for just listening. The repertory should include songs in both simple duple meter ($\frac{2}{4}$) and compound duple meter ($\frac{6}{8}$).

Rhymes, too, should have a place in the repertory—nursery rhymes and children's poetry can be a rich source for musical learning. Through this growing repertory of songs and verses musical development can be fostered.

Specifically a music program for early childhood classes should provide experiences from which children can discover that

1. music can be *louder* or *softer* (principles of dynamics);
2. music can be *faster* or *slower* (principles of tempo);
3. the size and material of the sound source can affect the quality of the sound produced (timbre);
4. sounds can be *longer* or *shorter* (principles of rhythm);
5. there is a regularly occurring underlying *beat* in music;
6. some beats have a feeling of stress (accent);
7. some songs are "stepping or marching" songs ($\frac{2}{4}$, $\frac{4}{4}$), while others are "skipping or galloping" songs ($\frac{6}{8}$);
8. there are places in the music for taking a breath (phrase);
9. in a song some phrases may be the *same,* other may be *different* (form);
10. pitches may move *higher* or *lower* or may *repeat* (melody).

These are the ten basic concept inferences toward which the teacher should be working during the year or years of preschool education. They are the major conceptual learning of the nursery school years in Hungary and they can comprise the framework for such musical training in North America. They are arranged here from the simplest and easiest to the most complex and difficult. They relate directly to what research has shown about the order in which young children acquire musical skills.[2, 3] In brief they may be stated as:

1. loud-soft	4. long-short
2. fast-slow	5. beat
3. timbre	6. accent (duple meters)

[2]Sinor, *loc. cit.*
[3]Harvard University's "Project Zero."

7. simple vs. compound duple meter   9. form
8. phrase   10. melody

Preschool children should not be expected to verbalize these concepts, rather they should be led to demonstrate their understanding. All concepts fundamental to the above ten areas of learning may be taught through singing and moving. All may be approached with children as "play."

Loud-Soft

Developmental psychology tells us that the first musical phenomenon to generate a response from children is dynamic level—the loudness or softness of music.

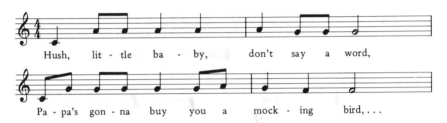

At the end of several lessons the teacher sings this song very softly to the children, without comment, as something for them to listen to. Later, when if has been heard a number of times, the children are invited to join in singing it. The teacher then asks the children what *kind* of song they think it is; how it makes them feel. The word "lullaby" may or may not emerge, but the words "sleepy," "quiet," and "soft" probably will. There should be some discussion as to *why* the song is soft: it is to make the baby go to sleep.

The teacher then asks the class to sing it louder. Care should be taken that *only* the dynamic level is changed; pitch and tempo must remain the same. The class does this and discovers that it does not seem "right" when sung loud. They will sense this only if the song is very familiar to them as a "soft" song.

The "soft" song should then be compared with a song of very different character—one the children have been singing in a louder voice.

This teaching pattern should be followed a number of times, using different musical examples. In this way the terms *loud* and *soft* may be taught and will be associated with the correct dynamic levels. If a child responds with an incorrect term, such as "hard" for loud or "quiet" for soft, the teacher should calmly supply the correct word and have the child repeat it. Consistent and accurate vocabulary is one key to effective teaching.

Fast-Slow

A known and loved quick-moving game song is an ideal vehicle for focusing children's attention on tempo.

Here we go 'round the mul - ber - ry bush, the
mul - ber - ry bush, the mul - ber - ry bush. . .

"Let's go faster . . . faster still . . . now slower . . . slower . . ." Young children have difficulty maintaining steady movement at a slow tempo, but this very difficulty helps them understand the uses of tempo.

"Which tempo feels best? . . . The slower tempo or the faster tempo? . . . Charles, show us how you like to skip for this game . . . Did Charles skip *faster* or *slower* than we did?" Again, this activity should be repeated many times with different musical materials.

One objective of lessons such as this is the development of a musical vocabulary. Four- and five-year-olds *can* learn that the fastness or slowness of music is *tempo* and that some songs sound better in a faster tempo, while others seem more "right" in a slower tempo. The words "faster," "slower" and "tempo" must be used frequently and with numerous songs. Later, individual children should be asked to sing favorite songs.

"Did Nancy sing her song in a faster tempo or a slower tempo than John sang it?"

Timbre

Children recognize voices and other sounds around them from a very early age. What they are responding to in most instances is the timbre or tone color of the sounds. This natural ability of children to focus on timbral differences may be nurtured in the classroom.

Down came John-ny, Down came he, He is hid-ing the but-ton and the key.

One child who is "it" hides his or her eyes. Another child passes around the circle and gives a key to one child and a button to another. All the other children clasp their hands in front of them as if they were holding the objects. At the end of the song the class sings

s m m s s
Who has the but - ton?

And the child with the button responds

s   m   m   s   s
I   have the but - ton.

The class then sings

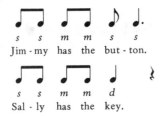

s   m   m   d
Who   has the key?

And the child with the key responds

s   m   m   d
I   have the key.

The child who is "it" now opens his or her eyes and must name the child with the button and the child with the key—from the sound of their voices:

s   s   m   m   s   s
Jim - my has the but - ton.

s   s   m   m   d
Sal - ly has the key.

When children first play this game, many mistakes are made, many incorrect guesses are hazarded. It has been the author's experience that within a month children have become so good at knowing each other's voices that they begin to resort to disguising their sounds. The quality that makes voices easily recognizable is *timbre*.

Instruments too may be used in timbre games. Children should after a time be able to identify sounds as wood, metal, or skin, and, later, more specifically, as sticks, wood block, hand drum, triangle, or tambourine without seeing the sound source. The teacher or a child strikes the instrument behind a desk where it can be heard but not seen.

Long-Short

In identifying some sounds as longer and others as shorter, children are actually focusing on rhythm:

Rain,   rain,   go   a - way
long   long   short short long

In Hungary the words *nagy* (big) and *kisci* (little) are used, but in English this can lead to some conceptual confusion. Eighth notes are *not smaller* than quarter notes; their duration is shorter. For this reason this author has opted to use instead the words *long* and *short*. Such usage also conforms to the common English understanding of rhythm as longer and shorter sounds and silences over the beat.

Children may sing short (4-beat) motives from songs, using the words long and short, or children's names may be sung, their rhythms clapped, and their sounds identified as longer and shorter:

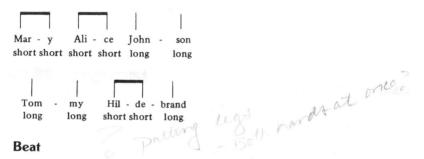

Mar - y   Ali - ce   John - son
short short short short long   long

Tom - my   Hil - de - brand
long   long   short short long

Beat

Stepping evenly to a beat is an activity that requires considerable skill and should be preceded by careful preparation. The earliest experiences with beat are best done in a controlled situation, with children perhaps sitting on the floor in a circle and patting the beat on their laps with large motions in imitation of the teacher. At first, few will "feel" the beat—they simply imitate. However, if such beat tapping is a regular part of each music period, some children will soon be able to sing familiar songs and tap the beat independently, without teacher guidance.

Only when most children can show the beat correctly with large patting motions on their laps, while singing known songs, should the teacher expect them to transfer the beat to their stepping. This is not to say that children should not have been moving to music previously. They will have been stepping, galloping, and skipping during many of their singing games and acting out with rhythmic motions the meanings of many of their songs. Such movement, however, is rarely accurately performed to the beat by children. Specific response to beat is a learned skill that requires time and practice.

When first having children consciously attempt to step to the beat, it is helpful to have them sing songs that are extremely familiar to them and continue to perform the large beat-tapping motions with their arms. Their feet then tend to move in unison with their arms.

The tempo at which earliest beat-stepping experiences are attempted must be the child's natural walking tempo, not the teacher's. Children's legs are shorter, and their natural stepping tempo is faster than that of adults.

The word *beat* can be taught to refer to what the children step and tap.

Accent

When children are tapping and stepping the beat accurately to many songs it is possible to focus their attention on stressed or accented beats.

Bounce high,   bounce low,   Bounce the ball to   Shi - loh.

The teacher demonstrates:

"Pretend you have a beach ball in your hands—bounce it and catch it." All bounce and catch imaginary beach balls while singing.

(Bounce - catch,   Bounce - catch   Bounce - catch   Bounce - catch)

"Now hide your hands behind your back and put the bouncing ball in your voices." The result of this activity is an exaggeratedly strong accented beat. However, when children have discovered *accent* in one song, they are able to discover it in others.

Simple and Compound Duple Meter

In Hungary the meter of children's songs and, indeed, of most adult folk music is $\frac{2}{4}$:

s   s   m   m   s   m   s   s   m
Csi - ga - bi - ga   told   ki   szar - va - dat

The earliest experiences with moving to music are reinforced by a language which is strongly simple duple in its stress patterns.

In English the linguistic and musical metric pattern is neither so straightforward nor so simple. While Hungarian speech always begins with a stressed syllable, English far more frequently begins with an unstressed one (an upbeat). While Hungarian moves in simple and direct patterns of twos, English tends to move in iambic verse, unstressed beats followed by stressed:

A   frog   he would   a - woo - ing go

The most cursory examination of any book of nursery rhymes will show them to be predominantly in $\frac{6}{8}$ and to begin with upbeats; and the traditional songs of English-speaking children exist in almost equal numbers in simple and compound meters. Indeed, in some instances the same song may be found in one region in simple meter:

Ring   a - round   the   ro - sy

and in another, in compound:

Ring   a-round   the   ro - sy

The spontaneous singing of young English-speaking children often moves freely back and forth between $\frac{2}{4}$ and $\frac{6}{8}$ from phrase to phrase.

Because of these differences between the North American setting and the Hungarian model, different teaching techniques must be employed. North American teachers cannot simply ignore some 50 percent of the musical and linguistic heritage of the children they teach. From the earliest stages this different musical material must be included; and preparation must be begun, even at the nursery school level, for feeling, responding to, and distinguishing between simple and compound meters.

The distinction most easily made by children is that some songs (those in $\frac{2}{4}$) are "stepping songs," while others (those in $\frac{6}{8}$) are "skipping songs." At the beginning the teacher simply moves in the appropriate manner and the children imitate. Later, the teacher may say, "This is a stepping song" or "This is a skipping song" before beginning the movement.

When the children have been led through many stepping songs and many skipping songs with movement, they can begin to make decisions about new songs—to identify whether they are stepping music or skipping music. This can only be done, however, if they actually experiment with movement to the song. The five-year-old cannot as a rule simply hear or sing a song and identify its metric nature; that skill is acquired later.

A word should probably be said here about the skill of skipping. Few three- or four-year-olds can skip, and many five-year-olds have some difficulty with it. At the five-year level, those who cannot actually skip can usually perform a gallop-like step in which the same foot is always hopping in front, with the other more or less sliding after. While it is perhaps useful to have a child who skips well take another, who is having problems, by the hand and skip with him or her, not too much time should be spent attempting to "teach" skipping. It appears to be, like walking, a developmental skill. While it is good to provide skipping models for children, most will skip when they are physically ready to, and not before.

Phrase

A musical *phrase* is a short musical thought, usually four to eight beats in length. Phrase endings are the natural breathing places in music:

d   d   d   m   d   d   d   m   d   d   m   s   s   breathing
Rock-y moun-tain, rock - y moun-tain, rock - y moun-tain   high,   place

Feeling for phrase is best taught by example. The teacher should be careful to phrase well in singing and to teach new songs phrasewise, never in shorter segments. It is best not to attempt to draw definitions of phrase from children. Even "where we breathe in music'' has little meaning for the five-year-olds who are largely unconscious of their breathing.

There are several ways through which the teacher may reinforce the meaning of phrase. He or she may have children change stepping direction in singing games at each phrase ending, or the children can be guided to make an arc-shaped motion from left to right with the right arm for each phrase:

advantage

Teacher

This latter has the advantage that the children produce in space the actual musical symbol for a phrase. The teacher must, of course, show the arc from right to left if the children are to mirror it and perform it from left to right—the direction of reading.

The most important aspect to phrase teaching at this level, however, remains the vocal modeling of the teacher and the use of the word ''phrase'' to identify the part the teacher wishes to have sung:

''Sing the first *phrase* after me.''

Form

If five-year-olds are correctly identifying phrases and can count ''how many phrases go by in this song,'' they can be taught the first elements of *form*:

''Is the second phrase the *same* as the first, or is it *different*?'' Only the words ''same'' and ''different'' are used at this stage and musical examples must be chosen in which the *same* parts are exactly alike and the *different* parts are very different:

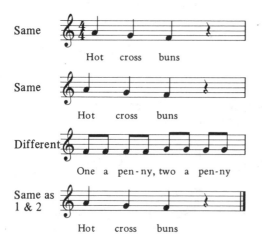

Children can diagram the forms of songs they know well, using felt squares and circles on a felt board. "Hot Cross Buns" would be shown as:

☐
☐
◯
☐

Melody

Young children's acquisition of melody has been the subject of considerable research in recent years. One such study, Project Zero at Harvard University, under the co-direction of Howard Gardner,[4] reports that while very young children can reproduce specific pitches with considerable accuracy, intervals and melodic fragments come considerably later, and the earliest intervals are generally major seconds and minor thirds. By age three, according to Gardner, "children embark on a seemingly systematic drill of each of those intervals as they appear in fragments" and begin to add fourths and fifths. By the end of the third year children appear to have a sense of the rhythmic structure of songs and reproduce fragments of songs, and by four they attempt to reproduce whole songs, although usually without stability of key or tonality. Only at five or six years of age does key stability appear to exist to any extent and are specific intervals sung correctly.

That these findings are true for the United States has certainly been borne out in this author's teaching experience; but that they are developmental rather than cultural is questionable. Most three-year-old children in Hungarian nursery schools exhibit the melodic skills listed as found at the six-year-old level in the United States. It would appear that if children sing and are sung to daily from an early age, they acquire accurate singing earlier.

However, in North American situations the reality is that children entering the schools at four and five are exactly as the Harvard study indicates—unable to maintain key stability, able to reproduce only fragments of melodies or general melodic contour.

The most important teaching mode for acquisition of melody is teacher modeling. Initially, songs should be chosen with simple repetitive segments where the children may join in.

Here,   Blue!   You   good dog   you.

Any complete song should be sung *to* children a number of times before children are asked to sing it. General hand levels (*not* specific hand signs) where pitches are

4Howard Gardner, "Do Babies Sing a Universal Song?" *Psychology Today* 15, no. 12 (December, 1981), pp. 70–76.

higher or lower and where they repeat are strong visual aids to children searching for the melody.

The teacher may discover that some children who have difficulty singing in tune within a group can actually reproduce melody fairly correctly alone or with just the teacher's voice. It is important to give children opportunities to sing alone, and with one or two others, as well as with the group.

Particular time and attention must be given to the starting pitches of songs. Often, children sing out of tune simply because they have inadequate opportunity to hear the given starting pitch.

If the song is short, the teacher should sing it through before asking the children to sing. If it is longer, he or she should sing at least one complete phrase. This helps to establish the tonality. After either of these introductions the teacher should give the starting pitch again and hold it while the children attempt to find it.

Fastening the terms "higher" and "lower" to pitches should, in this author's opinion, be postponed until singing is quite accurate. More effective are physical demonstrations—stretching and bending for obvious higher and lower parts of the music, and use of the aforementioned hand levels. Introduced too early, the terms *higher* and *lower* may become confused in children's minds with the terms "louder" and "softer"—a semantic problem peculiar to English, in which popular usage interchanges the words for dynamic level with the words for pitch: "Turn that TV down lower!"

Only when the vocabulary of dynamics is extremely secure should pitch terminology be introduced.

"Let's sing [the example] again. This time we shall sing it in a *higher place.*" (The teacher sings a phrase in the new key.)

Many familiar songs should be sung in "higher" places and "lower" places before attention is focused on *higher* and *lower* sounds within any one song.

CONCLUSION

The program of music education set out in the preceding pages can be the work of one year of kindergarten or can be more thoroughly accomplished over three years of nursery school. It should be particularly noted that few symbolic associations are suggested—the teaching is almost entirely aural-oral-kinesthetic at these levels.

If children can sing well, step the beat accurately, clap rhythms, apply dynamic and tempo judgments to their songs, and show where sounds are higher and where lower, and if, in addition, they have a repertory of some thirty songs, then the symbolic learning—the musical reading and writing—will progress rapidly in the following years from this solid foundation.

If, furthermore, the children have *enjoyed* their singing classes, if a spirit of play has permeated their lessons, then the attitude essential to further learning will have been well established.

A SUGGESTED REPERTORY OF SONGS
FOR FIVE-YEAR-OLDS[5]

In the following list the songs marked * are traditional singing games.

Loud-Soft and Fast-Slow

Bye Baby Bunting
Sleep Baby Sleep
Hush Little Baby
This Old Man

Hop Old Squirrel
Clap Your Hands
Bye Low, Baby Oh
* Bow Wow Wow

Timbre

Down Came Johnny
Cuckoo

Lucy Locket

Rhythm Clapping and Beat Tapping

The Wishing Song
The Counting Song
Rain, Rain, Go Away

Bounce High
Hot Cross Buns

Stepping Songs and Skipping Songs

* Ring Around the Rosy

* A-Tisket, A-Tasket
* Rise, Sally, Rise

* Here Comes a Bluebird

See Saw, Margery
Daw
* Looby Loo
* Here We Go Round
the Mulberry Bush
* Sally Go Round the
Sun

Listening Songs

Fox Went Out
Bought Me a Cat
It Rained a Mist

Stars Shinin'
Old Blue

WHAT IS A FEASIBLE PROGRAM FOR GRADE ONE IN
NORTH AMERICAN SCHOOLS?

What, specifically, can be accomplished with first graders in the framework of the
Kodály Method? First, it is necessary to review the learnings of the nursery school
and kindergarten years, i.e., in-tune singing, feeling for beat and accent in duple me-

[5]Although each song is listed under one area, most may be used for several teaching purposes. For example: all may be used to work on singing skills; many can be used for identifying phrases; and a number
listed under "Loud-Soft" and "Stepping Songs" may be used for clapping rhythms.

ter, ability to identify rhythm patterns of familiar songs, and ability to step and clap rhythm and beat, as well as the understanding of the concepts of high-low, loud-soft, fast-slow. In addition, it is necessary to add to the repertory of songs and singing games of small range and easy rhythms from which material will be drawn.

Two familiar nursery rhymes, good for teaching duple meter and later for deriving rhythm pattern and accent, are

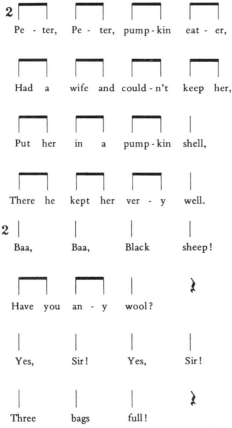

Children may 1) say these in rhythm; 2) step the beat; 3) clap the rhythm (the way the words go); 4) play the rhythm on hand drum or rhythm sticks while stepping the beat; and 5) clap the rhythm while thinking the words but not saying them aloud. These activities, in order of increasing difficulty, aid in the development of a rhythmic sense as well as of inner hearing and concentration.

Concurrently with training in rhythm and beat, attention must be given to in-tune singing. It is essential that there be much individual singing and tone matching in first grade. One simple way to encourage each child to match pitch is to have him sing his name, echoing the teacher on a *so-mi* or *so-mi-la* pattern.

Example:

Later the teacher may sing questions to which the child creates an answer:

Teacher:

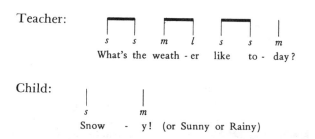

> *s   s   m   l   s   s   m*
> What's the weath - er like to - day?

Child:

> *s   m*
> Snow - y! (or Sunny or Rainy)

The simpler the required response, the more likely the child with pitch problems is to sing it correctly. In working with an individual child with a pitch problem the teacher should ask him to sing softly so that the child can hear the teacher's voice along with his. Often, out-of-tune singers sing so loudly they cannot hear others and so are unaware that they are not in tune. Of course, it goes without saying that never, under any circumstances, should an out-of-tune singer be discouraged from singing. Some children require more time to find their voices than others, but if there is no physiological disability in hearing or speech, any child can be taught to sing correctly in tune. In Hungary the author never heard an out-of-tune singer above second grade.

The earliest material used for teaching children to sing accurately and in tune should be authentic children's singing games and folk music of the proper ambit, i.e., within a range of five or six notes centering around F or F♯. F♯ was found to be the usual center tone children chose when singing independently.[6] The half step *fa-mi* will occur in some of the material, since many American children's songs contain a descending line at the end: *s f m r d,* making the song pentachordal, or, *l s f m r d,* making it hexachordal. However, the basic core of the teaching material should omit the half steps *fa* and *ti,* since research has shown that they are difficult for young children to sing in tune.[7] This is not to imply that songs with half steps, or, for that matter, songs of wider range, are not to be included in the repertory. Some songs with *fa* and *ti* must be taught, and there should, as well, be a few songs with notes beyond the most comfortable singing range of the children. If children cannot *say* the letter *r* correctly ("See the wabbit wun!") parents do not eliminate all *r*'s from their own speech. Instead, they pronounce *r*'s carefully, distinctly, and correctly. They provide a model for learning: "See the *rabbit run!*" So it is with singing. While most songs should be within the comfortable tessitura of young singers, some songs must include the difficult-to-sing minor seconds and some must extend the range a bit. Only if these sounds exist in the children's experience will they ever acquire them.

The songs taught at this point by rote will be used later for making specific tonal and rhythm patterns conscious knowledge to the children, so it is important to keep in mind the possible future pedagogical use of the material when choosing it.

[6]Gladys Moorhead and Donald Pond, *Music of Young Children* (Santa Barbara, Calif.: Pillsbury Foundation for Advanced Music Education, 1941–1951), Vol. I, Chart, p. 15.
[7]Marilyn P. Zimmerman, *Musical Characteristics of Children* (Washington, D.C.: Music Educators National Conference, 1971), pp. 8, 23–26.

For example, the three-note song, "Bye, Baby Bunting" may be used for several teaching purposes:

Bye,   Bab - y   Bunt - ing,   etc.

The children may use a rocking motion to show the beat. They may sing the rhythm with rhythm duration syllables: ta ti-ti ta ta. They may find the new note *la* in the song. However, at the initial teaching the song should be taught entirely by rote and its words and soft lullaby quality emphasized. Only later, when it is well known, should it be put to its other pedagogical uses.

The children's growing repertory of songs should be performed in a variety of ways. In order to reinforce the concepts of high and low, the children might stand and stoop for the obvious high and low sequences in songs; for loud-soft they might perform the same song in a range of dynamics from soft to loud, or, in the case of a march, step softly as if the parade were far away, then louder as it approaches, then very loud as it reaches the reviewing stand. The same sort of exercise may be done for fast-slow, having the children become a train starting slowly, then building up speed, and finally slowing down to a stop as they come into the station. Later it is useful to combine concepts. Ask a child to play the drum so that it sounds fast and soft, or the xylophone so that it sounds high and slow.

Since children may be entering first grade from a variety of backgrounds, the teacher will have to assess their musical skills before beginning any teaching of notation. It should go without saying that for a child who cannot sing a minor third accurately to call what he or she *is* singing *so-mi* is patently absurd.

The first rhythmic and melodic patterns taught to children are drawn from their own singing games and songs. As it happens, in North America these are quite closely related in melodic and rhythmic structure to those taught in Hungary and, indeed, to early childhood songs over much of the English-speaking world. Our simplest children's song material is based on the minor third *(so-mi)*, often with the addition of an unstressed beat on the fourth above the *mi, la*. One Hungarian children's song, for example, goes:

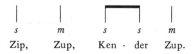

s   *m*   *s*   *s*   *m*
Zip,   Zup,   Ken - der   Zup.

This is identical to the American children's song:

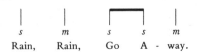

s   *m*   *s*   *s*   *m*
Rain,   Rain,   Go   A - way.

The American children's chant "One, Two, Tie My Shoe," sung by children entirely on *so-mi,* gives repeatedly the rhythm pattern

ta   ta   ti - ti   ta

like the opening phrase of the Hungarian children's songs

Hint - a   Pa - lin   ta
Re - tes   Ke - re - kes

RHYTHMIC LEARNING FOR GRADE ONE

Two other familiar duple-meter songs of limited range and simple rhythm are "Ring Around the Rosy" and "Lucy Locket Lost Her Pocket." These songs and others of equal simplicity, learned in preschool classes, may now be used in grade one to teach both the rhythm patterns of  ta ti - ti and rest and the tonal patterns of *so-mi* and *la.*

    The earliest notation should be highly graphic and should relate very directly to what is being sung. For example, in showing beat, hearts cut out of felt and arranged on a felt board may be used:

The procedure for introducing this "picture" of beat might be:

> Teacher: "Put the beat on your laps as you sing 'Ring Around the Rosy.' " (All do.) "What can you think of in your home that makes a sound like the beat?"
> Children's answers might include: "dishwasher," "washing machine," "clock."
> Teacher: "What do you have in your own *body* that makes a beat?"
> Children will answer: *"Heart."*
> Teacher: "Let's put hearts on the felt board to show the beats in the first phrase of our song. How many beats go by in the first phrase?"
> (Children must perform the first phrase again, tapping the beats to discover the answer.)

One child comes to the felt board and places four hearts, left to right, to diagram the beats of the first phrase, and others take turns pointing to the "beats" as the class sings. Beat should be diagrammed in this way for a number of songs.

    When children are having no difficulty discerning how many beats are in the first phrases of numerous songs and can diagram them with ease on the felt board, the teacher may move to pictorial notations of rhythm. Because they have been tapping the beat and clapping the rhythm for some time before this, it is a simple matter for the children to recognize where there is one sound on a beat, where there are two sounds on a beat, and where there is silence on a beat in the first phrases of familiar songs. Felt cutouts related to the subject of the song may be placed by the children on the felt board over the "beats" (hearts):

It is sometimes useful to have children physically demonstrate the rhythm of the song by having one child group others into the rhythm pattern:

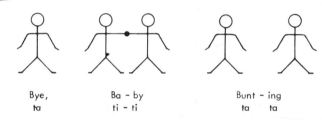

Where children hear and diagram *one* sound on one beat, its sound is given as "ta" and its notation as | . Where they hear and diagram *two* sounds on one beat, the sounds are called "ti-ti" and are shown as.

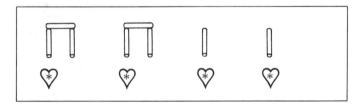

The ta's and ti's may then be sung as an additional verse to familiar duple-meter songs.

　　Children do not "know" quarter notes and eighth notes simply because they have figured out the opening motive of two or three songs. They must be led systematically through all the common patterns of these notes in their songs. For each, they should be led to discover which beats have one sound, which two, and which none. As each new pattern is introduced, the children should write or construct it.

Rhythm patterns to be introduced in grade one, in teaching order:

　　|　　　|　　　|　　　|

　　|　　　|　　　⌐¬　　|

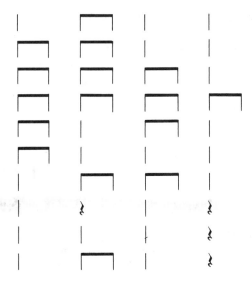

Since many first grade children are not facile with pencil and paper, bundles of sticks provide a simple and quick means for them to take rhythmic dictation. Thin dowels may be cut to five-inch lengths and arranged in bundles of twenty or so per child. They have the advantage of being more visible at a glance to the teacher than paper and pencil work. Such rhythm pattern sticks are used in Hungary and are available commercially in the United States.

One procedure for rhythm dictation in first grade might be for the class to 1) sing the song with words; 2) repeat it, singing ta's and ti's; 3) construct the pattern they have just sung with the rhythm pattern sticks:

4) sing the song again, this time pointing to the sticks.

An intermediate step which may prove helpful for children who encounter difficulty is to have them tap the song rhythm, moving the writing hand across the desk from left to right. This will give the exact placement for the sticks.

After each new pattern is presented, a flash card showing that pattern should be introduced:

These are chanted by the children rather than sung, and great care must be taken by the teacher to ensure that they are spoken in strict rhythm.

On the first exposure, the teacher may point to guide children's eyes left to right, but at all subsequent practice there should be no such guidance. The objective of flash practice is instant total pattern grasp. Just as one does not encourage children to read words letter by letter, one does not teach music reading note by note. By the time children have been working with flash cards for a few weeks the teacher should be able to show each card very briefly, then hide it while the children say its pattern:

Teacher (holding up the card): "One, two, ready, *read!*"
(On the word "two" the card should be out of sight.)

Later, children will be able to look at card #1, remember it, and say it while studying card #2, and so on through the twelve patterns taught in first grade. This is "reading ahead," a skill necessary to all musicians.

The disk game provides practice in differentiating between rhythm and beat:

Children sing and tap the beat of a familiar song.
When the teacher holds up a red disk the children switch to clapping the rhythm.
When he or she holds up a blue disk, they return to the beat.

The disks should be changed several times during the song. Again, the teacher may simply clap the rhythm of a familiar song and ask the children what it is. When they have become proficient at this, individual children may take the place of the teacher.

After ta and ti-ti, the quarter rest may be introduced either through a familiar song or through a nursery rhyme. "Pease Porridge Hot" is a good one:

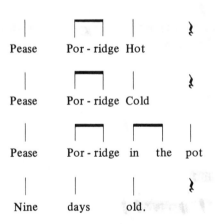

The rest is taught as one beat of silence. When clapping a rhythm pattern, the children should make a forceful but silent motion with the hands for the rest. They may tap their shoulders or simply swing their arms out, but the feeling of a definite beat must be there. In Hungary the rest is drawn simply as a $\angle$.

Once the quarter note, eighth note, and rest symbols have been thoroughly learned, the repeat may be introduced. Children will readily grasp the idea that by placing a sign after a measure or a phrase they can avoid writing or constructing it twice. They may use the sign even when responding orally by saying

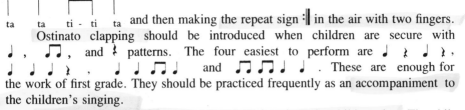

ta   ta   ti - ti   ta   and then making the repeat sign ⫶‖ in the air with two fingers. Ostinato clapping should be introduced when children are secure with ♩ , ♫ , and ♩ patterns. The four easiest to perform are ♩ ♩ ♩ ♩ , ♩ ♩ ♩ ♩ , ♩ ♩ ♫ ♩ and ♫ ♫ ♩ ♩ . These are enough for the work of first grade. They should be practiced frequently as an accompaniment to the children's singing.

To introduce an ostinato the teacher first claps it as the children sing. The children must correctly identify it and say it in ti's and ta's. Then they clap it as the teacher sings. At a later lesson half the class claps the ostinato while the other half sings; the two parts then reverse. When this can be done with ease, the children may try to sing and clap at the same time. The ability to think two different musical thoughts at the same time is not an easy skill to acquire, but it is a necessary one.

The concept of measure takes a little longer, but it may be included in first grade. Accented and unaccented beats will have been introduced in the preschool years. In first grade this should be reviewed and reinforced. This may be done by singing a duple-meter song, stressing the accented beats. Children should be asked whether all the beats sound the same. They will hear that some beats are louder than others. They can physically demonstrate the accented beats by marching, stepping heavily on the louder beats. Using felt hearts again the children may place accent marks under the "louder" beats while singing a song:

See   saw   up and   down
♡   ♡   ♡   ♡
>   >

The children may already be familiar with this mark—it is the symbol for "greater than" in mathematics.

There should be some practice with this before proceeding to bar lines and measures, but once the concept of regular accented and unaccented beats is understood, it is a short step to the function of the bar line. It may be explained to children that to make music easier to read, musicians draw lines before each accented beat, and the space between these lines is known as a "measure."

At this point the teacher should direct the children's attention to the fact that *every* "measure" has two beats—that the music is "moving in two's"—and there is a "2" at the beginning for this reason.

This should be done only with the most common meter of children's songs—the simple duple meter—in first grade. That is not to say that only duple-meter songs should be taught in first grade. On the contrary, it is essential to teach some songs in $\frac{4}{4}$ and $\frac{6}{8}$ since so much of North American musical heritage lies in these meters. However, the music reading material of first grade should be restricted to $\frac{2}{4}$ and even the aural derivations should be restricted to simple and compound duple.

Later in the year, first graders may be led to discover that in compound duple meter ($\frac{6}{8}$)—the songs they know as "skipping songs"—the movement is also in two's:

That duple meter is the basic meter of early childhood has been demonstrated in numerous experimental studies of which The Pillsbury Report was one of the earliest.[8] Only by obtaining a firm foundation in duple meter will the child later be able to comprehend more complicated metric patterns.

MELODIC LEARNING FOR GRADE ONE

When the children can distinguish between higher and lower pitches and can sing their simplest songs well in tune, they are ready to begin learning melodic patterns. They will have sung many songs beginning with the minor third, *so-mi*. One of these, without any rhythmic complications, may be selected to introduce this interval:

The teacher should use only the first four beats—the first phrase—to make the new pattern conscious knowledge to the children.

Beginning with four felt shapes in a row across the felt board

the teacher may:

1. have the children show with large arm motions where the sounds are higher and where lower in the phrase;
2. ask one of the children to push the stars around to show where the higher and lower sounds are:

> The child who does this should sing the phrase while doing this. (The resulting picture will not accurately represent the minor third. Children invariably push the stars far up for the higher sounds and far down for the lower ones.)

[8]Moorhead and Pond, Volume I, Chart, p. 12.

3. Then slip a piece of elastic over the felt board, creating a "line" across the middle, and ask that the higher sounds be placed *above* the "line," but touching it, and the lower sounds *below* the "line," but touching it. The result is a much more accurate picture of the minor third relationship:

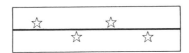

4. In subsequent lessons and with numerous other songs, add two additional elastic-band "lines," so that the stars, snails, umbrellas, or other song subject cutouts are actually showing the melody on a partial staff in the "spaces" between the "lines":

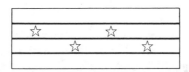

The terms "lines" and "spaces" should be used.

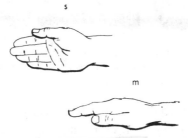

At this point the *solfa* syllables may be sung and the hand signs for *so* and *mi* introduced:

Before the position of *so-mi* on the full staff can be taught, it is necessary to spend some lessons helping the children become familiar with the musical staff and the terminology associated with it. For this a large felt demonstration staff for the teacher and individual felt staves of a size to fit comfortably on each child's desk are invaluable. Both felt staves and magnetic staff boards are common in Hungarian schools. Here felt staves may be made easily and inexpensively out of cut felt and staff lines with magic marker, iron-on tape, or stitching. Each staff should have an envelope attached to hold stemless felt notes. There are commercial magnetic staff boards available here, but to date all are too complicated, with stemmed notes, G-clefs, sharps, flats, etc. They could be useful in fourth grade, but not in first.

The first fact that children should be led to discover is that the staff has five lines and four spaces. They must be told that the lines and spaces of a staff are counted from the bottom up, like climbing a ladder; the child's natural tendency is to count from the top down, as in numbering a spelling paper.

Children have already constructed the *so-mi* patterns of familiar songs on the large three-line demonstration staff. These are now transferred to the third and second spaces of the five-line staff, and felt notes are substituted at this point for the roses, stars, and snails used previously:

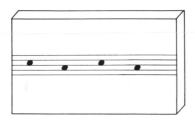

Tunes are sung with words in *solfa* and are constructed on the large demonstrator staff and on the children's small desk staves. Each time a pattern is constructed the children "check" it by singing the phrase first with words and then with *so-mi* while pointing to the notes.

The next step is to define what is meant by "on a line" when referring to the staff. In writing their names, children write the letters sitting on top of the line, but a note "on the line" must have the line running directly through it. This must be learned and practiced with felt staves or individual magnetic staff boards. A game can be made of it, combining the idea of "on a line" with the idea of counting staff lines from bottom to top. The children take one note from their envelopes and as the teacher calls "fourth line, first line, third line," each child places his note on the staff.

If children have difficulty perceiving the meaning of "on a line" in music, the teacher might construct a large staff on the floor using masking tape. The children can then practice being notes "on a line" or "in a space."

All of this simply enables children to move notes correctly and with facility on the lines and spaces of the staff. It is a necessary step in the development of a musical vocabulary, but there is little musical learning involved unless the teacher very consciously has the children sing each pattern as it is constructed.

The earliest work on staff is shown in only three key placements: C, F, and G, since only in these keys is no key signature needed for the pentatonic scale. Children construct the initial patterns of all their *so-mi* songs in spaces on C–A (the key of F), and on lines on G–E (the key of C) and on D–B (the key of G).

When singing these patterns from notation the teacher must be careful to pitch them correctly—second-space A *must* be sung at 440—*do* is movable from key to key, C–A is not. The latter are absolute pitches and must be sung as such when children are looking at notation.

Once introduced, the *so-mi* interval must be reinforced through additional songs that present it in a variety of rhythmic patterns. New song material may be read by the children from the board, from books, or from teacher-made charts, or may be taught by rote and the rhythmic and melodic notation derived by the class. With teacher guidance the derived notation may be constructed on felt staves or written on the chalkboard.

One order for deriving such a melodic and rhythmic notation might be as follows:

The children

1. sing the song with words, clapping the rhythm:

Cuck - oo,   where are   you?

2. sing the song again, this time with rhythm duration syllables:

ta   ta   ti - ti   ta

3. derive the rhythm at desks with sticks;
4. place rhythm on the chalkboard or demonstration staff in stick notation:

5. sing the song again, this time with *so-mi* and hand signs. The teacher must then place a staff on the chalkboard or demonstration staff and give the position of *so*:

s

After this has been done the melody may easily be derived in staff notation on the board and on the individual felt staves.

At some time during the early lessons on the *so-mi* pattern it is helpful for the children to verbalize the rule that

1. when *so* lives in a space, *mi* lives in the space below;
2. when *so* lives on a line, *mi* lives on the line below.

It must be kept in mind that the interval *s-m* is actually two patterns, one descending, *s-m*, and one ascending, *m-s*. The ascending one is more difficult for children. Care must be taken to provide practice in both patterns through song material selection.

Only when the children are secure in their aural recognition, singing, and writing of the *so-mi* interval should the next new note *la* and its associated patterns be identified for them. The children, of course, will have been singing many songs including the note *la*. From these, one containing only *so, mi,* and *la* should be chosen for deriving the *la*. Ideally, the new pattern should be contained in the first phrase of the basic teaching song.

The intervals to be taught are: *so-la, la-so, mi-la,* and *la-mi.* Each must be taught through known song material and reinforced with new song material. A good introductory song for the *so-la* interval is the children's game "Lucy Locket":

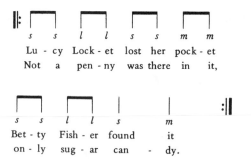

s	s	l	l	s	s	m	m
Lu - cy	Lock - et	lost	her	pock - et
Not	a	pen - ny	was	there	in	it,

s	s	l	l	s		m		
Bet - ty	Fish - er	found	it
on - ly	sug - ar	can - dy.

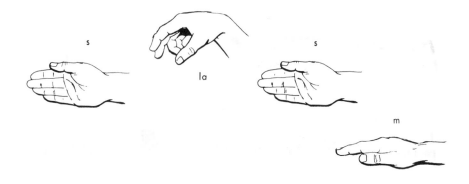

One song useful for the *mi-la* interval is

s	m	l	s	m
Bye,	Bab - y	Bunt - ing

s	s	m	l	s	m
Dad - dy's	gone	a - hunt - ing.

The same procedure used for teaching the *so-mi* interval should be followed. Nothing is intellectualized until it is first known by ear. The process is always (1) auditory to (2) writing or constructing to (3) reading.

IMPROVISING IN THE CLASSROOM

From the youngest ages children improvise. They make up tunes to play by and tunes to lull themselves to sleep. Only when teachers try to force this creativity do children appear to "dry up." A teacher who knows how to grasp and use the child's natural creative instincts can achieve remarkable results with even the youngest children.

The sense of play must permeate all early attempts at improvisation. If the teacher is smiling and relaxed, if he or she offers occasionally absurd questions and answers, the children will not be afraid to be imaginative.

In a kindergarten class in Halifax, being taught by Riet Vink, the author observed the following exchange:

Teacher:

How did you come to school to-day?

Child:

I rode an el-eph-ant all the way!

? Should they use only M S L

The same teacher allowed the children to ask her questions . . . any kind they wished, as long as they were sung. She sang the answers to each.

The earliest classroom attempts at vocal improvisation should be without any restriction other than that they be sung. Later, after children are responding freely, aspects of musical form may be applied:

"Can you make your answer in the same number of beats as my question?"

With rhythm, also, children should be encouraged to use their ta and ti-ti vocabulary to create different rhythm patterns. Rhythm "conversations" can be held in which each child tries to "say" something different in four beats.

? Clapping

CONCLUSION

This, generally, is as much new material as can be taught successfully to first-grade classes in American schools with music twice a week. The importance of knowing these tonal and rhythm patterns well cannot be too greatly emphasized.

By the end of first grade children should be able to sing familiar two- and three-note songs in tune correctly with words, rhythm duration syllables, *solfa* syllables, and hand signs. They should be able to follow the teacher's hand signs, hearing mentally and identifying the tune he or she is showing. They should be able to follow simple two-hand singing—i.e., the teacher shows *mi* with one hand and *so-la-so* with the other; the class is divided into two groups, one of which sings the *mi* while the other sings *so-la-so*. It is important that children hear intervals in this fashion—one note with the other. They should also be able to write or construct with felt staves and sticks any of the songs within their three-note reading repertory.

During the year they should also have learned many rote songs of wider range. Some of these will be used for new rhythmic learnings in later grades, others will have been included simply for their aesthetic value, to broaden the children's musical experience.

With all, children must never be given the feeling that music is mechanical. To this end, dynamics and phrasing must be considered in all singing, and attention must be given to singing in a variety of tempi. Games which accompany the songs should be played frequently. To the children, they are the reason for the songs. There is little point in giving children the skills with which to understand music if at the same time they are not given the opportunity to enjoy making music.

A SUGGESTED SONG LIST FOR GRADE ONE
(ARRANGED BY TEACHING PURPOSE)

These songs may already be known by the children from their preschool singing experiences. Some are suggested for more than one purpose. In all, thirty to forty will be new songs to be learned in first grade. An asterisk (*) indicates a song for which there is a game.[9]

For introducing rhythm patterns

♩ ♩ ♩ ♩	* Snail Snail Star Light	Good Night Bounce High	
♩ ♩ ♫ ♩	See Saw, Up and Down Blue Bells, Cockle Shells	Rain, Rain Counting Song	
♩ ♫ ♩ ♩	Bye Baby Bunting Hey Betty Martin	* Here Comes a Bluebird Go Tell Aunt Rhody	
♫ ♫ ♩ ♩	* Ring Around the Rosy * Little Sally Water	* Button You Must Wander	
♫ ♫ ♫ ♩	Old MacDonald Had a Farm Closet Key	Engine Engine #9 (rhyme)	
♫ ♫ ♫ ♫	Icha Backa, Soda Cracker Lucy Locket	Peter, Peter, Pumpkin Eater (rhyme)	
♫ ♩ ♫ ♩	* This Old Man	* Teddy Bear, Teddy Bear	
♫ ♩ ♩ ♩	Lemonade		
♩ ♩ ♩ 𝄾	Hot Cross Buns Hop, Old Squirrel	* Bow Wow Wow	
♩ ♫ ♩ 𝄾	Pease Porridge Hot		

Songs for $\frac{6}{8}$ meter

Hickety Tickety, Bumble Bee Hill Dill * Oliver Twist * The Farmer in the Dell	* Old Roger * I'm the King of the Castle Fiddle-de-de

Rhymes for $\frac{6}{8}$ meter

Pussycat, Pussycat Hey Diddle Diddle Jack and Jill	To Market, to Market Humpty Dumpty

[9]Directions for these and other games may be found in: Lois Choksy and David Brummit, *120 Singing Games and Dances* (Englewood Cliffs, N.J.: Prentice-Hall, 1987).

For introducing tonal patterns

s-m-s-m:

Star Light   Snail Snail
Good Night

s-m-ss-m:

Counting Song   See Saw, Up and Down
Rain, Rain   Bye Low, Baby Oh
Cuckoo
Blue Bells, Cockle Shells

s-l-s-m:

Bounce High   * The Mill Wheel
* Plainses Clapsies

ss-ll-ss-mm:

* Lucy Locket

s-ml-s-m:

Bye, Baby Bunting

ss-ml-s-m:

* Ring Around the Rosy   * Little Sally Water

The *m-l* interval occurs in the second phrase of most of the songs listed under *s-m*.

For preparing later rhythmic and tonal pattern learnings

𝅗𝅥 *half-note*

Who's That?   * Here Comes a Bluebird
Hey, Come Along

do

I See the Moon   * Ring Around the Rosy
* Knock the Cymbals   * Bow Wow Wow

re

Hop Old Squirrel   * Here Comes a Bluebird
* Button You Must Wander

Songs for listening
(The children will sing along with these after repeated hearings, but the teacher's purpose is the encouragement of good listening skills.)

Frog Went A-Courtin'   Skin and Bones
Old Blue   Fox Went Out
Who Killed Cock Robin?

Rhythmic Learning in First Grade

MONTH	PREPARE THE NEW LEARNING	MAKE THE CHILDREN CONSCIOUSLY AWARE OF THE NEW LEARNING	REINFORCE THE NEW LEARNING THROUGH PRACTICE
September	beat accent rhythm patterns $\mid\ \mid\ \mid\ \mid$ $\mid\ \mid\ \sqcap\ \mid$	beat ♡ ♡ ♡ ♡ shown on demo staff	Identifying longer & shorter sounds. Demonstrating beat with stepping & tapping
October	accent rhythm patterns $\mid\ \sqcap\ \mid\ \mid$, $\sqcap\sqcap\sqcap\mid$ $\sqcap\sqcap\mid\ \mid$, $\sqcap\sqcap\sqcap\sqcap$	accent (demonstrated in stepping) rhythm patterns $\mid\ \mid\ \mid\ \mid$ $\mid\ \mid\ \sqcap\ \mid$	beat ♡ ♡ ♡ ♡ accent
November	rhythm patterns $\sqcap\mid\ \mid\ \mid$, $\mid\ \sqcap\sqcap\mid$ $\sqcap\mid\ \sqcap\mid$, $\mid$ z $\mid$ z	rhythm patterns $\mid\ \mid\ \mid\ \mid$, $\sqcap\sqcap\sqcap\mid$ $\sqcap\sqcap\mid\ \mid$, $\sqcap\sqcap\sqcap\sqcap$	beat, accent, rhythm patterns $\mid\ \mid\mid\mid$, $\mid\ \sqcap\mid\ \mid$
December	rhythm patterns $\mid\ \mid\ \mid$ z $\mid\ \sqcap\ \mid$ z	rhythm patterns $\sqcap\mid\ \mid\ \mid$, $\mid\ \sqcap\sqcap\mid$ $\sqcap\mid\ \sqcap\mid$, $\mid$ z $\mid$ z	beat, accent, rhythm patterns $\mid\ \sqcap\ \mid\ \mid$, $\sqcap\sqcap\sqcap\mid$ $\sqcap\sqcap\mid\ \mid$, $\sqcap\sqcap\sqcap\sqcap$
January	ostinato $\mid$ z $\mid$ z $\mid\ \mid\ \mid$ z	rhythm patterns $\mid\ \mid\ \mid$ z $\mid\ \sqcap\ \mid$ z ostinato $\mid$ z $\mid$ z	beat, accent, rhythm patterns $\sqcap\mid\ \mid\ \mid$, $\mid\ \sqcap\sqcap\mid$ $\sqcap\mid\ \sqcap\mid$, $\mid$ z $\mid$ z
February	ostinato $\mid\ \mid\ \sqcap\mid$ meter, measure	ostinato $\mid\ \mid\ \mid$ z	beat, accent, rhythm patterns $\mid\ \mid\ \mid$ z $\mid\ \sqcap\mid$ z ostinato $\mid$ z $\mid$ z
March	ostinato $\sqcap\sqcap\mid\ \mid$	$\frac{2}{4}$ meter, measure, bar lines, repeat	beat, accent, ostinato $\mid\ \mid\ \mid$ z
April	♩ (half note)	ostinato $\sqcap\sqcap\mid\ \mid$	$\frac{2}{4}$ meter, measure, bar lines, repeat. ostinato $\mid\ \mid\ \sqcap\mid$
May	♩ (half note)	nothing new introduced	$\frac{2}{4}$ meter, measure, bar lines, repeat. ostinato $\sqcap\sqcap\mid\ \mid$

Melodic Learning in First Grade

MONTH	PREPARE THE NEW LEARNING	MAKE THE CHILDREN CONSCIOUSLY AWARE OF THE NEW LEARNING	REINFORCE THE NEW LEARNING THROUGH PRACTICE
September	higher & lower pitches *s-m*		
October	higher & lower pitches *s-m*	Identify when songs are sung "in a higher place" & when "in a lower place"	
November	higher & lower pitches *l-s-m*	Identify highest & lowest notes in songs. Show higher & lower sounds with arm & body motions	Sing songs at different pitch levels. Identify each as "higher" or "lower" than the previous singing of same song
December	higher & lower pitches *l-s-m*	Show with arm motions the higher & lower sounds in two-note *s-m* songs	
January	*l-s-m* staff	Diagram the higher & lower sounds *(s-m)* on a felt demo board, one-line & three-line staff. Introduce syllables *s-m* & hand signs	Diagram phrases of *s-m* songs on 3-line demo staff
February	Melodic patterns *s-m-s-m* *s-m-ss-m*	Introduce the full staff. Construct *s-m* phrases on full staff: *s-m-s-m* & *s-m-ss-m*	Construct *s-m* phrases of songs on staff on F-, C- & G-*do*
March	Melodic patterns *s-l-s-m* *ss-ll-ss-mm*	Introduce syllable *la* & hand sign in *s-l-s-m* pattern	Construct melodic patterns *s-m-s-m* & *s-m-ss-m* in F-, C- & G-*do*. Read phrases or songs using *so* & *mi*
April	Melodic patterns *s-ml-s-m* *ss-ml-ss-m*	Introduce *m-l* pattern	Construct melodic patterns *s-l-s-m* & *ss-ll-ss-mm* in F-, C- & G-*do*
May	Begin to prepare for new notes *do* & *re*		Construct melodic patterns with *m-l* on staff. Read whole songs which contain only *la, so* & *mi* in familiar patterns

4
Kodály for North American Schools: Grade Two

In his original conception of the method, Kodály considered that one of the strengths of the movable-*do* as a tool was that it did not restrict vocal sight-singing to key. The minor third, *so-mi*, is identified by its intervallic relationship, its sound, its function in the scale of the song in question, and its placement on the staff: space-space $\overset{s\ \ m}{\equiv}$ or line-line $\underset{s\ \ m}{\equiv}$ in *any* key. This was a simple enough concept, he thought, for children to grasp. He considered it unnecessary and undesirable in an approach aimed at vocal musical literacy to restrict young children to specific keys. A child knowing only the five tones of the pentaton, *do, re, mi, so, la,* could read them in any placement on the staff and in any clef, once told where *do* was. His idea was to reduce the complex musical page to the simplest musical elements, while still enabling children to read patterns encompassing the entire staff.

In recent years, however, a change has taken place in the official curriculum as practiced by teachers throughout Hungary. Today children in grades one and two are restricted to the keys of C, F, and G. All their reading and writing exercises are in these three keys. One rationale given for this change in procedure is that students need a firm key-centered foundation as preparation for instrumental music reading. Since the Kodály Method was never intended to be one primarily of preparation for instrumental study but, rather, a vocal method aimed at universal music literacy, this insistence on key-centeredness seems out of character. It is doubtful that the advantage of easier instrumental reading at third or fourth grade is worth the inhibition of a wider range of vocal reading in the lower grades.

There may be, however, a more valid reason for restricting early instruction to the keys of C, F, and G. In these keys no key signature is required for pentatonic songs. The B♭ in the key of F is unnecessary since there is no *fa* in the pentaton; the F♯ in the key of G is unnecessary since there is no *ti*. Therefore, in looking at a musical page the child does not see anything incorrect (such as the absence of a key signature in the key of D where the *mi* would call for a sharp) or see on the page anything he does not understand, as he would if a key signature were to be written but not explained. Key signatures can be taught meaningfully only as the scale half-steps *fa* and *ti* are introduced.

In view of this, perhaps it is best to restrict children's early reading and writing exercises to C, F, and G. Then, when the syllable *fa* is taught in the key of F or the syllable *ti* in the key of G, the one flat or one sharp in the key signature may be introduced in such a way that it has a very real and specific meaning, and is not simply a memorized gimmick, as it so often becomes for beginning music students. In any case, North American teachers must decide whether they wish to limit early reading and writing to the keys of C, F, and G or whether they prefer to use the entire staff, simply leaving key signature unexplained until later. In the following chapters it will be assumed that key signature is not introduced until the syllables *fa* and *ti* are taught.

WHAT IS A FEASIBLE PROGRAM FOR GRADE TWO IN NORTH AMERICAN SCHOOLS?

If the first grade has successfully completed the work outlined, in the second grade the children should be ready to learn the remaining notes of the basic pentaton, *do* and *re,* and to add to their working vocabulary in rhythm ties, the fermata ⌢, half notes ♩, an understanding of $\frac{4}{4}$ meter, and further experience with $\frac{6}{8}$ meter.

While this seems a small amount of new material, remember that with each new note introduced there is an increasing number of intervals to be taught from the song material. To be correctly taught, each interval must be found in a prominent place in several familiar song examples and then reinforced with new song material. The actual number of intervallic patterns a child must learn for the basic pentaton is twenty:

Tonal Patterns of the Basic Pentaton

New note

s-m	*s-m, m-s*
l	*l-s, s-l, l-m, m-l*
d	*d-s, s-d, d-m, m-d, d-l, l-d*
r	*r-s, s-r, r-m, m-r, r-l, l-r, r-d, d-r*

Each of these intervals must be practiced many times in the context of song material and isolated and practiced with hand signs. One tone may be sustained by a part of the class while the others sing the second tone. Only by hearing the two tones together can children develop intervallic hearing. Hand signs should be used by the teacher and by the children in this interval work. Visualization in space is an important aid to correct hearing and singing. The Kodály book *Let Us Sing Correctly* gives many good musical examples of exercises for intervallic training. These may be used by the teacher for reinforcement, but the basic teaching material should be songs.

The first new tone to be taught in second grade is *do,* the tonal center of most folk music of the Western world. Actually, very few songs built on the early childhood chanting tones *so-mi-la* include *do,* and almost all English language folk songs with *do* also include *re.* For this reason the author recommends teaching *do* from such limited song material as does exist, and then moving on quickly to the teaching of *re.* Even so, in order to have enough song material for preparing and reinforcing the learning it will be necessary to use *do-mi-so* phrases from some songs that include *re* in other phrases.

Two Possible Procedures for Introducing *do*

A possible song for making *do* conscious knowledge to children is "Ring Around the Rosy." It contains only the three notes the children already know, except for the last note of the song: *do*. The actions for the singing game have the children "all fall down" on the final note, physically representing the lower position of the *do* relative to the *so*, *la*, and *mi* in the song:

The teacher should

1. have them sing the first part of the phrase with *so-mi* and hand signs:
2. lead the children to compare the *so-mi* sound with the sound of the last note, by singing first the *so-mi*, then "All fall *down!*"
3. ask: "Is our new note higher or lower than *so*?" "Higher or lower than *mi*?" If the children successfully identify the new note as lower than both *so* and *mi*, the teacher may give the hand sign and the new *solfa* syllable *do*.

To show the actual position of *do* on the staff it is better to use a song with a *so-mi-do* pattern. Children construct patterns with a space-space-space or line-line-line relationship more easily than patterns in which the middle space or line must be skipped. It is recommended also that the pattern be shown first in F-*do*, since children perceive notes in spaces more readily than notes on lines at this early stage.

Following is an alternate procedure for introducing *do*, using a *so-mi-do* pattern song.

The song is

1. sung with words.
2. hummed, with hands indicating relative pitch; the teacher may give the *do* hand sign, but not yet the name or the staff position.
3. sung in *solfa* with hand signs, using *hum* for the unknown note:

so

mi

hum

4. placed on the chalkboard in staff notation as follows:

s	m	s	m	?	?	?
Fuz - zy	Wuz - zy		was	a	bear	

5. sung, following the staff notation, using hand signs and humming the unknown note.

At this point the teacher may sing the song using the name of the new note, *do*. The children are now ready to sing the entire song from the staff notation on the board. This should be followed by having the children construct the *so-mi-do* pattern on felt staves or on large-lined staff paper.

After the children seem very secure in the sound and position of *do* the teacher should change *so* to the fourth line of the staff and have the class make the necessary changes in *mi* and *do*. It is important to change the singing pitch when changing key this way. Even at a subconscious level children should be helped to associate a note with its actual pitch. If a child is looking at a note in the first space of the treble clef, he should hear that note as F whether its movable *solfa* designation is *do, mi, so,* or any other.

After *do* has been presented in a space (key of F) and on a line (key of G) the children should be led to verbalize a rule about the placement of *do*:

1. When *so* and *mi* are in spaces, *do* is in the space below *mi*.
2. When *so* and *mi* are on lines, *do* is on the line below *mi*.

Once this rule is understood, the concept of ledger lines may be introduced. When constructing the *so-mi-do* pattern in the key of C, the child can readily see that there is no line for *do*:

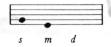

s m d

However, the rule says *do* must be on a line. The construction of a short line under the staff just for the *do* makes sense to children:

s m d

In the lessons that follow there should be much practice identifying *do* in familiar songs. The teacher might sing a song on a neutral syllable, being careful to choose those songs within the cognitive vocabulary of the children, i.e., those containing the notes *do, mi, so,* and *la.* The children, individually and in groups, sing the songs back a phrase at a time, using hand signs and finding *do,* the new note, in each song. The phrase or phrases containing *do* are then constructed on staves. After this, the children should see the song in print in one of their school music books, wherever possible, and should sing from the book using both words and *solfa* syllables.

The last step in the procedure is actual music reading. For this the material must be chosen very carefully. It must contain no rhythmic difficulties and no tonal patterns other than those already familiar through known songs, since it is to be a total reading experience in which both rhythm and melody are to be read. If this kind of reading material is not available in the grade singing books the teacher may have to duplicate a song for her class. This is necessary only at the early stages. Once children have all the notes of the extended pentaton, there is some suitable material available in most school song series.

The New Note *re*

One song ideally suited for the teaching of *re* is "Here Comes a Bluebird":

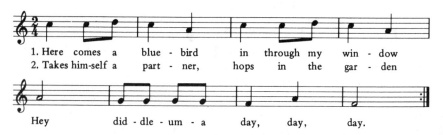

1. Here comes a blue - bird in through my win - dow
2. Takes him-self a part - ner, hops in the gar - den

Hey did - dle - um - a day, day, day.

The first and third phrases contain only the notes known very well by the children, *so, mi* and *la,* while the second and fourth phrases end with *do-mi-do,* also known by the children. The process then might be the following:

1. Have the children sing the first and third phrases in *solfa,* showing hand signs, and the second and fourth on a neutral syllable, "loo," or a hummed note.
2. Have them focus on the parts that go "day, day, day" to discover that this pattern is *do-mi-do.*
3. From the final *do* have them sing to find what the *first* note of the last phrase is. *[mi]*
4. Next, have them sing the entire last phrase, substituting a hummed sound for the unknown note:

mi   hum_____ do   mi   do

At this point the teacher must ask the question: "Is the new note higher or lower than *do*? than *mi*?" If the children aurally perceive that the new note is higher than *do* and lower than *mi,* the teacher may give its *solfa* syllable, *re,* and its hand sign.

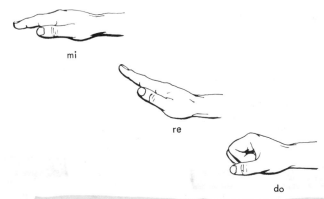

mi

re

do

If the teacher then places the known parts of the song on the chalkboard in staff notation, the children, having felt the position of *re* with hand signs, can easily derive its position on the staff

m   r   d

and can express the rule that:

1. If *mi* and *do* are on spaces, *re* is on the line between.
2. If *mi* and *do* are on lines, *re* is on the space between.

Once *re* is presented, there are many folk songs within the children's aural, reading, and writing capabilities.

It is important that musical examples be used for all the basic pentatonic intervals. Many of these intervals may be found in children's songs and folk songs. However, for some of the less common ones—the fourth from *re* to *so*, or *mi* to *la*, for example—the Kodály Choral Method book *Fifty Nursery Songs* offers some delightful songs for children, specifically composed by Kodály to reinforce the learning of the less common intervals. These small books, intended for use by nursery school teachers in Hungary, could in North America provide supplementary music reading material in the pentaton. It is regrettable that the title "Nursery Songs" makes it an impractical volume to hand out to second-grade American children who consider themselves far above the nursery stage. The songs contained in the book are not at all nursery-like in character. For example, the following is an excellent beginning reading song:

(p. 42)

or this one, with its stressed *mi-la* interval:

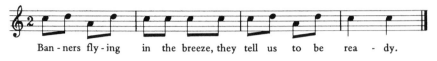

Ban - ners fly - ing   in the breeze, they tell us   to be   rea - dy.

Copyright 1962 by Zoltán Kodály.   —etc. (p. 42)
Copyright assigned to Boosey & Hawkes, Inc.
English edition Copyright 1964, Revised Version Copyright 1970, by Boosey & Hawkes.

In addition to the work on specific intervals, children's inner hearing of melodic line and phrase must be cultivated. This may be aided through various games and exercises. The class could sing a well-known song first with words and then with *solfa* syllables and hand signs. At a signal from the teacher the children stop singing but continue thinking the melody and using hand signs. At a second signal from the teacher the class resumes singing aloud. This kind of inner-hearing exercise is vital to the development of basic musicianship. For additional reading practice, flash cards may be made of song phrases, from which children can sing the phrase in *solfa* and identify the song.

Melodic dictation at this stage should be primarily oral. That is, the teacher sings a melodic phrase on a neutral syllable and the child sings it back in *solfa* and with hand signs. There should be much individual work of this kind in second grade. Music writing should be restricted to phrases of well-known songs. If the rhythm and *solfa* notation is derived on the chalkboard by teacher and class together, the children should then be able individually to place the notation correctly on the staff. For example:

The teacher might have the children sing "The Closet Key" song first in rhythm duration syllables and then in *solfa* and place what they sing on the board:

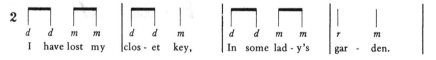

d   d   m   m | d   d   m | d   d   m   m | r   m
I have lost my | clos - et key,| In some lad - y's | gar - den.

The children should then be able to transfer this notation to staff notation in C, F, or G. In dictation it is important always to use a motif or phrase, never just a measure. Teacher and children must not lose sight of the musical nature of the experience.

RHYTHMIC LEARNING FOR GRADE TWO

In the rhythm learning material for the grade, $\frac{4}{4}$ meter presents little difficulty. The children have marched, stepped, clapped, and tapped the beat of $\frac{2}{4}$ meter throughout first grade, indicating accented and unaccented beats with their motions. They have demonstrated, without verbalizing, the function of the bar line, i.e., how to define where the stressed beat or accent falls in music. It is important now that they put this understanding into words, so that they may apply it to the new situation—$\frac{4}{4}$ meter.

They may come up with such statements as:*

> The loud beat is always called "one."
> The loud beat always comes right after the bar line.
> To count beats in a measure you go from one loud beat until you come to the next loud beat.

When children have shown this level of understanding, the teacher may sing a known $\frac{4}{4}$ song, emphasizing the accented beats slightly.

Example:

The children should sing the song and step the beat, stamping on the accented beat, or simply tap the beat as they sing, making the accented beat louder. From this they will be able to derive that there are four beats in a measure. The teacher can show on the board the example:

The time signature should be shown on the children's music at this level simply as the number of beats in a measure: two for $\frac{2}{4}$ and four for $\frac{4}{4}$. The bottom number has no meaning for them since the quarter note is the only beat note they know and to them it is "ta." Its mathematical value is not yet relevant to them. One other possible way to write the meter sign so that it will not confuse children is ♩₂ or ♩₄. This can be understood by children as two or four beats in a measure, "ta" being equal to one beat.

The Tie and the Half Note

The tie is an extremely important device for teaching all sounds of longer duration. For this reason some time should be devoted to teaching it at this level.

Using a song such as "Jim Along Josie":

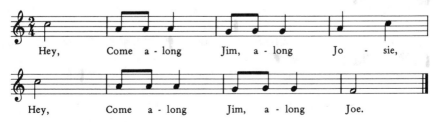

*These were actual statements made by second-graders.

1. The children sing the song and tap the beat to discover "how many beats go by in the first phrase."[8]
2. These are diagrammed on the chalkboard for the first phrase.
3. The children then show the notes by tapping laps on accented beats and shoulders on unaccented ones. Bar lines are placed in the correct places and the meter sign is placed at the beginning of the board example:

4. Next, the rhythm for measures two, three, and four is clapped, sung with ti's and ta's, and placed on the board above the beats:

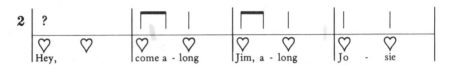

5. The children must then focus on the word "Hey" and try to derive notation for that measure. They usually first suggest ♩ 𝄽. They should be instructed to sing it again to see whether their voices really "rest" on the second beat. When they realize that the rest is incorrect, they usually suggest ♩ ♩.. They know they must "fill two beats" and that they have only one sound. The teacher must guide them to understand that the one sound is a *longer* sound; that it lasts for two beats. Once they have grasped this, the notation for "tie" may be shown:

Only after discovering two-beat sounds in several other songs and notating phrases with tied quarter notes should they be shown the shorter way of showing one sound on two beats—the half note: ♩.[1]

In Hungary the rhythm-duration syllable ta is extended to two beats, "ta-ah," for half notes and to four beats, "ta-ah-ah-ah," for whole notes. There should be no emphasis in the singing on the separate beats of a two- or four-beat ta; the syllable should simply be sung smoothly as the child taps his hand lightly on his desk to maintain the beat. In actual practice the author has found that most children do separate sounds beat by beat on ta-ah and tend to accent the second syllable, even in Hungary. To avoid this, a different syllable, "too," is now being used in a number of places, and instead of clapping the half note in rhythm, the hands make a long sliding motion, one against the other. These two devices together have corrected the problem for the author and for a number of other teachers. In addition, it is helpful to sing

[1]For further lessons on the half note and on the use of ties see: Lois Choksy, Robert M. Abramson, Avon E. Gillespie, and David Woods, *Teaching Music in the Twentieth Century* (Englewood Cliffs, N.J.: Prentice-Hall, 1986), pp. 176–79.

rather than chant rhythms with half notes. When singing, children rarely place incorrect stresses:

| ta | ta | ta | ta | ti - ti | ti - ti | too |

Half notes may then be found in familiar songs simply by beat-tapping and determining how many beats a note is sustained.

The fermata ⌒ may be taught in second grade, through any song in which the hold is artistically effective. The refrain of "Old Blue" is particularly good for this:

| Here, | Blue, | you | good | dog | you! |

Since the rhythms of this line of this song are not in the cognitive vocabulary of the children, only the "Here, Blue" part should be shown on the board and written by the children:

Here, Blue

Much work must be done in this grade to encourage the ability to think, sing, write, and read rhythms correctly. The sticks used in first grade for constructing rhythm patterns may still be used, but the children also should begin to take rhythm dictation with pencil and paper. One procedure for beginning this might be as follows:

1. The teacher sings a familiar song with words in a highly rhythmic fashion while the children listen and think ta's and ti's.
2. The children clap the rhythm and sing the song with ta's and ti's instead of words.
3. The teacher places the complete rhythm notation on the board *as* the children are singing it (for example, "The Closet Key"),

and asks: "How can we change this so that we do not have to write so much?"

4. Children will see that a repeat may be used after the fourth bar:

5. The children then read the rhythm from the board in speaking rather than singing voices. (This is always an added problem because children find it difficult to dissociate the

rhythm from the known melody. However, this is a necessary step if they are to be able to apply known rhythms to new song material.)

6. The children close their eyes and the teacher erases one measure. The children open their eyes and say the exercise, including the missing measure.

7. The above procedure is repeated until nothing is left on the board and the children are chanting the entire exercise by memory.

8. The children reconstruct the memorized pattern on paper.

Later, when the children have become proficient at this sort of writing exercise, the song rhythm placed on the board may be altered at steps 6 and 7 before being erased. This means that the children would actually be memorizing and writing previously unknown rhythm patterns rather than those drawn from familiar songs.

There should also be frequent aural rhythm dictation in which the teacher claps or taps a pattern of two to four measures in length and the class or an individual child repeats the pattern, clapping and chanting ta's, ti's and too's.

Compound Meter

In first grade children have determined that both stepping songs ($\frac{2}{4}$) and skipping songs ($\frac{6}{8}$) move in twos:

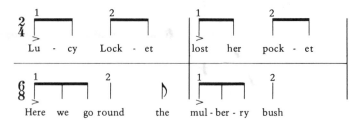

In second grade the children are led to discover that the subdivision over the beat, the "pulses," move in *twos* in stepping music and in *threes* in skipping music. This subdivision into two pulses or three pulses over the felt beat is the principal difference between all simple meters and all compound ones. It is easily perceivable by seven-year-olds if approached through ostinato.

"Is 'Bounce High' a stepping song or a skipping song?" [stepping; $\frac{2}{4}$]

"Put an ostinato of ti's in your hands while you sing 'Bounce High.' "

Ostinato:

(The teacher taps the beat audibly during this.)

"How many ti's are you clapping over each beat?" [2]

"There are *two* pulses over each beat in stepping music."

"Now let's sing 'Mulberry Bush.' Is it a stepping or a skipping song?" [skipping; $\frac{6}{8}$]

"Put an ostinato of ti's in your hands as you sing it."

Ostinato:

Here we go round the mul - ber - ry bush, the etc.

(The teacher maintains an audible two beats to the measure during the singing.)
"How many ti's were you clapping over each beat?" [3]
"In skipping music there are *three* pulses over each beat."
"If we show two ti's as ⊓, how do you think we should show three ti's?"
The children usually show ⊓⊓.

To reinforce this learning, simple eighth-note ostinati should be used to accompany both simple and compound meter songs, and the children should notate these patterns ⊓ or ⊓⊓.

Conducting will help establish more firmly the duple feeling of both $\frac{2}{4}$ and $\frac{6}{8}$. Seven-year-olds can conduct a straightforward two-beat pattern, down, up as they sing.

IMPROVISING AND COMPOSING

Seven-year-olds who have had experience in vocal improvising in kindergarten and grade one can extend that experience in grade two and can even begin composing, writing down in notation some of their musical ideas.

Rhythmic "conversations" should be continued, using longer phrases, and may now include the newly learned half note:

Teacher claps and chants:

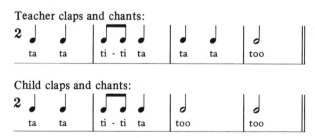

The only restriction on the child's response is that it must be of the same length as the teacher's.

The above exercise involves only speaking and clapping. Another may involve the whole class reading part of the exercise and individual children supplying a missing measure or measures, either vocally or by writing before saying.

When the children can do the latter they are ready to create with forms, a-a-b-a, a-a-b-b, a-b-a-b, a-b-a-c. Initially the teacher supplies the "a" phrase and individual children the "b" and "c" phrases.

It is only a small step from this to improvisation in rondo form, a-b-a-c-a-d-a. The teacher or the class may choose an "a" phrase, which is placed on the board:

Individual children then supply the "b," "c," and "d" phrases. The entire class performs the "a" phrase at each occurrence.

Rhythm *composition* may also be begun toward the end of grade two. A guide sheet such as the following will help children with this activity.

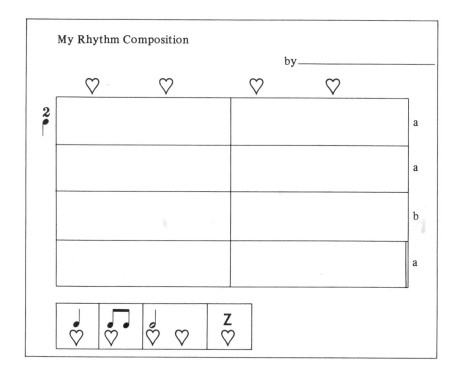

Children should perform anything they compose. Only in this way can the teacher be sure they are thinking the sounds as they write them.

Creative activities can also be done with melody in grade two. If children have improvised tunes to answer questions in grade one, in grade two such improvisations can take the form of genuine musical question-answer phrases, with the question phrase, sung by the teacher, ending on *re* or *so* and the answer phrase, sung by the children, ending on *do*.

Example:

Question phrase:

Children's melodic improvisations will closely follow the teacher's model at first. Later, with encouragement, they will become more adventurous.

There are other musical areas in which creativity also can be nurtured. Singing games can be created to accompany songs that do not have traditional ones. New verses can be invented for loved songs.

Creative activities take more time than some other kinds of musical learning mentioned in this chapter; however, if the language of music is ever to belong to children, such activities must be a basic part of the curriculum.

CONCLUSION

As in first grade much attention should be devoted to individual response both in singing and in rhythm work. Children need the opportunity to hear themselves occasionally without thirty other voices. It helps them to become more aware of their singing voices when they sing alone and when they listen to others sing alone. There should be very few out-of-tune singers left by the end of second grade if the teacher has spent enough time working individually with the children. All song material sung during the year must be performed with attention to the artistry and beauty of the material. It is necessary to take music apart to find where the bar lines go or where the *so-mi* interval occurs, but it is essential to put it back together and to make music of it again in each lesson. A beautiful singing tone, with attention to phrasing and dynamics, must be continually stressed if the music lesson is to be truly musical.

SUGGESTED SONG LIST FOR GRADE TWO (ARRANGED BY TEACHING PURPOSE)

(Some songs are suggested for more than one teaching purpose. An asterisk (*) indicates songs for which there are traditional games.)

For presenting *do*

s-d:
* Ring Around the Rosy
* Rise, Sally, Rise

Mother, Mother
Johnny Caught a Flea

d-s:
Curfew Song

s-m-d:
I See the Moon

Fuzzy Wuzzy

Songs with *s-m-d* or *d-m-s* phrases, but containing additional notes:

New River Train
Knock the Cymbals
* Bow Wow Wow
Rocky Mountain

* Sally Go Round the Sun
Dinah
Love Somebody
When You Get a Good Thing

For presenting *re*

m-r-d or *d-r-m:*
Hot Cross-Buns
Hop Old Squirrel ·
* Go 'Round the Mountain
Frog in the Meadow

* Long-Legged Sailor
Closet Key
Grandma Grunts

s–m-r-d:
Merrily We Roll Along
Who's That?
Old Blue
Jim Along Josie

Mighty Pretty Motion
Sleep, Baby, Sleep
* How Many Miles to Babylon?
* Swing a Lady Uptom

l-s–m-r-d:
* Here Comes a Bluebird
* Willowbee

* Button
* Great Big House in New Orleans
Fed My Horse in a Poplar Trough

For preparing low *la* (with *do* tonal center)

Old Mr. Rabbit
Jim Along Josie (#2)
Down Came a Lady

Cumberland Gap
The Bell Cow

For preparing the low *la* tonal center (minor)

Who Killed Cock Robin?
Old House
Canoe Song

Skin and Bones
I Got a Letter
Land of the Silver Birch

For preparing low *so*

* Draw a Bucket of Water
* Sailing on the Ocean
Hold My Mule

* Shake Them 'Simmons Down
There's a Hole in My Bucket
* Charley Over the Ocean

For presenting the Half Note ♩

Who's That?
Rocky Mountain
* Here Comes a Bluebird
* Cut the Cake
Do, Do Pity My Case

Jim Along Josie
Knock the Cymbals
Cumberland Gap
* Great Big House in New Orleans
Bye Bye Baby

For experiencing ⁶⁄₈ meter

* Oats, Peas, Beans and Barley Grow
* Old Roger
Fiddle-de-de
I Saw Three Ships

* The Allee Allee O
Skin and Bones
It Rained a Mist

For ⁴⁄₄ meter

Rain Come Wet Me
* Draw a Bucket of Water
* I've Been to Haarlem

* Bow Wow Wow
* Sailing on the Ocean

Songs for listening

It Rained a Mist
The Old Sow
Cotton-Eye Joe

The Merry Golden Tree
There Was a Little Oak

Rhythmic Learning in Second Grade

MONTH	PREPARE THE NEW LEARNING	MAKE THE CHILDREN CONSCIOUSLY AWARE OF THE NEW LEARNING	REINFORCE THE NEW LEARNING THROUGH PRACTICE
September	Ties & the half note. $\frac{6}{8}$ meter, $\frac{4}{4}$ meter		Review all rhythm patterns learned in first grade
October	Ties & the half note. $\frac{6}{8}$ meter, $\frac{4}{4}$ meter. Pulses in compound meter: ♫ ♫	Stepping songs move in 2's. Pulses of stepping songs move in 2's over the beat:	Review beat, accent & $\frac{2}{4}$ meter
November	Ties & the half note. $\frac{6}{8}$ meter, $\frac{4}{4}$ meter	Skipping songs move in 2's. Pulses of skipping songs move in 3's over the beat:	Review $\frac{2}{4}$ & $\frac{6}{8}$ as stepping songs & skipping songs
December	Ties & the half note. $\frac{4}{4}$ meter	Conduct $\frac{2}{4}$ & $\frac{6}{8}$ songs in 2's:	Distinguish between simple & compound meter songs by the pulses ♩ or ♫. Conduct both in 2's
January	$\frac{4}{4}$ meter, half note	Ties:	Conduct $\frac{2}{4}$ & $\frac{6}{8}$ songs in 2's. Notate using ties
February	$\frac{4}{4}$ meter, ⌒	Two ta's tied are equal to a half note: ♩ ♩ = ♩	Use half notes in music writing. Read rhythms with half notes
March	Patterns to be taught in grade 3: ♩. ♪	$\frac{4}{4}$ meter, derived from accented beats ⌒	Read & write songs in $\frac{4}{4}$
April	♩. ♪ ♪♩ ♪	Conducting $\frac{4}{4}$	Conduct $\frac{4}{4}$ songs
May	♩. ♪ ♪♩ ♪ ♪♩.	Separated eighth notes — shown on flash cards; all patterns taught in grade 1. ex.: ♩ ♩ ♪♪♪	Read & write familiar rhythm patterns using separated eighth notes

Melodic Learning in Second Grade

MONTH	PREPARE THE NEW LEARNING	MAKE THE CHILDREN CONSCIOUSLY AWARE OF THE NEW LEARNING	REINFORCE THE NEW LEARNING THROUGH PRACTICE
September	*do* & *re*	*do* in the *s-d* pattern. *Solfa* syllables & hand signs	Review patterns of *l–s—m*, learned in grade 1
October	*do* & *re*	*do* in the *s—m—d* ↓ ↑ patterns on staff in F-, C- & G-*do* placements	*s-d* ↓ pattern. Sing songs in *solfa* & show hand signs
November	*re* in *m-r-d* ↓ ↑ patterns.	*re* in *m-r-d* ↓ ↑ patterns. *Solfa* & hand signs; on staff in F-, C-, & G-*do*	Sing in *solfa* & with hand signs *s—m—d* ↓ ↑ patterns & phrases in songs. Notate *s—m—d* phrases. Read *s—m—d* phrases
December	*re* in *s—m-r-d* ↓ ↑ & *l-s—m-r-d* ↓ ↑ patterns	*re* in *s—m-r-d* ↓ ↑ & *l-s—m-r-d* ↓ ↑ patterns in songs	Sing in *solfa* songs with *m-r-d*. Show hand signs. Write *m-r-d* phrases. Read *m-r-d* songs
January	*re* in *m-r-m* & *d-r-d* patterns	*re* in *m-r-m* & *d-r-d* patterns in songs	Sing with *solfa* & hand signs *s—m-r-d* & *l-s—m-r-d* songs. Notate. Read. Improvise with *m-r-d*
February	New tonal learnings for grade 3: low *la* in *do* tonal center songs	*re* in *s-r* ↓ ↑ patterns in songs	Sing with *solfa* & hand signs songs with the patterns *m-r-m* & *d-r-d*. Notate. Read. Improvise answer phrases with *m-r-d*
March	low *so* in the *s,-l,-d* pattern		Sing with *solfa* & hand signs songs with *s-r*. Notate. Improvise answer phrases with *s—m-r-d*
April	low *so* in the *s,-d* pattern		Notate, read & improvise answer phrases with all the notes of the basic pentaton: *l-s—m-r-d*
May	low *la* as a tonal center—the minor mode		

5
Kodály for North American Schools: Grade Three

In the third grade, rhythmic learning should include, in simple meter, new quarter–eighth note patterns ♩ ♪, ♪♩ ♪, ♪♩. and ♪♩ 𝄾, and in compound meter, ♩ ♪♩ ♪ and ♩. ♩. Standard numerical meter signs may be introduced for $\frac{2}{4}$ and $\frac{4}{4}$, and the meter sign ℂ for common meter should also be shown.

In melodic learning the children should be given the remaining notes of the extended pentaton—low *so*, low *la*, high *do*. This will expand the intervallic vocabulary to a possible fifty-six combinations:

TONAL PATTERNS OF THE EXTENDED PENTATON

New note

s-m	*s-m, m-s*
l	*l-s, s-l, l-m, m-l*
d	*d-s, s-d, d-m, m-d, d-l, l-d*
r	*r-s, s-r, r-m, m-r, r-l, l-r, r-d, d-r*
l₁	*l₁-s, s-l₁, l₁-m, m-l₁, l₁-l, l-l₁, l₁-d, d-l₁, l₁-r, r-l₁*
s₁	*s₁-s, s-s₁, s₁-m, m-s₁, s₁-l, l-s₁, s₁-d, d-s₁, s₁-r, r-s₁, s₁-l₁, l₁-s₁*
d'	*d'-s, s-d', d'-m, m-d', d'-l, l-d', d'-d, d-d', d'-r, r-d', d'-l₁, l₁-d', d'-s₁, s₁-d'*

While some of these intervals are uncommon and unsingable for children, the great majority may be found in folk or composed song material, and must be practiced both through songs and in isolation as intervals.

If absolute note names are to be taught, this is the level at which to begin. The determining factor as to whether or not to teach absolute note names must certainly be teaching time. If there is sufficient teaching time, surely it is good that the children be aware of absolute note names and be able to work with them as they do with *solfa*. However, in the teaching situation where there is never enough time to cover the basic grade material, they may be omitted. Absolute note names are unnecessary to vocal sight reading. Given *do,* a singer with a firm *solfa* background can read anything. The purpose of knowing the absolute note names is primarily to prepare for instrumental lessons which commonly begin in the fourth or fifth grade. If note names are not taught by the vocal music teacher in third grade, those children who study instruments will learn them later. There is, of course, the advantage of better and more complete musicianship when children know both *solfa* syllables and absolute note names.

In Hungary the distinction between *solfa* syllables and absolute note names in writing is made by using only lower-case letters for the syllables and upper-case ones for the names. For example:

sol-fa	absolutes	
d'	C	F
t	B	E
l	A	D
s	G	C
f	F	B♭
m	E	A
r	D	G
d	C	F

In this way one may indicate *do* in the key of D as D—*d* without confusion.

HOW TO TEACH ABSOLUTE NOTE NAMES

The children may have learned the names and staff positions of some pitches incidentally in grades one and two.

The A-440 tuning fork, used by many Kodály teachers to pitch songs, may be struck and placed against the chalkboard to amplify its sound, so that children can sing its pitch. The author begins each music lesson in this way, with the children listening for the tuning fork pitch and then singing "A." The tuning fork's end is touched to the second space of a staff drawn on the board:

so that pitch, name and place are all associated in the children's minds. After hearing and singing this for a time, children actually memorize the sound of A, so that the teacher may begin a class by saying: "Who would like to give us the A today?" The pitch sung by a child should, of course, be checked with the tuning fork.

The name, place and pitch of G may be learned when children first draw G-clef signs and discover they are called "G-clef" because they circle around the G-line:

G

They discover that the G-line sounds one step lower than tuning fork A.

In second grade children will have notated tonal patterns and songs in three key placements. If the teacher has referred to these keys as F-*do*, G-*do* and C-*do* and shown the place of each of these repeatedly, those absolute names are also known and place on staff is associated with them.

In third grade these incidental learnings are formalized and the remainder of the notes are introduced much in the same manner as *solfa* was introduced in first grade—through well-known songs of very limited range. The first song should be a three-note one on *do-re-mi* in the key of F, one that the children can already read fluently in *solfa*, such as "Hot Cross Buns" or "The Closet Key." In these there is a clear stepwise descending *m-r-d* passage.

Example:

Hot   Cross   Buns!
mi - re - do
A   G   F

The children have to be told that the musical alphabet goes only as high as G and then starts over again. The entire familiar song used to teach A-G-F should then be placed on the chalkboard and sung with words, with *solfa*, and with absolute names. The singing is an essential step. It is imperative that at this early stage specific pitch be associated with the absolute names. It is a simple matter for children to memorize F-A-C-E for the spaces and E-G-B-D-F for the lines of the staff, but they should not be allowed to do this. The intellectual knowledge of note names means nothing if it is not accompanied by sure knowledge of relative sounds.

After the children have become proficient at singing their *m-r-d* songs in F with absolute names, the teacher may move on to the key of G, still using only *m-r-d* three-note songs. Only one new note, B, will be needed. Later the procedure should be repeated for the key of C. At this point children will know by both sight and sound the notes from middle C to B. Others may be added as the children seem ready for them.

One effective visual aid for learning absolute note names, which may be constructed by the teacher, is a set of magnetic *solfa* discs and corresponding absolute note name indicators shaped like xylophone bars; these may be arranged on the chalkboard by children and then used for pointing out three-note songs in F-, C-, and G-*do*.[1]

For example, the following figure illustrates the use of the magnetic *solfa* discs and absolute note name indicators for "Hot Cross Buns" in F-*do* and C-*do*:

[1]These were designed and tested at The University of Calgary by graduate students Louise Karlsson, Robert Wilkie, and Jeanette Panagapka.

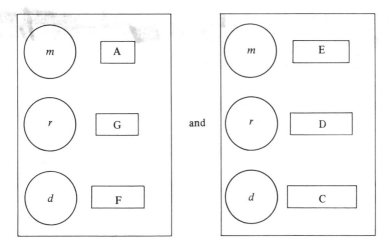

The special value of these is that the children see that *do* moves but the F or C does not. The succeedingly smaller bars representing absolute notes from lowest to highest also reinforce the pitch concept of shorter bars–higher sound, longer bars–lower sound.

They should be used only for three-note, tetratonic, and pentatonic songs at this point, and there should always be a gap between *mi* and *so* and between *do* and low *la,* and their related absolute notes, visually representing the minor third interval. This is a readiness step for the later learnings about key signature.

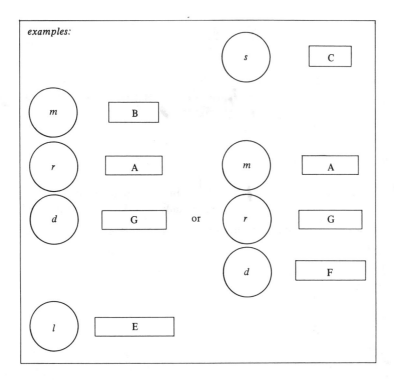

The teacher would do well to construct all needed absolute name bars at one time in order to be sure their sizes are graduated from the lowest notes eventually needed (A below middle C) to the highest (high G), with all sharps and flats needed for key signatures. One simple way of doing this is shown in the following diagram.

G
F♯   G♭
F
E
D♯   E♭
D
C♯   D♭
C
B
A♯   B♭
A
G♯   A♭
G
F♯   G♭
F
E
D♯   E♭
D
C♯   D♭
C
B
A♯   B♭
A

Once absolute note names have been introduced, this knowledge may be transferred to instrumental experience. This is a good time to introduce class recorder instruction and the playing of barred instruments.

NEW RHYTHM LEARNING

The three basic rhythm patterns to be taught in third grade occur in numerous songs and are closely related to each other conceptually. Until this time the children's conscious knowledge has included only even arrangements of sounds, ♩ and ♫, and sounds lasting longer than a beat, ♩ . Now they will discover that there can be "uneven arrangements of sounds over beats":

Chairs to mend, Old chairs to mend, Mack - er - el, Fresh

Mack - er - el, An - y old rags an - y old rags?

All of these are taught through ostinato and ties.

Procedure

The ostinato ♩ ♫♩ ♩ is taught and practiced with the above song until it can be performed without difficulty. It is shown on the chalkboard with separated eighth notes: ♩ ♪♪♩ ♩. When the children are secure with the ostinato pattern and singing, the teacher asks:

"Is our ostinato the same as our singing rhythm in the first phrase?" [No, it is different]
"Where is it different?" [On the first word, "Chairs"]
"How is it different?" ["Chairs" is a longer sound]
"How can we change the notation of our ostinato, using a tie, so that when we perform it, it will sound the same as our singing rhythm?"

The children should be able to show: ♩ ♪♪♩ ♩ ♩ . When they have done this, and checked it by singing, the teacher may show

The sung or spoken syllable for the dotted quarter in Hungary used to be "ta-i." This created a problem in that children made two distinct sounds rather than one longer sound. In North America, and more recently in Hungary too, the syllable "tam" has been substituted for this note:

♩. ♪♩ ♩ │♩. ♪♩ │

tam ti ta ta tam ti too

The next most common rhythm in English language folk song is ♪♩ ♪ simple syncopation. It is found in numerous singing games and dances and in many spirituals.

Example:

Ain't I rock can - dy, Ain't I rock can - dy,

Ain't I rock can - dy, Al - a - ba - ma gal!

Like the dotted quarter-eighth pattern, this is taught through the use of ostinato and ties. The ostinato ♫ ♫ ♩ ♩ is practiced with the song until it can be performed well. It is shown on the chalkboard with separated eighth notes: ♪♪♪♪♪♩ ♩ and the following questions are asked:

"Is our ostinato the same as our singing rhythm?" [no]

"Where is it different? On which word? How is it different?" The children usually have to sing and clap again to discover that the word "I" is longer.

"How can we change the notation of our ostinato, using a tie, so that when we perform it, it will sound the same as our singing rhythm?" The children should be able to show

Ain't I__ rock can - dy

They know that ♩♩ is the same as ♩ , so the pattern may now be shown as ♪♩ ♪♩ ♩ . If the children should place the tie in an incorrect place, the rhythm can be performed as it would sound. For example,

Ain't__ I rock can - dy

In this way the class will quickly hear and correct the mistake. The pattern ♪♩ ♪ may be read either as "ti-ta-ti" or as "syn-co-pa."

For both of the above rhythm patterns, and for the next one, the same procedure is followed and, indeed, the same questions, worded in the same way, are asked. This consistency is quite deliberate. The children are not just being given a new rhythmic pattern, they are being taught a *process* through which to "figure out" such patterns for themselves in the future. They are being given aural relationships rather than mathematical equivalents: "The dot is worth half the value of the note preceding it."

The rhythm patterns ♪♩. and ♪♩𝄾 tend to occur in songs which also include the above syncopation pattern ♪♩ ♪, a pattern to which they are closely related. The ostinato through which to teach them must contain ♪♩ ♪ over the ♪ ♩. or ♪♩𝄾 pattern and must match the song pattern in the rest of the phrase.

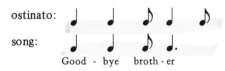
ostinato: ♩   ♩   ♪ ♩   ♪
song: ♩   ♩   ♪ ♩.
Good - bye broth - er

The questions asked are exactly as above, with the last one—"How can we change the notation of our ostinato, using a tie, so that when we perform it, it will sound the same as our singing rhythm?"—resulting in

ostinato: ♩   ♩   ♪ ♩   ♪
Good - bye broth - er___

Children have already learned that ♩ ♪ may be shown as ♩. and is spoken as tam. The pattern ♪♩. is spoken as ti-tam.

The learning of these three rhythm patterns should be reinforced through singing, reading and writing many songs containing them, and also through using them in improvisation and composition.

The whole note might be taught at this time as it occurs in

"I Got a Letter":

o | o ‖
oh,   yes

or "Rattlesnake":

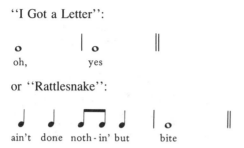

ain't done noth-in' but bite

The children are asked to tap the beat to see "how many beats go by" as they sing "oh" and as they sing "yes," or as they sing "bite." If they agree that there are four, the teacher should elicit from them ways of showing one sound lasting for four beats. They will probably show ♩ ♩ ♩ ♩ and ♩ ♩ . The new note "o" is then given and its syllable "toe" sung:

ta   ta   ti ti ta   toe

Whole notes are rare in children's music, and whole rests even rarer. One possible way to reinforce the duration of the whole note is through two-hand singing. Following the teacher's hand signs one group might sustain a note for four beats while the second group moves on each quarter note beat:

s   l   s   m
m_____

Many exercises of this sort may be found in the Kodály volume "Let Us Sing Correctly." However, if teaching time is short, since the whole note and the whole rest occur so rarely in children's song material, they can be omitted from the teaching plan until a later grade with little effect on reading ability.

Compound Meter

The other principal rhythmic learning of grade three involves the most common ⁶⁄₈ patterns ♩♪♩♪ and ♩.♩. . Children have had the ♪♪♪ ♪♪♪ pattern in grade two. Once they have realized in simple meter that ♪ ♪ ♪ or ♩ ♪ may be shown as ♩., that knowledge may be transferred to their experience with compound meter:

Oh   dear   what can the   mat - ter   be?

Taking "what can the matter be" as an ostinato, the children will discover that "Oh, dear" is

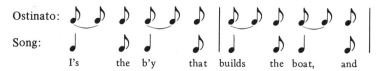

Oh _____ dear _____   Oh,   dear

Using the same ostinato they can derive the ♩♪ pattern from the song "I's the B'y":

Ostinato:

Song:

I's   the b'y   that builds   the boat,   and

Children will need practice with these rhythms for fluency. They should sing many $\frac{6}{8}$ songs, using rhythm syllables. Flash cards do not work well for $\frac{6}{8}$ patterns. To contain a phrase, the card has to be too long for ease of handling. The author has found that a simple chart, such as the one following, can be useful for practicing $\frac{6}{8}$ rhythms before reading new song material. The teacher may indicate which pattern or part of a pattern is to be read, and can skip from one pattern to another either at the beginning or in the middle, thus creating a number of different patterns.

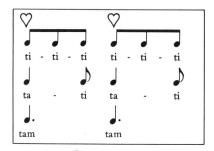

ti - ti - ti   ti - ti - ti

ta - ti   ta - ti

tam   tam

It is in third grade also that the "beat" note for $\frac{6}{8}$ is discovered to be the dotted quarter.

The meter sign will be shown in children's notation as $\frac{2}{\bullet}$. This continues the procedure of showing simple meters first as simply "2" or "4" and later as $\frac{2}{\bullet}$ or $\frac{4}{\bullet}$.

In third grade the standard rhythmic vocabulary—quarter note, eighth note, half note—is introduced and used interchangeably with ta's and ti's when referring to those notes. However, all rhythm reading continues to be done with duration sylla-bles. Standard rhythm names cannot be spoken in correct rhythm: "quar-ter"—a two-syllable word for one sound.

After the introduction of the term "quarter note," simple meter signs may be shown as $\frac{2}{4}$ and $\frac{4}{4}$, the bottom "4" representing the "quarter note beat."

The reason for delaying for so long a numerical lower part for meter signature is that if this is introduced in grade one or two, when children are reading only simple meter songs, they may form the mistaken notion that the "beat note" is always ta, a quarter note. By waiting until grade three to identify the beat note as ♩ in some songs ($\frac{2}{4}$ and $\frac{4}{4}$) and as ♩. in others ($\frac{6}{8}$) the way is more open to other possible beat notes, ♪ ($\frac{3}{8}$) or ♩ ($\frac{2}{2}$).

Rhythmic Dictation

Rhythm dictation exercises now become somewhat longer and more involved. Starting with simple four-beat exercises, the children will gradually develop to the point where by the end of third grade they should be able to retain and repeat accu-rately exercises of sixteen beats.

An early example of a rhythm tapped by the teacher, to be clapped and chanted back by one child, is:

2 | | | ⌐⌐ | ||
ta   ta   ti ti ta

Later, two well-known rhythm patterns are connected and the child is asked to repeat the eight-beat exercise after the teacher taps it:

2 | | | ⌐⌐ | | | | | | ⁊ ||
ta   ta   ti ti ta   ta   ta   ta

The first few times a sixteen-beat exercise is attempted, the last eight beats should be a simple repeat of the first eight:

2 | | | ⌐ | | | | | | ⁊   :||

Only when the children are doing this well should an alteration be made, and then, only one:

↑
alteration

In this way children can be trained to hear and categorize rhythm patterns of considerable length. It is not necessary that such exercises be written by the children. Oral recitation of them and final placement on the chalkboard for the entire class to see and perform are sufficient.

NEW TONAL LEARNINGS

Low *la (l,)* should be the first note of the extended pentaton taught. It is introduced through *do*-tonal center (major) song material since this mode is more familiar to children than the minor mode with its *la* tonal center. *La* is best introduced to children through a song in which it is the only note unfamiliar to the children—for example, in the last phrase of the song "Rattlesnake."

RATTLESNAKE

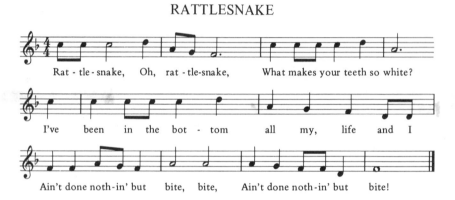

Rat - tle - snake,   Oh,   rat - tle-snake,   What makes your teeth so white?

I've   been   in   the   bot - tom   all   my,   life   and   I

Ain't done noth-in' but   bite,   bite,   Ain't done noth-in' but   bite!

In leading children to discover the new note low *la,* "Rattlesnake" is an excellent vehicle because the entire first part of the song is built on basic pentatonic tonal patterns with which the children are very secure.

Teaching Process

1. The last part of the song is sung in ti's, ta's, too's and toe's (the whole note) and its rhythm is placed on the board:

2. The children sing the last two phrases with words and *show* the last note *do* with a hand sign. (The last note of most songs is the most secure note, the one the children recognize most readily.)

3. From the final note *do* the children sing the beginning of the preceding phrase, "ain't done," and find that that is *do* as well.

4. They then sing that phrase and the beginning of the last phrase in *solfa* as the teacher places the *solfa* on the board with a question mark at the unknown note:

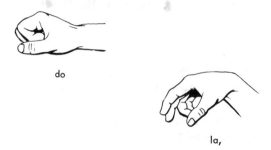

5. The teacher asks: "Is the new note higher or lower than *do?*"
6. If the children perceive the sound as lower, the teacher may give its name, hand sign, and position on staff in the keys of F, C, and G. The sign for low *la* is exactly as for *la* except that the hand is positioned below the *do*:

do

la,

The song "Jim Along Josie" (#2) can be used in exactly the same manner as either a song through which to present low *la* or as one through which to reinforce learning.

JIM ALONG JOSIE (#2)

Hey, come a - long_____ Jim, a - long Jos - ie,

Hey, come a - long_____ Jim, a - long Joe.

It is good to have more than one song planned through which to make new notes conscious knowledge to children. Under ideal circumstances a half-dozen "preparation" songs, plus one to present the learning, and several more to reinforce and assess children's acquisition of the learning should be enough; but children are not machines, and the unexpected occurs with great regularity in classrooms.

Having successfully used "Rattlesnake" in exactly the manner given above with several classes, the author attempted the same lesson with another class, only to reach the question "Is the new note higher or lower than *do?*" and find the children almost evenly divided as to the answer. Since this class had never previously exhibited any difficulty in distinguishing between higher and lower pitches, there were no clues to the nature of the problem. Only after several further lessons and three new "make conscious" songs did the reason for the problem come from one child: "It *must* be higher than *do* because *nothing* is lower than *do!*" These children were using intellect rather than ears. Somewhere in their past experience the major scale beginning and ending on *do* had been so firmly entrenched that they were ready to disbelieve their own hearing—they simply rejected the possibility of notes below *do.*

Once the relative position of *la,* has been established as:

On the line below *do* when *do* is on a line,
In the space below *do* when *do* is in a space,

the children easily derive that low *so* is in the staff position immediately below low *la.* It is easiest to introduce low *so* through a song containing both the low *la* and the low *so,* so that children may discover the *so* from its position below *la,*. An example of a *l,*-s, song is the singing game "I've Been to Haarlem":

```
d     d   d   l,   s,    d     d   d   l,   s,
I've been to Haar-lem,   I've been to Do-ver
```

The strong *do-la,*-so, motif in the first two measures and an uncomplicated rhythm make this pentatonic song a good choice. There are many examples of *do-la,*-so, and *so,*-la,-do patterns in North American folk music. Many more pentatonic North American folk songs seem to be built around the scale from low *so* to *mi* or from low *so* to high *la* than from *do* to *do'.*

After the children can work easily with songs containing low *so* and low *la,* songs with only the low *so* may be examined. For practicing low *so* in a song without low *la,* an easy example is "Hush, Little Baby." Each new phrase starts with low *so:*

```
s,    m
Hush  lit-tle    ba - by,     don't  say  a    word.

s,   s,   r
Mam-my's gon-na  buy  you  a   mock - in'      bird.
```

Both the *so,*-mi and *so,*-re intervals exist in this song, and because of its many verses there is ample opportunity for practice on both intervals.

For the *so,*-do interval the verse of "Goodbye, Old Paint" uses *so,* as the upbeat leading to *do* for each verse. The hand sign for low *so* is as for *so,* only in the position below low *la:*

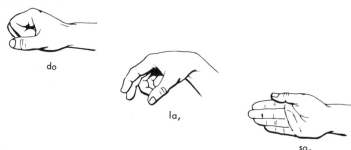

do

la,

so,

Notes below *do* are indicated in writing with a subprime, for example: low *la* = *l₁*, low *so* = *s₁*.

Upbeat

A word must be said here about teaching the upbeat since the most common occurrences of the tonal pattern low *so* to *do* is as an anacrusis.

One song that has worked well for the author in teaching upbeat is the following Appalachian riddle song with its nonsense verse that sounds almost like Latin, but is not:

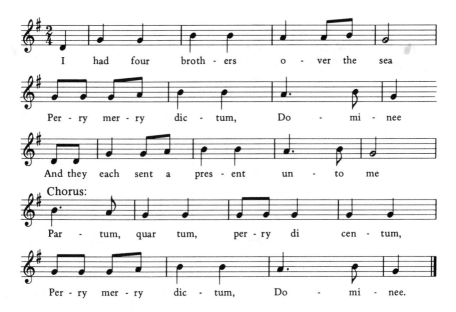

"Begin conducting in twos on the chorus part. When you get to the end, go immediately back to the beginning and continue singing and conducting." When the children reach the beginning ("I"), the teacher stops them and asks:

"What kind of beat are you conducting?" [An upbeat.]

"What kind of beat do the songs we usually conduct begin on?" [A downbeat.]

In this way the first association with the word "upbeat" comes from the physical action of raising the arm in a conducting gesture. Such an approach helps make more sense of the notation for upbeat to children.

At later lessons the children may sing, and tap the accented beats for other songs beginning with upbeats and find in their notation:

"Which measure is incomplete?"

"Where is the rest of that measure?"

With a sight-singing vocabulary extending from low *so* to high *la* there are literally hundreds of pentatonic songs easily available from which to choose the children's singing material. Many can be found right in the school song series. The teacher should carefully preview each song to determine whether all of it is within the learned abilities of the children, rhythmically and melodically. Even in instances where a problem exists with part of a song, it can often be used if the teacher gives the difficult section by rote. Usually there is some part of the song that is easily within the reading vocabulary of children in third grade. For the music teacher willing to turn to folk music collections for her song material, there is a vast number of published collections, many specifically aimed at children.

High *do (d')* may be introduced through the cumulative song "Had Me a Bird":

d'	*d'*	*d'*	*s*	*s*	*s*	*d'*	*d'*	*s*
Had	me	a	bird	and	the	bird	pleased	me.

The range of this pentatonic song is *do* to high *do,* and its rhythms are simple.

High *do* is not so much a new note as an old friend in a new placement. The hand sign is the same, simply raised to a position above *la*:

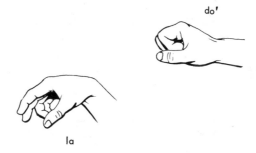

do'

la

As with each new tone, the children should sing the *d'* in the context of familiar songs, making the new hand sign. They should then see it on the staff, draw it on staff paper in melodic dictation, and, last, recognize it in a new song.

The Minor Mode

Children should have been singing some songs of minor character since first grade. They will have sensed the differences in mood and color of these songs. In third grade, with the new note low *la* in their tonal vocabulary, they can begin to classify songs as to whether they are *do* tonal center, of *Major* character, or *la* tonal center, of *minor* character.

For beginning this classification songs built largely on major or minor triads are particularly helpful:

Rock- y moun - tain high

Old   House,   Tear it   down,   Who's

Pulling the triads from these two songs and others like them, divide the class into three groups. First, have them sing a *do-mi-so* chord, one group entering at a time, following the teacher's hand sign. Then sing a *la-do-mi* chord, beginning on the same pitch. Without understanding the construction of a major or minor chord, the children will nevertheless hear the differences in the two chords, and if their attention is directed to each note in turn, they may realize that the middle note (the third of the triad) is lower in the *la*-centered chord.

Whenever a new pentatonic song is sung the notes needed should be placed on the chalkboard, either on the staff (as for "Old Blue"):

or as a tonal ladder (as for "Swing Low, Sweet Chariot"):

l

s

m

r

d

l₁

s₁

Only those notes actually needed for the song should be placed on the chalkboard. When constructing a tonal ladder care should be taken that space is left where the step and a half occurs (where the *fa* and *ti* are missing).

It is a very graphic aid to young children to have them "be" the notes of the tonal ladder. The larger children should represent the lower notes, and, as the "notes" ascend in pitch, the children should be smaller.[2] In this way the concept of high and low is correctly reinforced.

Now with the full pentaton in the children's singing vocabulary, the Kodály Book *333 Elementary Exercises in Sight-Singing* may be a useful addition to the lesson, since it provides exercise on tonal patterns not as commonly encountered in song material and yet with which the children must be fluent if they are to progress easily to the next steps in the sequence. In choosing an exercise the teacher should be sure

---

[2]This conceptualization of pitch may be compared with the pitch-size relationship existing in resonator bells and in organ pipes.

of its pertinence to the specific lesson being taught. For example, if the children have had difficulty with *re-la,* there are specific examples for reinforcing this interval.

There are numerous techniques for making these essentially exercise-like compositions more interesting. They may be sung or clapped in canon, sung as question and answer by pairs of children, or sung by the group against a simple rhythm ostinato. For third grade, however, they should be used sparingly, and only when specifically useful to the learning of a skill which needs additional reinforcement.

Some of these tunes will be familiar to the children if the Kodály Nursery Songs were used in second grade. When asked to compose his Nursery Book, Kodály simply chose from his "333" those that seemed most appropriate, and to these a Hungarian poet contributed the words.

Although the melodic skill teaching material for third grade should be pentatonic, other song material must be taught as well. It takes some time to teach children to sing *mi-fa* and *ti-do* half steps in tune. A certain amount of rote song material for the grade must include these intervals in preparation for their introduction on the conscious level in fourth grade; indeed, the *fa* and *ti* will have occurred in pentachordal and hexachordal rote material since first grade.

Singing should also include increasing numbers of songs with melodic ostinati and descants and should also include rounds and canons. Children may create their own ostinati and descants.

The two notes *so-mi* in varying rhythms may be sung effectively against any *do*-pentaton song. By experimenting, children will discover other pleasing combinations. A simple ascending and descending pentatonic scale descant may be used in the same manner, as for example, with "Cotton-Eye Joe":

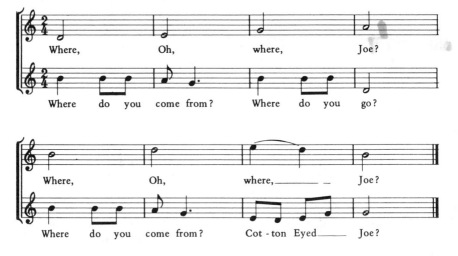

Canon singing should also be introduced at this point if it has not been previously. To do this the teacher chooses a song the children sing very securely. It need not be designated as a "round" or "canon." Many tetratonic and pentatonic songs lend themselves to canon singing; for example, "I Got a Letter":

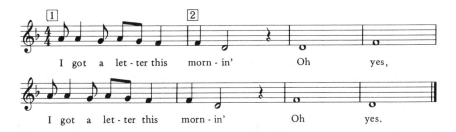

I got a let-ter this morn-in' Oh yes,

I got a let-ter this morn-in' Oh yes.

After the children start to sing the teacher sings the second part softly. The children are led to discuss what happened, and then they try singing the second part while the teacher sings the first. When they can do this well, the class may be divided with half on one part and half on the other. Later, small groups or pairs of children should sing the two parts. The children must at all times be encouraged to listen to each other and to fit their singing together.

Rhythm canon games may also be played once the principles of canon singing are understood.

When the children are repeating four-measure rhythms well, the teacher should place one from a familiar song on the chalkboard and ask the children to clap it. When they have clapped it once correctly, the teacher should ask them to repeat it. This time the exercise should be tapped one measure behind in round style. When it is completed the children should be asked to describe what happened. The words "round" and "canon" should be mentioned, and the class may divide into sections to read the exercise in canon style. Line drawings on the chalkboard exercise may help children know when to start:

IMPROVISING AND COMPOSING

The third-grade child with a solid background of Kodály training is capable of creating in every aspect of music: text, movement, rhythm, melody, and harmony.

The easiest of these is text. Children may alter songs by substituting words and finding rhyming words:

"Whistle, daughter, whistle and you shall have a _____."
"I can't whistle, mother, because _____ _____ _____ _____."

Some examples: "sheep" . . . "I am asleep"
"pig" . . . "I am too big"
"fish" . . . "I do not wish . . . to"

One class came up with twenty-two verses for the above song.

A bit more difficult, but still possible at this age, is the changing of a text so that it suits some special occasion, such as writing Halloween or Christmas words to a folk song tune, or celebrating some event in school life by fitting a verse about it to a loved song. These latter activities consume a considerable amount of time if attempted during a music period, but classroom teachers can make them a part of language classes, and they are often highly cooperative and happy to receive such specific suggestions.

In the area of movement, children have by third grade experienced circle games and dances involving acting out, chasing, partner choosing, and arch forming. They have also probably played singing games in which there is interaction between two lines facing each other in contra-dance formation. They have moved in steps, slides, runs, tiptoes, skips, and gallops. They are aware of the possibilities of body position in space and of weight in movement. This then is the movement vocabulary children bring to the creation of new singing games and dances.

Children love to move. Often one of the first questions as a new song is being taught is, "Does it have a game?" This is the teacher's cue to say "No, but we can certainly make one up for it."[3]

In rhythm improvisation and composition the techniques begun in grade two of creating rhythms within forms are continued and are expanded to include the newly learned rhythm patterns of ♩ ♪, ♪♩ ♪ and ♪ ♩· .

Melodic improvisation, still largely question-answer phrases, should include the new notes low *la* and low *so*. Children may begin to compose and write down melodies now also—but such written composition follows considerably behind the music reading vocabulary. Given a specific rhythm and told which tone set to use (*m-r-d*, for example) and in what form to write (a-a-b-a or a-a-b-b, for instance) the third-grade child will have little difficulty composing. One direction this author has found to be absolutely essential is: "Be ready to sing your composition to the class." Only in this way can the teacher be assured that children are thinking sound as they notate.

To speak of "harmony" in a third-grade context may seem a bit overambitious. However, the foundations for theory must be laid early, and through creative activities they can be made enjoyable. The word "harmony" is used here to mean two or more musical ideas occurring simultaneously. Ostinati, descants and canons all contribute to the child's ability to deal with multiple musical ideas; and it is this latter skill that is needed for understanding theory at higher levels.

The simplest two-part improvisations are ostinati to be clapped, sung, or played on instruments to accompany songs. Children can create melodic ostinati by taking one phrase or motif from a song and using it as an accompaniment for that song. For example, to accompany "Ring Around the Rosy":

♩	♩	and	♩	♩	♩
s	m		s	s	d
Ros -	y		all	fall	down

The tonal center may also be used as a second part for some songs. Children set words that fit with the song. For "Old House" they might sing:

‖: ♪ ♩·   ♩ :‖

l_1 l_1 l_1
Tear it   down!

[3]For further information on creating dances with children see: Lois Choksy and David Brummitt, *120 Singing Games and Dances* (Englewood Cliffs, N.J., Prentice-Hall, 1987).

Not every attempt at creating a second part will "sound good." Indeed, children's and teachers' opinions as to what does "sound good" may at times differ. If the children create it, the children like it, and the children can perform it accurately, the teacher should attempt to suspend his or her somewhat more sophisticated tastes for the duration of that performance. The surest way to stifle any creative impulse is to attempt to "fix" the product.

MUSIC LISTENING

Throughout the early grades in Kodály programs, careful, attentive listening is encouraged. Because for the youngest children the voice is the most immediate instrument, the earliest listening experiences are the teacher's singing and the classmates' singing. Later, instruments—violin, trumpet, clarinet, flute—are introduced one at a time, wherever possible through live performance in the classroom by a teacher, an older child, or a parent. Children draw inferences about playing mode and the effect of instrument size and material on pitch and timbre.

In the third grade these experiences are extended to cover the basic instruments of the symphony orchestra and the children listen to orchestral settings of folk songs they have sung, such as Aaron Copland's "Simple Gifts" in his ballet suite *Appalachian Spring*.

No great amount of time is spent listening to records. The "listening experience" on record or tape is preceded by much singing of the theme to be listened to and is followed by further singing and analysis. All listening in a Kodály program is approached through singing.

CONCLUSION

As at every grade level care must be taken that children are singing correctly, in tune, and with good tone quality. It is important that each music period end with good singing rather than with skill teaching, music writing, or some other activity less likely to encourage a love of music in the young child. The basis of the music program is singing, and the music period should begin and end with a song musically performed.

SUGGESTED SONG LIST FOR GRADE THREE (ARRANGED BY TEACHING PURPOSE)

Some songs are suggested for more than one teaching purpose. An asterisk (*) indicates songs for which there are traditional games; two asterisks (**) indicate songs which may be sung in canon.

For rhythm patterns

♩. ♪:

** Chairs to Mend   The Bell Cow
* Stoopin' on the Window   Old Gray Goose
* Toodala   Perry Merry Dictum Dominee
                                    In the Bleak Midwinter

♪♩ ♪:

* Alabama Girl   Land of the Silver Birch
** I Got a Letter   Hop Up, My Ladies
New River Train   Do Lord
** Weevily Wheat
Nobody Knows

♪ ♩.:

Cotton-Eye Joe   Goodbye Brother
I Saw the Light

♩ ♪♪ ♪ and ♩. ♩. in ⁶⁄₈

I's the B'y   Bonavist' Harbour
It Rained a Mist   I Saw Three Ships
Joseph Dearest, Joseph Mild   ** Row, Row, Row Your Boat
* Oats, Peas, Beans and Barley Grow Oh Dear, What Can the Matter Be?

For low la *(with* do *tonal center)*

Rattlesnake   Old Mr. Rabbit
The Bell Cow   Cumberland Gap
Jim Along Josie (#2)

For low la *(with* la *tonal center)*

Land of the Silver Birch   ** I Got a Letter
Old House   Who Killed Cock Robin?

For low so

* I've Been to Haarlem   Cotton-Eye Joe
Old Gray Goose   Here She Comes So Fresh and Fair
Perry Merry Dictum Dominee   Hush, Little Baby
Swapping Song   Sweep Away
My Old Hammer   Mary Had a Baby
The Sally Buck   ** Lady Come Down and See
Frog Went A-Courtin'

Songs to prepare for learning fa *and* ti *in grade four*

Whistle, Daughter, Whistle   I's the B'y
Bonavist' Harbour   Stars Shinin'
New River Train   ** Brother John
Yankee Doodle   Aunt Rhody

Songs to prepare for ♩♩♩♩, ♩ ♩♩ *and* ♩♩ ♩ *in grade four*

  * Paw Paw Patch   * Old Brass Wagon
    Billy Came Over the Main White Ocean

Songs to prepare for ¾ *meter in grade 4*

    Lavender's Blue   ** Music Alone Shall Live

Some suggested listening

Song	Related Composition
Simple Gifts	Appalachian Spring (Aaron Copland)
Goodbye, Old Paint	Billy the Kid (Aaron Copland)
Greensleeves	Fantasia on Greensleeves (R. Vaughan Williams)
Peter Emberly	Miramichi Ballad (Kelsey Jones)

Other suggested listening

A Young Person's Guide to the Orchestra (Benjamin Britten)

Rhythmic Learning in Third Grade

MONTH	PREPARE THE NEW LEARNING	MAKE THE CHILDREN CONSCIOUSLY AWARE OF THE NEW LEARNING	REINFORCE THE NEW LEARNING THROUGH PRACTICE
September	Uneven arrangements of sounds over beats ♩. ♪		Review rhythmic learnings of grade 2: separated eighth-note patterns ♩ ♪♪ ♩ ♩ Conducting in 2's & 4's
October	♩. ♪ ♪♩ ♪ ○ upbeat	Present standard musical terms for rhythm durations: quarter note ♩ eighth note ♪ half note ♩	Review the use of the tie to extend duration, & half notes: ♩‿♩ = ♩
November	♩. ♪ ♪♩ ♪ ♪♩. upbeat	♩♩♩♩ = ○ ♩‿♩ = ○ (spoken "toe") Term: whole note ²₂ now shown as ²₄ ⁴₂ now shown as ⁴₄ & **C**	Review ostinato patterns ♩ ♪♪♩ ♩ & ♪♪ ♪♪♩ ♩ Notate & read songs with standard meter signs ²₄, ⁴₄ & **C**

MONTH	PREPARE THE NEW LEARNING	MAKE THE CHILDREN CONSCIOUSLY AWARE OF THE NEW LEARNING	REINFORCE THE NEW LEARNING THROUGH PRACTICE
December	𝅘𝅥. 𝅘𝅥𝅮 𝅘𝅥𝅮𝅘𝅥 𝅘𝅥𝅮 𝅘𝅥𝅮𝅘𝅥.	Present upbeat in $\frac{2}{4}$ & $\frac{4}{4}$ songs through conducting	Review $\frac{6}{8}$ songs with initial patterns of ♫♫ ♫♫ Notate the ♫♫ ti ti ti pattern. Notate & read using whole notes: 𝅝 toe
January	Compound duple meter $\binom{6}{8}$ Patterns: 𝅘𝅥. 𝅘𝅥. 𝅘𝅥 𝅘𝅥𝅮 𝅘𝅥 𝅘𝅥𝅮	Present 𝅘𝅥. 𝅘𝅥𝅮 tum - ti	Conduct songs in $\frac{2}{4}$ & $\frac{4}{4}$ beginning with upbeats
February	𝅘𝅥. 𝅘𝅥. 𝅘𝅥 𝅘𝅥𝅮 𝅘𝅥 𝅘𝅥𝅮	Present 𝅘𝅥𝅮𝅘𝅥 𝅘𝅥𝅮 ti - ta - ti syn-co - pa 𝅘𝅥𝅮𝅘𝅥. ti - tum	Notate & read music with upbeats. Notate & read songs with 𝅘𝅥. 𝅘𝅥𝅮
March	Prepare for new learnings in grade 4 ♬♬ , ♫♬ ♫♫	Present compound duple meter patterns 𝅘𝅥 𝅘𝅥𝅮 𝅘𝅥 𝅘𝅥𝅮 ta - ti - ta - ti & 𝅘𝅥. 𝅘𝅥. tum - tum	Notate, read & improvise using 𝅘𝅥. 𝅘𝅥𝅮 & 𝅘𝅥𝅮𝅘𝅥 𝅘𝅥𝅮
April	♬♬ , ♫♬ ♫♫ $\frac{3}{4}$ meter	$\frac{2}{\cdot}$ as the meter sign for compound duple meter	Notate & read songs with 𝅘𝅥𝅮 𝅘𝅥. Read songs in compound duple meter
May	♬♬ , ♫♬ ♫♫ $\frac{3}{4}$ meter		Use compound duple meter in improvising

Melodic Learning in Third Grade

MONTH	PREPARE THE NEW LEARNING	MAKE THE CHILDREN CONSCIOUSLY AWARE OF THE NEW LEARNING	REINFORCE THE NEW LEARNING THROUGH PRACTICE
September	low *la* & low *so*		Review the basic pentatonic notes *l-s—m-r-d* in F, C, & G key placements
October	low *la* & low *so*	Present low *la* in *do*-tonal center songs; octave *l,-l*	Read, write, improvise & compose using basic pentatonic tones in F-, C- & G-*do*
November	low *so*	Present low *so* in the *s,-l,-d* & *d-l,-s,* patterns -*do* tonal center	Notate & read songs with low *la*
December	low *la* in minor mode songs, as tonal center	Present low *so* in the *s,-d* pattern	Notate & read songs with the *s,-l,-d* & *d-l,-s,* patterns
January	low *la* as a tonal center; minor mode	Less common intervals with low *la* & low *so*: *l,-r*, *l,-m*, *s,-r*, *s,-m*	Notate & read songs with the *s,-d* interval in them. Improvise using the *s,-l,-d* pattern
February	high *do*, high *re* & high *mi*	Present low *la* as the tonal center in minor	Notate, read & improvise using all known intervals of the extended pentatonic
March	New learnings for grade 4: *so*-pentatonic songs, *re*-pentatonic songs	Present high *do*; octave *d-d'*. high *re* & high *mi*	Aurally distinguish between *la*-tonal center songs & *do*-tonal center songs. Notate & read *la*-pentatonic songs
April	*so*-pentatonic songs, *re*-pentatonic songs, songs with *fa*, songs with *ti*		Notate & read songs with high *do (re', mi')*
May	*so*-pentatonic songs, *re*-pentatonic songs, songs with *fa* & *ti*		Notate, read, improvise & compose using the extended pentatonic scale—*do* tonal center

6
Kodály for North American Schools: Grade Four

In grade four the children's experience with pentatonic modes should be extended to include the *so* and *re* scales in which there are a number of English-language folk songs.

In this grade, too, *fa* and *ti* may be introduced, completing the tones making up the major and minor diatonic scales. The concepts of keys and key signatures will be a large part of the year's work. Key signatures for F, G, D, and B♭ should be introduced, and if the children's prior reading has been restricted to F, G, and C and their related minors, it should now be expanded to include D and B♭ major and their related minors, B and G.

RHYTHMIC LEARNING FOR GRADE FOUR

The rhythmic material for the grade consists of common sixteenth note patterns, ♪♪♪♪ , ♪ ♪♪ , and ♪♪ ♪ , the new meter $\frac{3}{4}$, simple triple, and rhythm patterns in that meter, and further experience with compound duple, including the introduction of the standard meter sign, $\frac{6}{8}$.

Sixteenth Notes

Sixteenth notes in groups of four ♪♪♪♪ and in combination with eighth notes ♪ ♪♪ and ♪♪ ♪ may be introduced early in fourth grade. A simple but effective folk song for teaching the four sixteenth notes pattern is "Old Brass Wagon":

Cir-cle to the left,   Old brass wag - on

The children should:

1. Sing and tap the beat to determine how many beats are in a measure.
2. Clap the rhythm for the part that goes "old brass wagon."

3. Sing that part in ti-ta's so that the teacher may place it on the chalkboard.
4. Decide what kind of note is on the word "left"—one sound on one beat—a ta. This is placed on the board as well:

At this point the teacher asks:

"How many sounds are we singing on the first beat?"

The children sing the phrase again to discover the answer: Four!

"When we sing four even sounds on one beat, they look like this: 🎵
They are called "sixteenth notes" because they are twice as fast as eighth notes. We sing them with the syllables[1]

ti - ka - ti - ka

The children should at this point practice notating the four sixteenth notes pattern and read further songs containing it before going on to patterns combining sixteenth and eighth notes.

To derive these patterns, an eighth note ostinato is useful:

Ostinato:

Rhythm:

Bil - ly came   o - ver the   main white   o - cean

"Is there any place in this phrase where we are clapping one sound but singing two?" ["Billy" and "over"]
    "When there are two sounds over one eighth note, one ti, what are they?" [sixteenth notes, tika:

ti - ka - ti

For the reverse of this pattern the same process is followed using a song such as "How Many Miles to Babylon?"

Ostinato:

Rhythm:

How   man - y miles   to   Bab - y - lon

[1] In Hungary the syllables "tiri-tiri" are used. However, Hungarian children strongly roll their *r* sounds, giving a crisp and distinct sound to each sixteenth note. English speaking children tend to swallow the *r* sound, producing an extremely unrhythmic voicing on this pattern. Instrumental music teacher and former Director of the Kodály Musical Training institute at Hartt School of Music, Jerry Jaccard, suggested the use of the above syllables. They have been used successfully by this author for several years now.

The new pattern is spoken as

ti - ti - ka

Triple Meter

Triple meter, $\frac{3}{4}$, is taught in the same manner as $\frac{2}{4}$ and $\frac{4}{4}$ by finding the accented beats and counting from them to discover how many beats are in each measure.

However, there are some potential problems in the teaching of $\frac{3}{4}$. It is not the most common meter in English language folk songs, so children's experience with it is probably less than with $\frac{2}{4}$, $\frac{4}{4}$ and $\frac{6}{8}$. Also, a large number of $\frac{3}{4}$ songs begin with an upbeat. Although children at this point have had the upbeat in duple and quadruple meters, to teach a new meter through songs with upbeats is not easy.

The author suggests that a small core of $\frac{3}{4}$ songs *without* upbeat be used for the initial teaching of this meter, and that only after the children can easily distinguish between duple and triple meter songs should triple meter with anacrusis be introduced.

There is one further problem in that some $\frac{3}{4}$ music tends to move *one* to the measure rather than three. This is particularly true of songs in fast tempo. For initial teaching of $\frac{3}{4}$, tempo must be slow or moderate. If a song does not lend itself to these tempi it should not be used for this purpose.

One possible beginning triple-meter song without upbeat is the Texan folk song "Billy Barlow":

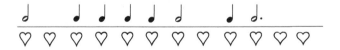

Let's   go   hunt - ing   says   Risk   -   y   Rob.

Other possibilities are "Lavender's Blue" and "My Country 'Tis of Thee."

Once they know the song well, children can be led to derive the meter by:

1. tapping accented beats louder;
2. calling the accented beats "one" and counting the beats between the accented beats.

The rhythm and beats may then be placed on the chalkboard as they are performed and sung:

One child should place the accent marks under the stressed beats and a second child could draw the bar lines where they belong before the stressed beats. When this much is done, the class can hear and see how many beats there are in a measure, and the number "3" should be placed at the left in the time-signature position.

The completed exercise:

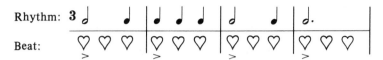

At this point the dotted half note may be introduced, using the same song. Children will feel the three beats of the final note of the song ♩. . This can be derived through tied notes:

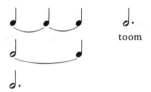

It is possible that fourth-grade children will have enough comprehension of fractional parts to perceive that ♩ is one half of ♩ and that a dot in music adds one-half the value of the note it follows. However, if this understanding does not come at this time, it is enough that children realized the dotted half, said "toom," lasts as long as three quarter notes tied or as a half note and quarter note tied.

Triple meter should be reinforced by movement and by conducting. A singing game such as "Coffee Grows on White Oak Trees" is excellent for helping children feel the difference between duple and triple. The first part of this song is in a moderate $\frac{3}{4}$ tempo and the children move with a waltz-like step to it, while the second part is in a fast duple with sharply contrasting square dance steps. To conduct $\frac{3}{4}$ children move arms down, out, up:

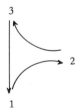

Conducting should be a regular part of all classes.

Compound Meter

It is in grade four that the teaching of $\frac{6}{8}$ meter—begun in kindergarten and first grade and continued throughout second and third—is completed and the standard meter sign is introduced.

The cowboy song "Go Slow, Little Dogies" is a good one for this purpose. It holds no tonal difficulties, being pentatonic, and it includes only the most common $\frac{6}{8}$ rhythm patterns: ♩♩♩ ♩♩♩ and ♩♪♩♪ .

"We have discovered that $\frac{2}{4}$ is $\frac{2}{4}$ and that $\frac{3}{4}$ is $\frac{3}{4}$. The quarter-note beat is represented in the meter sign by the "4" on the bottom. In "Go Slow, Little Dogies" and the other songs in the same meter we are feeling two beats to the measure, and our meter sign is $\frac{2}{4}$.. What number can we substitute for the dotted quarter?"

The children will make suggestions, but there will be no agreement among them.

"Musicians had the same problem with this meter that *you* are having. There *is* no number to equal the dotted quarter note, the beat note. If we cannot use the *beat* note as the lower part of the meter sign, is there anything else we could use? A regular recurring part?" [the pulse— ♩♩♩ ♩♩♩]

Go   slow   lit - tle   dog - ies,   stop   mil - ing   a - round,

"What number represents the pulse?" [8, for the eighth note]
"How many of these can we have in a measure?" [six]

The meter sign for this kind of music is shown first as $\frac{6}{\flat}$ and then as $\frac{6}{8}$, six pulses to the measure with the eighth note as the pulse.

The terms "compound meter" and "simple meter" may be taught at this time and the distinction made that in all simple meters the pulses move in twos over the beat, while in all compound meters the pulses move in threes over the beat:

Simple Meters

Compound Meters

Later, other compound meters will be introduced—$\frac{9}{8}$, $\frac{12}{8}$ and $\frac{6}{4}$—to reinforce this learning.

Children should now notate using $\frac{6}{8}$ meter, read from standard notation songs in $\frac{6}{8}$, and use $\frac{6}{8}$ in their creative exercises.

MELODIC LEARNING FOR GRADE FOUR

One problem that the author has found exists for some teachers is a seeming inability to work well within any mode other than the major diatonic scale. This is understandable since most music teachers have as a requirement of their profession a strong pianistic background. Such training has the effect of putting aural "blinders" on teachers who hear other modes and other scales as "altered scales" or "incomplete scales," and *hearing* them in this way, they *teach* them in this way. It is not possible in a book to correct the erroneous ear training of some generations, but tetratonic, pentatonic, pentachordal, and hexachordal scales are neither "incomplete" nor "gapped" scales—they are in their own forms quite perfect and complete. Children can and do perceive this if the teacher does not impose his or her own preconceived notions of tonality on them.

It is because of the above that the author feels it important to introduce *la*-pentatonic songs in third grade and the less common *so*-pentatonic and *re*-pentatonic modes in fourth grade. No child with sufficient experience in these modes will ever have to live within the straitjacket of nineteenth-century diatonic major-minor tonality.

THE RIDDLE SONG

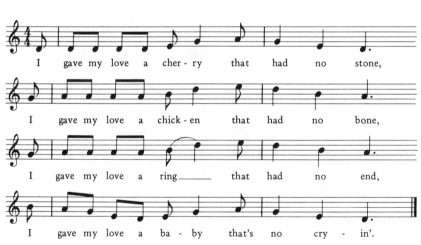

The above song is a beautiful Appalachian example of the *so*-pentatonic mode. It should be taught by rote to the children and its "riddle" discussed and enjoyed. It may be compared to another riddle song—"Perry Merry Dictum"—learned in grade three.

When the children are singing it well, the teacher may guide them to find out what its tone set, its scale, is. Given the sound of *do* (G), children should derive the *solfa* for phrases two and three. The teacher lists each *solfa* syllable on the board ladder style as the children sing it: first *do*, then *re*, *mi*, *so*, and *la*, shown as:

l

s

m

r

d

The children then complete the song to find on what note it ends, and the remaining pitches are added to the ladder:

l'

s'

m

r

d

l

(s)

The last note, *so,* the tonal center, the *key* note of this song, is circled. The children have discovered that a song does not have to end on *do* or even on *la;* that *so* too can be a tonal center.

They should practice singing the *so*-pentatonic scale and sing other songs in this mode, such as "Handsome Molly."

Re-pentatonic can be introduced in the same manner, using the song "Shady Grove":

Shad - y Grove,   my true love,   Shad - y Grove I   know;

Shad - y Grove,   my true love, I'm   bound for Shad - y   Grove.

In this instance C will be given as *do* and the third phrase derived first. The children will discover the scale to be:

d

l

s

m

(r)

with the final note, *re,* the tonal center. Other songs in this mode should be sung and their scales derived.

At this point the scales for all pentatonic modes should be sung from the same starting pitch:[2]

d'	*r'*	*m'*	*s'*	*l'*
	d	*r*		*s*
l		*d*	*m*	
s	*l*		*r*	*m*
	s	*l*	*d*	*r*
m		*s*		*d*
r	*m*		*l*	
ⓓ	ⓡ	ⓜ	ⓢ	ⓛ

The bottom three notes of each of these scales comprise the typical cadence for that pentatonic mode.

Children can become very proficient at singing these pentatonic scales. The aural skill of distinguishing between major seconds and minor thirds and singing each correctly in each scale is one that contributes much to later interval identification and understanding of scale construction, even though children do not at this point call them "major second" or "minor third" but refer to the former as a "whole step" and to the latter as a "step and a half."

INTRODUCING *FA* AND THE FLAT

Many of the rote songs of grade three will have included *fa*. From these, several should be selected which have the repeated *fa* in a strong position. For example, "Joseph Dearest, Joseph Mild" (third line):

f   f   f   s   f   m r

God will give you your re - ward,

or "New River Train" (third line):

m   m   d   r m   f   f   f f f   s   s   s

Same old train that＿ brought you here gon-na take you back,

Perhaps one of the best songs for initial teaching of *fa* is the American folk song "Whistle, Daughter, Daughter" which contains only the notes *so, fa, mi, re* and *do,* and contains *fa* in a descending line:

Whis - tle, Daugh-ter, whis - tle, and you shall have a   cow.
I can't whis -tle moth- er be - cause I don't know how.

[2]To the author's knowledge there are no North American folk songs in the *mi*-pentatonic mode. However, once children know the other pentatonic modes they will ask about this one, and can sing its scale.

Several teaching periods should be spent working on familiar rote songs including the *fa* before it is brought to the conscious awareness of the children, its notation shown, and its *solfa* name and hand sign given. Particular attention should be paid to in-tune singing of the *mi-fa* half step and to making children feel the smallness of the interval.

The initial lesson in which children see *fa* in staff notation should be in the key of C or G so that no key signature will be necessary. Using the above song, the steps might be as follows:

1. Teacher and children derive the *known solfa* notation on the chalkboard in contour notation, singing ''hmm'' for the unknown note:

2. Teacher then gives the hand sign for the new note. Class sings, again using ''hmm'' but with the correct hand sign.
3. Teacher sings the song through in *solfa* using the new syllable *fa*.
4. Class sings the song using the new syllable *fa*.

The lesson should be followed up by the children's writing the song in G-*do* staff notation, the *fa* in red for emphasis. As a guide, the teacher may place on the chalkboard:

The same exercise should then be written in C-*do*. A child might give placement of the first three notes on the board to help the class get started. At the end of the writing period the entire song should be placed in staff notation on the chalkboard so that there is immediate correction of any mistake.

In a subsequent lesson, after children are singing, reading, and writing *fa* easily in C- and G-*do*, it will be time to introduce the meaning of the one-flat key signature necessary for *fa* in F-*do*. In order to do this the children first sing the song in G-*do*. The teacher should focus the children's attention on the smallness of the *mi-fa* interval and identify it to them at this point as a "half step." This can be reinforced with *solfa* discs on the chalkboard:

Construct a scale of children in front of the class, being sure that the children representing *mi* and *fa* stand close together:

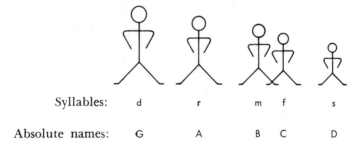

Syllables:	d	r	m	f	s
Absolute names:	G	A	B	C	D

Have the class sing the song with syllables while the teacher touches each child at those points in the song where his or her note occurs. The teacher is "playing" the song on the child-scale. Then have the children sing the absolute note names for each child in the scale, calling *do* G. The song should be sung again, this time with absolute note names as the teacher taps the child representing each note.

This may now be related to *solfa* discs and absolute note name bars on the chalkboard.

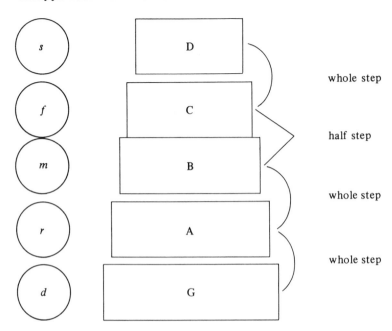

It is important that the scale pattern "whole-step, whole-step, half-step, whole-step" be impressed upon the children, and that they understand that *mi-fa* is a half step, forever, and that in absolutes B-C and E-F are always half-steps.

If they can sing the pattern of whole steps and half steps with ease—

do	to	*re*	is	a	whole	step,	*re*	to	*mi*	is	a	whole	step,
G	to	A	is	a	whole	step,	A	to	B	is	a	whole	step,

mi	to	*fa*	is	a	half	step,	*fa*	to	*so*	is	a	whole	step.
B	to	C	is	a	half	step,	C	to	D	is	a	whole	step.

—it is time to introduce the concept of the function of the flat in key signature.

Having the child-scale stand again, the teacher may suggest singing the song in F-*do,* and ask the children "What additional note will we need?" Another child will have to join the child-scale to be F. The class will probably realize that for this song in F the note D will not be needed, so that child may sit down. It is important that none of the other children have changed their positions. The scale will look like this:

The children should then sing the F-scale with *solfa* names and the teacher ask, "What is wrong with our scale?"

The children, who have been taught to expect the small step between *mi* and *fa,* will see that it is now between *fa* and *so.* Reverting to absolute names, the teacher should sing or play on a keyboard the song as it sounds in the key of F with a B♮. Children should both *see* that B next to C forms the wrong scale pattern and *hear* that B sounds "too high," that a lower sound is needed. The teacher asks:

"What must we do with B if it is too close to C?"

The children will suggest moving the B closer to A. The teacher may then say:

"B is an 'absolute' note; it is a half step from C forever. We need a new note that is related to B but is lower. The new note is 'B-flat.' It is on the same place on the staff as B, but because it has a flat sign in front of it, its sound is a half step lower than the sound of B."[3]

The above can be made clearer by using *solfa* discs and absolute note name bars on the chalkboard:

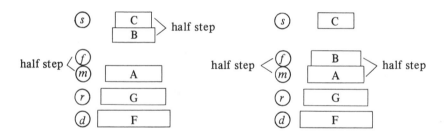

From this it is very evident that a new note, B♭, was necessary to make the half step in *solfa* and the half step in absolute note names occur at the same level of the scale ladder.

Using the same song examples, the *solfa* discs, and the absolute note name bars, the teacher may at this point introduce the new key "B♭-*do*":

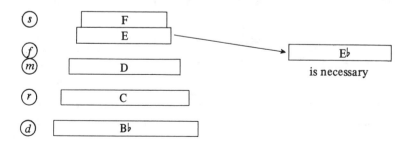

[3]The author believes children should not be told that a flat "lowers the pitch." B♭ is not a B lowered, but a totally new pitch with a different frequency. A flat sign gives us a new note, one half-step lower than the one usually shown on that line or in that space.

and the new key "E♭-*do*":

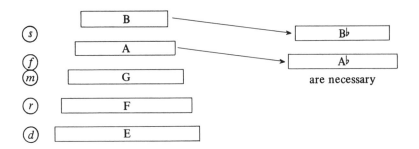

The children should be able to perceive both aurally and visually the need for flatted notes to produce the correct scale patterns.

They can also discover that the last flat in the key signature is always *fa*, and that by counting down four places they can tell where *do* is with any number of flats in the key signature:

—and they will eventually realize that the next-to-last flat is always *do*.

INTRODUCING *TI* AND THE SHARP

When the principle of scale construction for the lower tetrachord is firmly in place and children are working well with flats in key signature, the teacher may move on to the introduction of *ti* and the need for the sharp in some key signatures.

An excellent song for introducing *ti* is "Yankee Doodle":

The first phrase of this song *ends* with the new note *ti*, while the second phrase contains *ti* in the third measure as a part of the broken V chord and as the leading tone to *do*.

The procedure is much the same as for introducing *fa*. The rhythm and meter are first derived and placed on the board, then the *solfa* for the known notes is placed under the notation. The unknown note is highlighted by a question mark and the teacher asks:

"Is the new note higher or lower than *do*?'' [lower]
"Is the new note higher or lower than *la*?'' [higher]

At this point the syllable *ti* is given and the new hand sign shown:

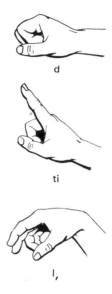

The hand sign for *ti* points up toward *do,* indicating the smallness of the step between the two notes. The song may then be written on the staff by the children in both F- and C-*do*. The smallness of the *ti-do* interval must be emphasized, and the children learn that *ti* to *do* is a half step like *mi* to *fa*.

When the *ti* is easily sung, recognized, and writen in F- and C-*do*, it is time to introduce the concept of sharp in key signature. A song using only the notes of the upper tetrachord is the easiest vehicle through which to do this:

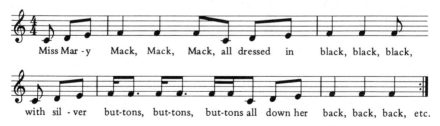

Again, a child-scale should be constructed:

In this case the *ti* and *do* must stand close together to point up the smallness of the interval.

The song should be sung in *solfa* and in absolute note names as the teacher taps in song order, the children representing each note. After singing the absolute note names in F, the teacher may ask the class: "What must we do to make these notes fit G-*do*?" The children will see that the fourth child, G, is now *do* and that this new *do* and the new *ti* (the third child) are no longer close together, as they must be:

This can be shown on the chalkboard also:

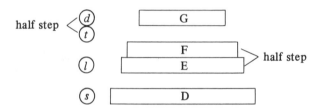

It is important that the teacher either sing or play the song with an F♯ at this point so that the children hear as well as see the need for a higher pitch. The new, higher note is F♯ and is shown on staff in the same place as F but with the sharp sign ♯ in front of it.

The class should then sing the song again in absolute note names in G-*do*, using the name F-sharp where it occurs.

Initially in the music writing of *ti* in G-*do* the sharp should be shown in the first space, where children sing it. Children may then be told that the one-sharp key signature always means G-*do*. In the lessons that follow, children can be shown that in printed music the one sharp is usually placed on the fifth line of the staff, rather than in the first space. If they understand that the one sharp in the key signature means that F is always sharped wherever it occurs in the song, the more usual key signature will present little added difficulty.

As scale patterns become firmly learned it may not be necessary to use children as scale steps. However, the more concrete the beginning steps, the better able the children will be to cope with more abstract learnings at later stages.

Using songs of wider range, the children can now derive the key signatures for D-*do* and A-*do*:

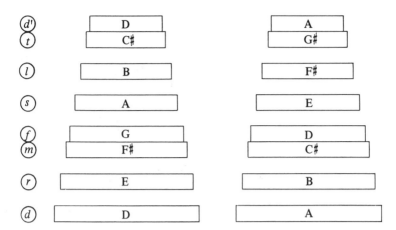

Through music writing and reading in these keys they will discover that the last sharp is always *ti,* a half step below *do.* Knowing this they will be able to "find *do*" even in keys not previously studied.

D - *do*   A - *do*   E - *do*

The fact that children can "find *do*" in any key does not mean that they will read and notate with equal facility in all keys. In each new key placement they must be prepared before reading. A "flying note"—a note head on a pointer—can be used to lead children through scale, intervals, and melodic turns of the song to be read before they open their books:

The "hand-staff"—the use of one's own hand as a reminder of staff placement of notes—is also extremely useful in practicing different key placements. To prepare the children for reading or notating in the key of D, for example, the teacher could lead them through the scale and various intervals, using the pointer finger of the right hand against the "lines" and "spaces" of the left hand:

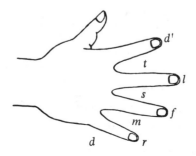

MINOR MODE SCALES

Ease in reading and writing in the minor will always follow at some distance reading and writing in the related major keys, simply because so much more song material exists in English in the major. Nevertheless, some effort should be expended to ensure that children do sing, read, and notate minor mode songs. Folk song material can be augmented by some of the beautiful composed songs in minor, such as this canon by Praetorious:

Rise up O   Flame___ and___ by___ thy___light   glow   ing,

Only the natural minor mode is used for reading and writing at this level, although some of the rote song material used may be in melodic or harmonic minor scales.

IMPROVISING AND COMPOSING

For all intents and purposes, children who have been in a consistent Kodály program since kindergarten are functionally musically literate by the end of grade four. However, genuine literacy implies the ability not just to read but also to express one's own thoughts verbally and on paper. True musical literacy implies the same skill. At any time, the musical vocabulary with which children improvise and compose is always smaller than the vocabulary with which they can read and notate, and that, in turn, is smaller still than the rote vocabulary. However, in all three of these levels–rote, reading-writing, and improvising-composing—creative activities can be a part of the music program.

At the "rote" level, new verses may be created and dances may be invented for songs far beyond the musical reading and writing vocabulary. These are legitimate forms of musical creativity.

One activity the author has found children to enjoy immensely at this rote-learning level is the "finish the song" game. Using a song the children have neither sung nor heard before, the teacher presents it by rote, all except for one phrase. The words and rhythm of that phrase are taught, but not its melody:

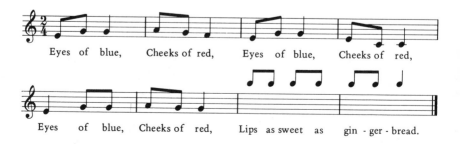

Eyes of blue,   Cheeks of red,   Eyes of blue,   Cheeks of red,

Eyes   of   blue,   Cheeks of red,   Lips as sweet as   gin - ger - bread.

Some of the phrases made up by fourth graders to end this song were:

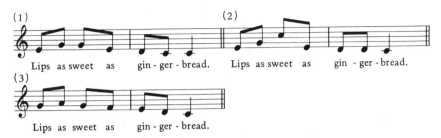

The actual ending of the folk song is:

It is not necessary even to teach this "correct" ending. The purpose of the exercise is the process, not the product.

At the reading and writing level—the level of the most recently learned notes—the creative activity must be much more structured. The teacher may ask a musical question incorporating the "new" note or pattern, and the students try to give answer phrases, also using the new note or pattern:

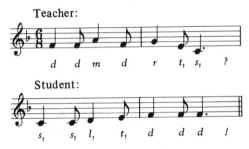

In such question-answer phrases the student usually takes the rhythm supplied by the teacher and, frequently, uses the last note given by the teacher (*re, ti* or *so*—the notes of the V chord) as his or her starting point.

Creating with pencil and paper—composing—should be done only with the notes and rhythms known best by the children. The vocabulary of composition follows by many months the reading and writing vocabulary, and by years the rote vocabulary.

In fourth grade children will probably be able to do some carefully guided composition using the *do*-pentatonic scale, given the meter, rhythm, and form. Usually with a child of this age only one aspect of the music is not given by the teacher. A melody may be given, all in whole notes, and the children asked to organize it into rhythm; or a rhythm may be given, a tone set established, and the children asked to compose a melody.

The most important ingredient for creativity in the classroom is an acceptant atmosphere. This does *not* mean uncritical acceptance of everything and anything children produce. A measure with seven beats in a $\frac{4}{4}$ song is incorrect. The student must change either the rhythm or the meter. It *does* mean that children's work is to be valued; that they know their efforts are being carefully studied by the teacher. To suggest a correction shows more interest and knowledge on the teacher's part than a word "Good!" scrawled across the top of a paper.

All compositions should be performed for the class. Music is sound, not just notes on paper. At the beginning, children should be allowed to sing their own compositions. Later, they should give them to other children to perform. It is amazing how much more clearly and accurately notation is done if someone else is going to have to read it.[4]

LISTENING TO MUSIC

At the fourth grade level in Hungary what might be called a structured "listening program" begins, and it begins with music of the Viennese Classical period, the music of Mozart and Haydn. It is felt that the flowing melodies and simple harmonies of these composers are a good starting point for children raised on a diet of folk song.

For the same reasons, these composers are the author's choice for early listening lessons; in years of working with young children the author has never had a class that did not appear to enjoy their music.

All listening in a Kodály classroom is approached through singing. Themes are sung in *solfa,* memorized, and notated before being heard from record or tape.

Sometimes listening might be initiated as a reading and writing exercise:

1. The teacher sings on "loo":

2. The children sing the melody back in *solfa* and the teacher places it on the chalkboard:

3. The children notate this in F-*do* on manuscript paper.
4. The children sing and memorize what they have written.
5. The teacher asks them to sing it again, and this time he or she sings a countermelody:

4For further suggestions on improvising and composing with children see: Lois Choksy, *The Kodály Context* (Englewood Cliffs, N.J.: Prentice-Hall, 1984) pp. 75-86.

The children will no doubt recognize this as "Twinkle, Twinkle, Little Star." This lower voice part was put to it by Mozart in his set of variations for keyboard on "Ah! Vous dirai-je, Maman." It has been given here in the key of F because children can sing both parts in that key; in the original it is in C-major. These Mozart variations are an excellent starting point for children. Knowing and singing both the melody and the harmonization, they can find one or the other of these in almost every variation.

For introducing the music of Haydn to children the possibilities are so many that choice of one or two is not easy. One work that has proven effective with children is his *Cello Concerto in D Major,* Op. 101. The slow movements of most Haydn symphonies are good material for teaching, as are some of the keyboard pieces and chamber music. One can hardly go wrong with any choice, but the author recommends avoiding those compositions whose principal appeal is that they have a story attached to them—*The Surprise* Symphony, *The Clock* Symphony, *The Farewell* Symphony. For too many years children have listened to amusing–and largely untrue—stories in "music appreciation" lessons rather than to music.

The author has one other favorite composition for teaching at this level: the last movement of The *Trout* Quintet by Schubert. The children can sing the Schubert lied, "The Trout," first, then hear recordings of it as sung by a soprano or baritone, and finally, hear the variations on the melody as Schubert incorporated it into his Quintet.

Only four listening examples have been suggested here. Others may certainly be used in addition to or in place of the ones suggested, but it must be realized that any listening example should be heard many times, not just once, and that it is preferable to listen in depth to one work than merely to "hear" many.

CONCLUSION

A well-rounded music program for grade four will include much singing in unison, in canon, and in two parts. Attention must be given, as always, to singing with artistry. Dynamics and tone quality should be stressed in each lesson.

Children should by the end of fourth grade have the skills of basic music literacy, although they will still be acquiring the skills needed for improvisation and composition.

Music listening will play a larger part than previously in these lessons, although it should always be an active rather than a passive listening.

Above all, children should be encouraged to feel the beauty of the music they make, not simply to understand the mechanics of it.

SUGGESTED SONG LIST FOR GRADE FOUR (ARRANGED BY TEACHING PURPOSE)

Some songs are suggested for more than one teaching purpose. An asterisk (*) indicates songs with traditional games or dances; two asterisks (**) indicate songs which may be sung in canon.

For rhythm patterns

♩♫♫♫

Love Somebody
* Old Brass Wagon
Shanghai Chicken

* Golden Ring Around Susan
Chicken on a Fence Post

♩♫♫ and ♫♫♩

* How Many Miles to Babylon?
* Skip to My Lou
The Old Chisholm Trail

Billy Came Over the Main White Ocean
* Paw Paw Patch

$\frac{3}{4}$ meter (without upbeat):

Billy Barlow
Rain, Come Wet Me
* Green Gravel
** Oh, How Lovely
** Rise Up, O Flame

Lavender's Blue
Scarborough Fair
** Music Alone Shall Live
* Coffee Grows on White Oak Trees
Derry Ding Dong Dason

$\frac{3}{4}$ meter (with upbeat):

Goodbye, Old Paint
Streets of Laredo

There's a Hole in My Bucket
Yonder Mountain

do-*pentatonic*

Blood on the Saddle
* Coffee Grows on White Oak Trees

The Sally Buck

la-*pentatonic*

Land of the Silver Birch
Big-Eyed Rabbit
Hush, My Babe

Wayfaring Stranger
Walter Jumped a Fox

so-*pentatonic*

I Gave My Love a Cherry
Johnson Boys
There was a Little Oak

Handsome Molly
Yonder She Comes

re-*pentatonic*

Shady Grove
* Old Betty Larkin

* Maria

Songs with fa *and without* ti

Whistle, Daughter, Whistle
Cradle Hymn
Christmas Greetings
I Saw Three Ships
Brother John
New River Train
Un Canadien errant

Stars Shinin'
It Rained a Mist
Fire Down Below
Joseph Dearest, Joseph Mild
The Alberta Homesteader
Ah! Si mon moine voulait danser!

Songs with **fa** *and* **ti**

Bonavist' Harbor
The Ryans and the Pittmans
Blow, Ye Winds in the Morning

Yankee Doodle
I's the B'y
The Kelligrews Soiree

Songs to prepare for grade five learnings

meters—$\frac{6}{4}$, $\frac{9}{8}$, $\frac{2}{2}$:

Down in the Valley ($\frac{9}{8}$)

Sailing on the Ocean ($\frac{2}{2}$)

My Willie Is Brave ($\frac{6}{4}$)

scales:
minor without alteration:
Brave Wolfe
The Birch Tree

Rise Up, O Flame
Rose Red

minor with *si*:
Ah, Poor Bird

Mam'zelle Zizi

Some suggested listening examples

Mozart: Variations on "Ah! Vous dirai-je, Maman"
        "Eine Kleine Nachtmusik" (second movement)
Haydn: Cello Concerto in D Major, op. 101, 3rd movement, Allegro (Rondo)
        The *Emperor* Quartet (last movement)
Schubert: Lied—"The Trout"
        The Trout Quintet (last movement)

Rhythmic Learning in Fourth Grade

MONTH	PREPARE THE NEW LEARNING	MAKE THE CHILDREN CONSCIOUSLY AWARE OF THE NEW LEARNING	REINFORCE THE NEW LEARNING THROUGH PRACTICE
September	♫♫ ♫ ♫		Ostinato of ♩♩ performed with simple meter songs; of ♩♩♩ performed with compound meter songs. Review terms "beat" & "pulse"
October	♫♫ ♫ ♫	Four even sounds on one beat as sixteenth notes as ♫♫ spoken as tika-tika	Review ♩. ♪, ♪♩ ♪ & ♪ ♩. Notate & read songs using ♫♫ tika-tika

MONTH	PREPARE THE NEW LEARNING	MAKE THE CHILDREN CONSCIOUSLY AWARE OF THE NEW LEARNING	REINFORCE THE NEW LEARNING THROUGH PRACTICE
November	$\frac{6}{8}$ standard meter sign	[♩♪♪♪ *ti ka-ti*] & [♪♩♪♪ *ti - ti ka*] derived from ostinato [♫ ♫ rhythm]	Notate & read songs using [rhythm figures], [rhythm], & [rhythm]. Improvise patterns with [rhythm]
December	$\frac{3}{4}$ meter & ♩.	Derive the meter sign for duple as $\underset{\flat}{\frac{6}{\bullet}} = \frac{6}{8}$ (taken from pulse note ♪ rather than beat note ♩.)	Notate, read & improvise using [rhythm], [rhythm] & [rhythm]
January	$\frac{3}{4}$ meter & ♩.		Read $\frac{6}{8}$ songs from standard notation. Use $\frac{6}{8}$-meter sign correctly in notating
February		Derive $\frac{3}{4}$ meter in songs without upbeat. ♩. as equal to ♩ ♩ ♩	Notate & read in $\frac{6}{8}$. Construct rhythm compositions in $\frac{6}{8}$ meter
March		$\frac{3}{4}$ in songs with upbeat	Conduct $\frac{3}{4}$ meter. Notate & read songs in $\frac{3}{4}$ meter
April	New learnings for grade 5: $\frac{6}{4}, \frac{9}{8}, \frac{2}{2} = \Phi$		Conduct $\frac{3}{4}$ songs beginning with upbeats. Notate & read $\frac{3}{4}$ songs with upbeats
May	New learnings for grade 5: $\frac{6}{4}, \frac{9}{8}, \frac{2}{2} = \Phi$		

Melodic Learning in Fourth Grade

September	*so*-pentatonic scales. New note: *fa*	*so* as tonal center in some songs. The *so*-pentatonic scale	Review *do*-pentatonic & *la*-pentatonic scales. Read & notate songs in these scales
October	*re*-pentatonic scale. New notes: *fa* & *ti*	*re* as tonal center in some songs. The *re*-pentatonic scale	Notate & read songs in *so*- & *re*-pentatonic

MONTH	PREPARE THE NEW LEARNING	MAKE THE CHILDREN CONSCIOUSLY AWARE OF THE NEW LEARNING	REINFORCE THE NEW LEARNING THROUGH PRACTICE
November	New notes: *fa* & *ti*. The *m-f* half step	Derive the place of *fa*, as higher than *mi* & lower than *so*. Learn its *solfa* syllable, hand sign & place on staff in C- & G-*do*	Sing all pentatonic scale from the same starting pitch, using *solfa* & hand signs. Identify "whole steps" & "step & a half" in each
December	Scale patterns of whole steps & half steps. New note: *ti*	Present the scale pattern "whole step, whole step, half step" for the lower tetrachord. Children learn that *m-f* is a half step "forever"	Notate & read songs with the new note *fa*. Show the tetrachord pattern with child scales & *solfa* discs
January	Scale patterns of whole steps & half steps. Term: "Key Signature." New note: *ti*	Discover the need for a new note, B♭, in the key of F to produce the correct tetrachord pattern in *solfa*	Practice singing whole step/half step scale arrangement from *do* to *so*. Notate in F-*do* using the flat sign
February	Scale patterns of whole steps & half steps. Key signatures for B♭- & E♭-*do*. New note: *ti*	Using *solfa* discs & absolute note name bars, construct scales on B♭ & on E♭ for *d-r-mf-s*, following tetrachord pattern. New keys: B♭-*do* & E♭-*do*	Read songs in F-*do* from standard notation & key signature. Practice "finding *do*" in other keys with flats in their key signatures
March	New note: *ti*. Upper tetrachord pattern. Scales of G-*do*, D-*do*, & A-*do*	Derive the place of *ti*, as lower than *do* & higher than *la*. Learn its *solfa* syllable, hand sign & place on staff in C- & F-*do*	Notate & read songs in F-, B♭- & E♭-*do*. Notate & read songs with ti in F- & C-*do*. Sing songs with ti in *solfa* & with hand signs
April	Prepare for grade 5 learning through songs in the natural minor scale	Present the scale pattern for the upper tetrachord: *s-l-td'*: whole step, whole step, half step. Children learn that *t-d'* is a half step "forever" & discover the need for a new note, F♯, in the key of G to produce the correct tetrachord pattern in *solfa*	Compare the two tetrachords. Notate & read songs in G-*do* with F♯
May	Natural minor scale. Harmonic minor scale	Using *solfa* discs & absolute note name bars, construct scales in G-, D- & A-*do*	Notate & read songs in G-, D- & A-*do*. Practice "finding *do*" from key signatures with sharps

7
Kodály for North American Schools: Grades Five and Six

Fifth and sixth grades are years of practice and of putting to use the skill and concept learnings of the first four grades. There is further material to be learned, but the foundation of music literacy has by now been laid, and the primary work of the last two elementary years should be the securing and the reinforcing of this literacy. The known skills and concepts must now be applied to increasingly sophisticated song material, including that of well-known composers. Part-singing should occupy a portion of every lesson.

GRADE FIVE

The new material for the grade includes, in rhythm, the dotted-eighth–sixteenth note patterns ♩.♪ (tim-ka) and ♪♩. (tik-um), cut time ($\frac{2}{2}$), compound meters $\frac{3}{8}$, $\frac{9}{8}$, $\frac{12}{8}$, and $\frac{6}{4}$, and rhythmic augmentation and diminution. Melodic learning should include classification of songs, by sight and sound, as belonging to major and minor scales, scale construction, major and minor interval identification, the natural ♮, and the sharped *so (si)* needed for harmonic minor. There should be some diagramming of song form and creation of simple melodies within known scales and forms. If absolute note names were introduced in grade three and reinforced in grade four, reading and writing in absolute notes may be expanded now to include all remaining keys.

Music theory will now begin to require more teaching time. Children should learn scale patterns for major and minor scales and sing and identify intervals by size and type, major or minor. Tonic, dominant, and subdominant chords and their inversions are introduced and are used to accompany singing.

Part singing should occupy a portion of every lesson, with descants, rounds and canons sung in three and four voices, and much other material sung in two parts.

The listening program extends, historically, from the music of Bach and Handel to the period of Beethoven.

RHYTHMIC LEARNING FOR GRADE FIVE

Augmentation and Diminution

As with all musical skills, augmentation and diminution are taught best through singing and hearing, deriving the visual symbols as an end step. They present little difficulty for children if taught through a well-known simple song such as the French round "Brother John." With the notation on the chalkboard, the class sings the round in the familiar way first.

Normal:

Then the teacher may ask: "How can we change this to make it twice as fast? What kind of notes will we begin with?" [eighth notes]. The class should perform the song in that way and then derive the notation for the "new" way on the chalkboard:

Diminished:

Once the "old" way and the "new" way are on the board, the class may try singing one against the other. Then, they will discern that yet another dimension can be added by doing the song slower:

Augmented:

The words "diminution" and "augmentation" may be introduced as they apply to rhythm, and the children should then try writing augmented and diminished rhythms to other easy familiar songs and to find examples of augmentation and diminution in the music they listen to.

Cut Time

In order to teach cut time *(alla breve)* to children it is necessary that they first be familiar with the symbol for $\frac{4}{4}$, common time (" **C** "). This should have been used in notating and reading in grades three and four, and may also be found in school series music books, frequently in marches. The children should be reminded that **C** is simply another way of writing $\frac{4}{4}$, that it means four beats in a measure, with each beat equal to a ta or quarter note. While it would be possible simply to tell children that the **₵** with a line through it means $\frac{2}{2}$—two beats in a measure and a half note equal to one beat—it would certainly be more meaningful to have them discover this for themselves by singing a cut-time song by rote, feeling the two beats per measure, and then looking at the song in their books to find the signature

One procedure for doing this might be: Have the children

1. sing the song and play the game for "Sailing on the Ocean":

Sail - ing   on   the   o - cean   the   tide   rolls   high

(This involves stepping the beat, two steps to a measure.)
2. identify the song as "moving in twos" and conduct it with a duple beat;
3. look at the notation on the board, without a meter sign:

4. sing it in ti-ta's while conducting as before.

At this point the teacher should ask:

"How many beats were we conducting for each measure?" [two]

One child should then come to the board and place the beats under the rhythm notation where they occur in conducting:

"If there are two beats in each measure, what must the top number in our meter sign be?" [2]

"What about the bottom number? What kind of note is equal to two ta's or four ti's?" [the half note, too]

"So what must the meter sign be?" [$\frac{2}{2}$; two beats in each measure, with each beat equal in duration to a half note]

Only when this is fully understood should the *alla breve* symbol, ¢, be introduced:

"When we are notating in $\frac{4}{4}$, how can we show the meter without using numbers?" [C]

"In $\frac{2}{2}$, cut time, we can show the meter the same way with a slash through it, ¢. Cut time is notated like $\frac{4}{4}$ but it is always stepped or conducted in twos."

Compound Meters $\frac{9}{8}$, $\frac{12}{8}$ and $\frac{6}{4}$

If children are secure in their understanding that

1. in all simple meters the subdivisions of the felt beat, the *pulses*, move in twos,
2. in all compound meters the subdivisions of the felt beat, the *pulses*, move in threes,

then extending their reading and writing vocabulary to the less common compound meters $\frac{9}{8}$, $\frac{12}{8}$, and $\frac{6}{4}$ will not be difficult.

Since the children have had much experience with simple triple ($\frac{3}{4}$) and simple quadruple ($\frac{4}{4}$) meters by this time, the related compound triple ($\frac{9}{8}$) and compound quadruple ($\frac{12}{8}$) meters should be introduced before the others.

By conducting, the children will discover that the felt beats in this song move in threes, beginning with an upbeat:

By tapping an ostinato of ti's they will find that the pulses also are in threes, making it a compound meter, $\frac{3}{?}$. They know that in $\frac{6}{8}$ the meter sign is shown for pulses ($\eighthnote$) rather than conducting beat ($\dottedquarter$) and so can deduce that the standard meter sign for $\frac{3}{?}$ must be $\frac{9}{?}$ or $\frac{9}{8}$.

The process for $\frac{12}{8}$ is exactly the same, with the conducting beat now in fours and the meter sign shown as $\frac{4}{?}$ before being derived as $\frac{12}{?}$ or $\frac{12}{8}$.

The meter $\frac{6}{4}$ may be approached similarly, although in this meter one may sometimes perceive six actual beats. Still, even at a slow tempo, the pulse movement is in threes (compound) rather than in twos (simple):

In folk songs some examples of $\frac{6}{4}$ may be found, as above, in the ballads of ancient tradition, while many more examples of $\frac{6}{4}$ are to be found in composed music.

Dotted-Eighth–Sixteenth Note Patterns

The dotted eighth followed by a sixteenth note ♪. ♪ , is fairly common in North American folk music, while the sixteenth followed by a dotted eighth note ♫. , is common in Hungary and comparatively rare here although it may be found in those songs that came to North America with Scottish settlers:

If   a   bod-y   meet   a   bod-y   com-in' through the   rye

Both should be learned from song material.

The traditional Southern song "Marching Down the Levee" is a possible one for introducing the dotted-eighth–sixteenth pattern:

We're march-in' down the   lev - ee,   We're   march-in' down the   lev - ee,

This pattern may be approached in two ways. First, by using rhythmic augmentation the teacher can help children perceive the aural relationship of ♪. ♪ to ♩. ♪ :

This can be reinforced by showing the eighth–sixteenth pattern as tied notes:

tim - ka

The Texas folk song "Rain, Come Wet Me" has the less common sixteenth–dotted-eighth pattern four times:

Rain,   come   wet____ me,   Sun,   come   dry____ me

This can be introduced similarly by using augmentation and, later, ties:

tik-um

MELODIC LEARNING FOR GRADE FIVE

Since the introduction of *la* in grade three, children have been aware of *do*-ending or major mode songs and of *la*-ending or minor mode songs. With the presentation of key signatures in grade four and the associated scale-construction activities, the half step and whole step concept was introduced. In fifth grade this knowledge should be applied to all music reading material. Children should, by looking at the key signature and the final note of a new song, be able to determine whether it is *do*- or *la*-centered and, by looking through the song, what its scale is. This scale should then be placed on the chalkboard and practiced with hand-singing before the song is read. Children should be given time to read any new song silently before being asked to sing at sight.

When the construction of basic major and minor scales holds no difficulty for the children, it is time to introduce the alterations that produce other scales. Basic whole-step–half-step patterns of the major and the minor scales are

	1	2	3 4	5	6	7 8
major:	*d*	*r*	*m f*	*s*	*l*	*t d'*
			½			½

	1	2 3	4	5 6	7	8
minor:	*l*	*t d*	*r*	*m f*	*s*	*l'*
		½		½		

The most common alteration in English-language folk song is probably the sharped *so*—*si*—needed for harmonic minor:

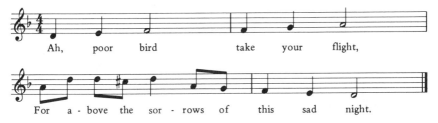

Ah,   poor   bird   take   your   flight,

For   a - bove   the   sor - rows   of   this   sad   night.

When the children know the above song well, but have not yet seen its notation, the teacher should have them sing it with *solfa* and hand signs. On the word "the" they will probably sing the correct pitch, but will call it "*so*". The teacher should then sing the melody for them with a *so* (C♮) rather than a *si* (C♯) and ask if it sounds correct. If the children can hear that the new note is higher than *so,* its *solfa* syllable, *si,* and its hand sign may be introduced:

si

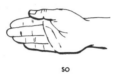

so

In practicing the *la'-si-la'* melodic turn, the teacher should have children compare it to the *do'-ti-do'* sound, using hand signs and beginning the two patterns on the same starting pitch.

The harmonic minor scale may then be introduced:

l'

si

f

m

r

d

t

l

and songs sung in this tone set, such as "Mam'zelle Zizi":

Don't you cry, Mam'-zelle Zi - zi,   Don't you cry, Mam'-zelle Zi - zi,

MUSIC THEORY FOR GRADE FIVE

Intervals. With scale steps firmly learned as "whole steps" and "half steps" and the difference between whole steps and half steps aurally perceived by children, it is now possible to introduce intervals: first, the seconds, then the thirds, major and minor.

It is interesting to note that the terms "major" and "minor" are not used in Hungary with respect to intervals. Rather, they use *nagy* (big) for major and *kicsi* (little) for minor. How much more descriptive these words actually are to children than our words "major" and "minor" which have little meaning outside their musical context. For this reason the author initially uses a dual vocabulary:

"big seconds, major seconds"
"little seconds, minor seconds"

until the idea of major intervals as larger and minor intervals as smaller is established.

At fifth grade children know the *solfa* for intervals; they can sing them correctly. It merely remains to label properly *what* they are singing. Exercises are useful for this purpose. While the very word "exercise" is anathema to some educators, it has been the author's experience that children enjoy these musical challenges much as they enjoy tongue twisters in language.

For seconds:

For thirds, singing in sequence is useful:

Rhythmic variation can add further interest to these drills:

To help children remember which thirds are major, the following melody helps:

At this point the teacher should begin to assess children's learning by singing major and minor seconds and thirds on "loo." The children should be able to sing these intervals back in correct *solfa* and identify them by size and type:

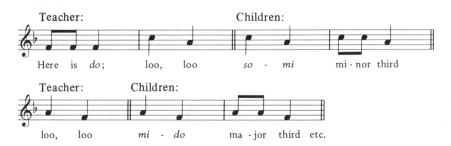

Children should keep lists in their notebooks of intervals categorized by size and type:

	Seconds		Thirds
Major	*Minor*	*Major*	*Minor*
d-r	m-f	d-m	r-f
r-m	t-d	f-l	m-s
f-s		s-t	l-d
s-l			t-r
l-t			

No great amount of time need be spent in any class period on intervals. They can be a form of vocalizing at the beginning of a class. Regular brief work will ensure that they are learned.

Chords.   In third grade, tonal centers *do* and *la* were used as ostinati to accompany songs, and triads were pulled from songs and sung over these root tones. In fourth grade the children should have discovered that in some places in some songs an accompaniment using only *do* did not seem to "fit"; that it was necessary in these instances to shift to *so*:

Example: "Skip to My Lou":

SKIP TO MY LOU

In fifth grade these incidental learnings are the basis for beginning instruction in harmony. Children should be shown that *do,* the first degree of the major scale, can also be shown by the Roman numeral for *one,* ''I.''[1]

The teacher may then have the class sing the notes of the triad on I as they occur in a familiar song:

... Rock - y moun - tain   high ...   *d   m   s*   I

''When we sing the third and fifth over any pitch the result is a *triad* or *chord.* Let's sing the I chord to accompany ''Brother John'':

Are   you   sleep - ing   are   you sleep - ing

Ding   dong   Ding   dong

The class is divided into three groups, each singing one of the chord tones as the teacher sings the melody. This can be done with a number of songs. Rounds and canons particularly lend themselves to this kind of one-chord harmonization.

Turning to a song such as ''I's the B'y'' the class should aurally determine where *do* (I) can be used in accompanying it and where *so* (V) is needed, and mark their music accordingly:

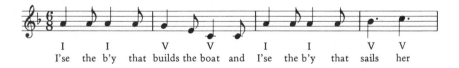

I   I   V   V   I   I   V   V
I'se   the b'y   that builds the boat   and   I'se   the b'y   that   sails   her

Then they should be guided to find the V chord in the melody and to sing it in three parts:

I'se   the b'y   that   builds   the boat   *r   t₁   s₁*   V

---

[1]This is easy to teach if children have had Roman numerals in mathematics class. Today, this is by no means certain. If they have not had this numbering system, it will have to be taught in the music class, since it is universally the way chords are indicated in music.

Inversions of these chords should be taught before going on to other chords. They will facilitate chordal accompaniment singing. The possible inversions are:

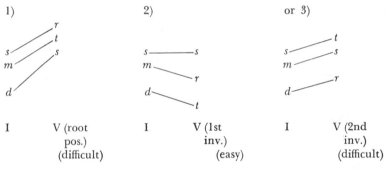

	m				*t*
d	*d*			*s*	*s*
s	*s*	*s*	*r*	*r*	*r*
m	*m*		*t*	*t*	
d			*s*		
root position	first inversion	second inversion	root position	first inversion	second inversion

I Chord   *V Chord*

Starting from the I chord in its root position, the class should decide which inversion of the V chord is easiest to sing:

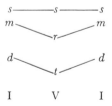

1)		2)		or 3)	
I	V (root pos.) (difficult)	I	V (1st inv.) (easy)	I	V (2nd inv.) (difficult)

The children see that the first inversion leads most comfortably to and from the tonic chord. They should then practice three-part chord singing from I to V to I until it is easy for them:

I   V   I

The parts should be shifted around the class so that all children have practice with the upper, middle, and lower voices.

When they can do this easily, these chords can be sung to accompany known songs. Many songs need only these two chords for an artistic harmonic accompaniment.

When the class can sing such chordal accompaniments using the I and V chords, the IV chord may be introduced. Like the I and V chords it should initially be taken from a song the children know:

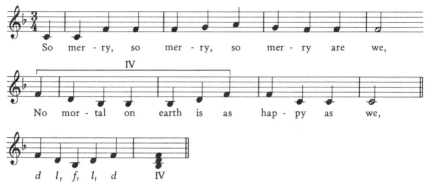

So mer-ry, so mer-ry, so mer-ry are we,

No mor-tal on earth is as hap-py as we,

d l₁ f₁ l₁ d   IV

Again the class should sing the chord with its inversions and decide which inversion moves most smoothly from the tonic and to the dominant. The progression will be

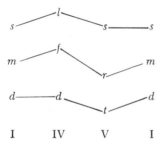

I   IV   V   I

With these three chords a very pleasant accompaniment may be sung to many of the songs the children know. One that contains both the I chord and the IV chord outlined in the melody is "Feller from Fortune" (also known as "Bonavist' Harbour"):

Lots of fish in Bo-na-vist'Har-bour, Lots of fish right in a-round here,

Triads should, of course, be practiced in minor as well as major. The same procedure should be used in introducing the basic chords and their inversions, and the progression from i to V and back will have to be taken from songs and practiced with three-part singing. The song "Mam'zelle Zizi" has both the tonic and the dominant chords outlined in its melody, and has them in the best progression for singing:[2]

Don't you cry Mam'-zelle Zi-zi,   Don't you cry Mam'-zelle Zi-zi,

l d m   i   si ti m   V₆

[2]By convention, small Roman numerals are used to indicate minor triads and capital Roman numerals to indicate major triads.

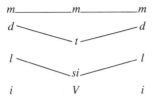

The subdominant is rarely called for in harmonizing folk songs in minor.

GRADE SIX

Rhythmic learning for grade six includes mixed meters, asymmetric meters, and triplets, while new melodic material includes melodic minor and the modes. The C and F clefs are introduced and used in reading and writing. In theory, children sing, construct, and read chords with sevenths, and add the new triads ii and vi to their working vocabulary. They expand their identification and classification of intervals to include perfect fourths and fifths and major and minor sixths and sevenths.

Their singing should be more often in parts than in unison and more often from the vocal works of great composers than from the folk song repertory; their music listening should include examples ranging from Baroque to Contemporary.

They should, by the end of sixth grade, be able to improvise vocally within the diatonic major scale and, given sufficient guidance, to compose small works.

RHYTHMIC LEARNING FOR GRADE SIX

Mixed Meters and Asymmetric Meters

Songs in which there are measures in a second meter appear to cause very little problem to sixth graders with a secure grounding in duple and triple meters. As with all musical learning the first experiences should be extremely obvious ones and should be approached aurally before being seen in notation. The dance ''Coffee Grows on White Oak Trees'' moves in threes throughout the A section and shifts to a rapid duple in the B section. Even young children can feel and hear this metric shift. When a meter changes for only a measure or two, aurally perceiving just what has happened is a bit more difficult:

Meter shifts from four to three, such as in the example above, are best discovered through singing and conducting before seeing notation. There will be uncertainty as to where the downbeat *is* in some measures. Children may even try to rearrange the meter so that it "fits" a regular conducting beat. All will feel that there is a problem. At this point seeing the notation and discovering that there are two meters in the song become a solution rather than a problem. There are not a great number of folk songs with shifting meters, but one may find good examples of it in songs by Benjamin Britten, Béla Bartók, and others.

Asymmetric meters, $\frac{5}{4}$, $\frac{7}{4}$, $\frac{5}{8}$, $\frac{7}{8}$, are also best approached through singing; but in this case the meter should be applied to a simple familiar song such as "Brother John" or "Aunt Rhody" before being introduced in new song material.

Children know that music moves in twos or in threes. A *five* meter must therefore be either $2+3$ or $3+2$, while a *seven* meter may be $3+2+2$, $2+3+2$, or $2+2+3$. Singing, the children tap a $3+2$:

✗ ✔ ✔ ✗ ✔
tap—clap—clap—tap—clap

or a $3+2+2$:

✗ ✔ ✔ ✗ ✔ ✗ ✔
tap—clap—clap—tap—clap—tap—clap

The original rhythm must be made to fit the new meter. What they usually sing, after a bit of experimenting, is:

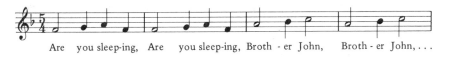

Are   you sleep-ing, Are   you sleep-ing, Broth - er John,   Broth - er John, . . .

or for $\frac{7}{4}$:

Are   you sleep-ing, Are   you sleep-ing, Broth - er John,   Broth - er John, . .

or for $\frac{7}{8}$:

Go   tell Aunt Rho - dy,   Go   tell Aunt Rho - dy . . .

When they can alter easy $\frac{4}{4}$ songs to fit asymetric meters, they will be able to read and sing folk songs or composed songs in them:

THE SHIP'S CARPENTEER

'Twas in Lis - burgh of late a— fair dam - sel did dwell,

Her wit and her beau - ty— no one could e'er tell . . .

Triplets

Triplets are extremely uncommon in English-language folk song. They usually occur as a single triple rhythmic figure in an otherwise quite straightforward duple or quadruple song, such as in the spiritual "Lonesome Valley":

No - bod - y else———— could walk it for Him

or as in the ballad "Handsome Molly":

I wish I was in Lon - don, or some oth-er sea port town . . .

The questions asked in deriving triplets are those that were asked earlier for eighth-note pairs or four-sixteenth-note groups:

"How many sounds are on the beat?"
"Are they even or uneven?"

The last question is particularly important since many people tend to perform triplets not as three *even* sounds over the beat but as ♪♪♩ . Children must be made aware of the difference. Triplets are spoken as

"tri - o - la"

Many examples of triplets may be found in composed music.

MELODIC LEARNING FOR GRADE SIX

If children have learned the basic tetrachord pattern in earlier grades, and can sing major, natural minor, and harmonic minor scales from the same starting pitch, and can identify songs in these scales, in sixth grade the modes may be introduced.

By starting at any point in the *solfa* scale, it is possible to sing a modal scale simply by singing up eight steps, being careful to maintain the half-steps between *mi* and *fa* and between *ti* and *do*:

do	to	*do'*	—	Ionian Mode
re	to	*re'*	—	Dorian Mode
mi	to	*mi'*	—	Phrygian Mode
fa	to	*fa'*	—	Lydian Mode
so	to	*so'*	—	Mixolydian Mode
la	to	*la'*	—	Aeolian Mode
ti	to	*ti'*	—	Lochrian Mode

The scale on *mi* is so rare in folk music of the Western world as to be of only academic interest; the scale on *fa* also is uncommon; the scale on *ti* is never used. Modal North American folk music tends to be Ionian (what one thinks of simply as "major"), Aeolian (what one thinks of as "natural minor"), Dorian, or Mixolydian; so that for practical purposes only two new modal scales need really be made familiar to children—the Dorian and the Mixolydian. However, it is sometimes easier for children to understand the construction of these two scales in the context of all modal scales.

Modal scales may be classified broadly as being either major or minor in character, depending upon whether the interval from the first to the third step of the scale is a major or a minor one. By considering all minor modes as *la*-centered and all major ones as *do*-centered, the alterations necessary to produce each mode become quickly apparent and form a pattern easy to remember.

Modes of Major Character

Ionian	Lydian	Mixolydian
d' ⟩	d' ⟩	d'
t	t	ta ⟩
		l
l	l	
s	s ⟩	s
f ⟩	fi	f ⟩
m	m	m
r	r	r
d	d	d
Ionian	Lydian	Mixolydian
(the "major" scale)	(the scale on *fa*)	(the scale on *so*)

Modes of Minor Character

l'	*l'*	*l'*
s	*s* ⟩	*s*
f ⟩	*fi*	*f* ⟩
m	*m*	*m*
r	*r*	*r*
d ⟩	*d* ⟩	*d*
t	*t*	*ta* ⟩
l	*l*	*l*

Aeolian	Dorian	Phrygian
(the natural minor scale)	(the scale on *re*)	(the scale on *mi*)

Essentially this means that by simply being able to 1) hear whether a scale is major or minor in character, and 2) hear the altered *fa* or *ti*, one may classify any song by mode.

A well-known American folk song in Mixolydian mode is "Old Joe Clark." The major-mode feeling of the song is unmistakable, and the flatted *ti* occurs repeatedly. Notice the strong major feeling of the chorus,

Round and round, old Joe Clark

and the repeatedly flatted seventh of the verse:

Old Joe Clark he had a house,

ta

The second phrase of the Newfoundland folk song "As I Roved Out," with its raised *fa*, is an example of the Dorian mode:

As   I   roved   out   one   fine   sum-mer's eve - nin'

To   view   the   flow'rs   and   to   take   the _____ air,

To simplify the entire thing for children:

The *la* scale + *fi* = Dorian Mode; the *la* scale + *ta* = Phrygian Mode.
The *do* scale + *ta* = Mixolydian Mode; the *do* scale + *fi* = Lydian Mode.

fi

As pentatonic modes were practiced singing from the same starting pitch in fourth and fifth grades, these diatonic modes will also become more familiar to children if their scales are practiced from the same beginning pitch. The changing of *fa* in natural minor to *fi* for Dorian or of *ti* in major to *ta* for Mixolydian in practicing scale singing makes children more aware of the crucial notes to listen for in determining the modes of songs. It is not unrealistic to expect sixth graders to be able to identify the mode of a new song with one or two listenings.[3]

Clefs

The word *clef* is French and ordinarily refers to a house key. The clef sign in music "unlocks" the music much as a house key unlocks a door. Each clef sign tells where one specific pitch is, and, knowing the place of one pitch, the music student can quickly deduce the others. There are three basic clefs: the G-clef, the F-clef, and the C-clef.

Throughout the early elementary years children read only in the G-clef. Correct placement of their voices dictates this. The G-clef specifies which line on the staff

---

[3]Reading modal songs from books is sometimes a problem. The correct key signature for a Dorian song ending on D is *no* sharps or flats; the correct key signature in Mixolydian ending on G is the same. Unfortunately, most publishers insist on placing the Dorian song in D-minor, with a key signature of one flat, and the Mixolydian one in G-major, with a key signature of one sharp. Then, wherever B occurs in the Dorian song or F occurs in the Mixolydian there is a ♮ sign, implying that the new note is an "accidental." Since this practice makes no sense at all, one is hard pressed to explain it to children.

is G above middle C by encircling that line:  ; the F-clef indicates by its

two dots which line is F below middle C: ; the C-clef indicates middle

C by the meeting of its two semicircles: . Any clef may indicate any staff

line, although for all practical purposes the most common clef placements are:

Treble   Bass   Alto   Tenor

It is good, toward the end of sixth grade, to introduce reading in clefs other than the G-clef. Boys' voices will be changing soon, if they have not already, and by the end of junior high school most of their music will be shown in F-clef. Changing clefs will hold no difficulty for children who sing easily in relative *solfa*. However, if absolute note names have been taught, they too should be practiced in F- and C-clefs. Each should be introduced through a song already known well in *solfa* in G-clef, for example, "Row, Row, Row Your Boat":

G clef:

F clef:

C clef:

Once the clefs have been introduced, some of the more familiar songs should be written by the children in the new clefs.

MUSIC THEORY FOR GRADE SIX

Intervals

Children's identification of intervals by sight and sound should be expanded in grade six to include perfect fourths and fifths and major and minor sixths and sevenths. Wherever possible examples should be drawn from song material. These may be categorized and placed in notebooks beside the lists of seconds and thirds begun in grade five:

	Fourths		*Fifths*	
Perfect	*Augmented*	*Perfect*	*Diminished*
d-f	*f-t*	*d-s*	*t-f*
r-s	[all whole	*r-l*	[contains 2
m-l	steps = an	*m-t*	half steps]
s-d	augmented	*f-d*	
l-r	fourth]	*s-r*	
t-m		*l-m*	

Children should be led to discover that the sixths are simply inversions of the thirds; the sevenths, of the seconds. From this systematization of intervals and their inversions, children should be able to deduce the following rules:

1. The inversion of a major interval is always minor.
2. The inversion of a perfect interval is always perfect.

Chords

Chords with sevenths may be introduced in sixth grade through a song in which the V_7 occurs:

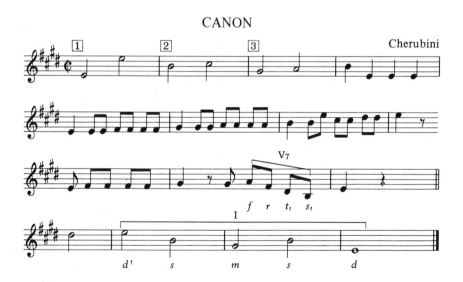

CANON

Cherubini

The class should sing notes ascending and descending as a broken chord and should be divided into four parts so that the children may hear the chord notes together:

f   r   t₁   s₁

Once they can sing the V_7 chord and have found the best inversion for singing a I—V_7—I progression,

s—s
m—f
d—t

I V_7

they can now accompany songs vocally with these chords.

Later they may practice singing seventh chords as they earlier practiced triads:

In previous grades children have been guided to find the harmonies implied in their folk songs and have been led to discover these same harmonies in their listening examples. Most folk songs in major or in harmonic minor may be chorded with I and V, with an occasional IV chord. For the less common triads ii and vi, the teaching material must be drawn from composed music; for example, from the very singable second movement theme of the Beethoven Piano Concerto #5 in E-flat Major:[4]

Most of this theme is harmonized in an extremely simple way using I and V and an occasional IV. However, at measure 7 and again at measure 10, at a point that sounds as if it is going to be a V—I cadence, the listener is offered instead a I-V-vi:

s _____ *s* _____ *l*
m _____ *r* _____ *m*
d _____ *t₁* _____ *d*

I   V   vi

[4]This example has been transposed to a good singing key for children. This must often be done with instrumental music.

The children, after knowing the melody, should first listen for the place where it sounds as if it is going to end, but doesn't; then they should sing the V—vi progression. Later, they may sing possible resolutions from the vi chord:

m ____	f ____	f ____	m
d ____	d ____	t ____	d
l, ____	l, ____	s, ____	s,
vi	IV	V₇	I

or

l ____	l ____	s ____	s
m ____	f ____	f ____	m
d ____	d ____	t, ____	d
vi	IV	V	I

Once they have sung these progressions they will become more alert to them in other listening examples.

The ii chord is perhaps a bit more difficult to perceive aurally, substituting as it so often does for IV. In the following listening example from the fifth movement of Beethoven's Symphony #6 there is an easily singable melody line accompanied in the second phrase by the equally singable harmonic progression I-vi-ii-V₇-I:

| V | I | vi | ii | V₇ | I |

Children may try substituting ii for IV in their folk song chording.

Pencil and paper should play very little part in the teaching of harmony in the elementary school. The order for teaching is aural-oral and everything should be voiced. The written harmony exercises so dear to the hearts of theory teachers will never be necessary for the great majority of students, and for those who will later need this ability, it will be quickly acquired if aural skill is present. The purpose of theory at this level is to enhance singing and listening.

MUSIC LISTENING IN GRADES FIVE AND SIX

In Hungary children are introduced first to the Viennese classical school and the composers Mozart and Haydn, and from there move both back and forward in time in succeeding school years. By eighth grade the Hungarian student in a "Singing School" has a fairly comprehensive knowledge of music history from early music to the late twentieth century and, more than knowing "history," knows *music* of all periods and styles.

This is accomplished in *daily* music lessons over a period of five years. It cannot be accomplished in the three upper-grade years of North American elementary schools, in which music is, in good situations, a twice a week occurrence.

Obviously, choices have to be made. However, the principle underlying the Kodály approach to music listening—that everything must be sung before being heard—*can* be applied; and the sequence beginning with Classical, moving back in time to the Baroque and earlier music and forward to the Romantic and later music is a most workable one, even with limited instructional time.

In North America few school systems dictate what is to be covered in curriculum in music; even fewer specify which composers and what music should be part of any listening program. Song series texts suggest listening lessons, but none appear to have any underlying rationale for their choices, and in such texts styles and periods are intermixed to the point that it would be very difficult to teach more from them than the most superficial aspects of the specific compositions given.

The author suggests that a music listening program for fifth and sixth grades be organized in four ways: by composer, by period or style, by form, and by instrumentation. By keeping all of these aspects in mind when making choices, the teacher can ensure well-rounded listening experiences.

The author's choices of composers are not always the same from year to year, but certain composers are always represented:

> in grade 4: Mozart, Haydn, Schubert
> in grade 5: Bach, Handel, Beethoven
> in grade 6: Brahms, Debussy (or Ravel), Stravinsky, Bartók

Further, a composer and a specific work is not "dropped" when the child moves from fourth to fifth grade. Rather, each composer, once introduced, is returned to in subsequent years. Sometimes the work originally introduced, or another section of that work, is studied in greater depth; at other times another work of the same composer is heard.

Always the work is introduced first through some singable section. When children "hear" it later, they listen to discover how the composer treated the thematic material, not "how the tune goes."

Opposite is a planning chart for some music listening experiences for fifth and sixth grade classes.

The choices listed above are by no means meant to be exclusive; they are simply ones the author has used successfully in the past two years with children of this age level. They do represent a number of periods, styles, forms, and instrumentations. They all have melodic lines that can be sung and all employ compositional devices children can identify, such as shifting from major to minor, using canonic entrances, or employing sequence.

Some part of every class period should be given to the music listening experience. This does not mean that children should listen to records every period. The teacher might easily spend part of three or four class periods getting the class ready to hear one recorded example, and part of another three or four to follow up that listening, before having them listen to that example again on recording.

Planning Chart for Music Listening Experiences

COMPOSER	PIECE	STYLE/PERIOD	FORM/GENRE	INSTRUMENTATION
Bach, J. S.	Little G-minor Fugue	Baroque	Fugue; polyphony	Organ; then orchestral transcription; then synthesizer
Bach, J. S.	Jesu, Joy of Man's Desiring	Baroque	Contrapuntal; melody & countermelody	Choir & organ; orchestral transcription; two-piano transcription
Handel, G. F.	The Royal Fireworks Minuet #2	Baroque	Suite; dance forms; minuet	Baroque orchestra; modern symphonic arrangements
Haydn, F.	Cello Concerto, op. 101, 3rd movement	Classical	Rondo	Cello & orchestra
Mozart, W. A.	Eine Kleine Nachtmusik (last movement)	Classical	Rondo	Classical string orchestra
Mozart, W. A.	Ah! Vous dirai-je, Maman	Classical	Theme & variations	Harpsichord; piano
Beethoven, L.	Symphony #6 (fifth movement)	Romantic	Symphony	Orchestra, increased in size
Schubert, F.	Lied: The Trout (The Trout Quintet, last movement)	Classical	Song form ABA; theme & variations	Piano/voice; violin; viola; cello; double bass; piano
Debussy, C.	Afternoon of a Faun	Impressionist	Tone poem	Orchestra
Stravinsky, I.	The Firebird	20th century	Ballet suite	Orchestra

In presenting the *andante* from Mozart's "Eine Kleine Nachtmusik," for example, the author first placed the rhythm on the board:

EINE KLEINE NACHTMUSIK

2nd movement *Andante*

Children spoke the rhythm in ti-ta's, derived its form (a-b-a-c), memorized it, and notated it. At a later lesson the melody—the violin part—was placed under the rhythm notation in *solfa* and read by the class:

¢ ♪ᵧ ♪ᵧ | ♩. 　♪ ♫ ♫ ♩ | ♫. ♪♩♪ᵧ |
　　m　　m　　m　　　s　f　r　f　l　　s　m　s

At this point the class could have notated it in C-*do* in manuscript books. Instead, in this instance, they were given copies of the theme notated on staff with only one phrase, the third, missing. They sang the whole theme and filled in the third phrase. This was easy for them since it is identical to the first. When the melody was memorized, the children attempted to harmonize it vocally using *do, fa* and *so* (I, IV, V).

At subsequent lessons the viola and cello parts were read and sung, and the three parts were then sung together and analyzed to determine how closely the class's harmonization followed that of Mozart. Only then did the children hear a tape of the composition.

At later listenings the children determined how many times this theme occurred, what the overall form of this movement was, and how dynamics and tempo were used in it to achieve unity and variety.

Few works can be covered in a year if they are approached in this fashion, but compositions studied in this manner are acquired for life—they become a part of the listener.[5]

IMPROVISING AND COMPOSING IN GRADES FIVE AND SIX

Children with four or five years of solid musicianship training behind them are ready for creative tasks at a fairly high level. The concepts they have drawn from singing and listening can now be applied in improvisation and composition. They can experiment vocally and on paper with such compositional techniques as

[5]For further suggestions on music listening see Chapter 5 of the author's *The Kodály Context*.

(a)   changing a known melody from major to minor:

GO TELL AUNT RHODY

(b)   using sequence to extend a melodic fragment:

(c)   augmenting or diminishing a rhythm; using the augmented or diminished version to create an accompaniment for the original:

(d)   composing a variation for a known tune over a known second voice part:
      (over the lower voice part of Mozart's "Variations on Ah! Vous dirai-je, Maman")

Any assignment in composition must be extremely specific. In order to have children in a musicianship class at Mount Royal Conservatory compose a "B Section" for the rondo in the Mozart Horn Concerto, Calgary music teacher Sharyn Favreau gave the following directions:

> Compose a B Section for the rondo in Mozart's Horn Concerto to the following harmony:

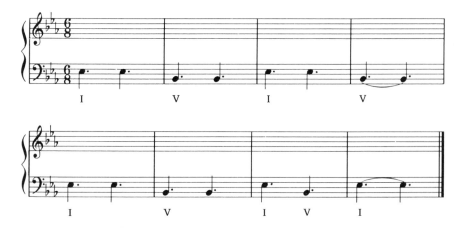

Step 1: Compose a rhythm using $\frac{6}{8}$ patterns— ♩. , ♩ ♪ , ♫♫ , etc.
Step 2: Compose a melody.
    a) Use question—answer phrases.
    b) Use notes from the I chord, *d-m-s,* E♭ G B♭, and from the V or V₇ chord,
       s,-t,-r-f, B♭ D F A♭.
    c) Sing as you write. Be able to sing your composition in class next week.

Two melodies composed by children[6] for this are shown below:

Not every child at fifth or sixth grade will be able to compose a section for a rondo, but with sufficient guidance any student who is musically literate can compose something:

Compose a third phrase for the following song:

[6]Respectively, Martha Baldwin, nine years old, and Rhys Yarrington, twelve years old.

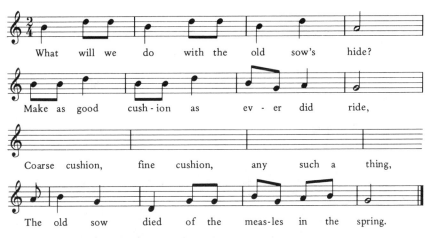

What will we do with the old sow's hide?

Make as good cush-ion as ev - er did ride,

Coarse cushion, fine cushion, any such a thing,

The old sow died of the meas-les in the spring.

1. Say the words aloud to decide what the rhythm should be.
2. Notate the rhythm using ♩, ♪, ♫ , and ♩ .
3. Use notes of the pentatonic scale, *l-s-m-r-d-l₁-s,* and end the phrase on *so* (as a question phrase).
4. Be ready to sing your phrase to the class.

There are as many possible third lines to this tune as there are children in a class. Children love to compose. It is up to the teacher to see that they have opportunity to do so.

PART SINGING IN GRADES FIVE AND SIX

Developing skill in part singing is part of every lesson from first grade. The simplest melodic ostinato with a nursery tune is one step toward eventual independence in singing one part while hearing others, in blending voices and adjusting to the other sounds being produced.

Rounds and canons are among the easiest kinds of part singing in which children can engage. The following one in natural minor is not difficult, but the harmonies produced by the three parts are very beautiful. It may be sung in *solfa* or on a neutral syllable. Many sets of words have been put to this old melody, but none seem to fit it particularly well. Children might enjoy creating a text for it.

CANON IN C-MINOR

Anon.

Many canons are by well-known composers. The following one, with both words and music by the early English composer Henry Purcell, is built on a simple C-major scale and is one fifth graders in the author's classes have enjoyed:

KNOWLEDGE AND WISDOM

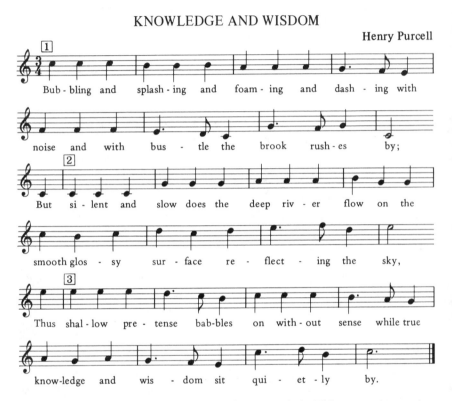

Voices in canon do not always begin on the same pitch. This canon, by another early English composer William Byrd, has the second voice enter a fourth below the first, while the third voice enters at the same pitch as the first:

NON NOBIS DOMINE

Children should learn this piece in unison and attempt the three parts only when they know the melody well. The *solfa* for the voice at the fourth may be realized in two ways:

It is not a very large step from canon singing of this kind to more complex pieces with canonic imitation, such as this charming small chorus by Kodály:

FROM "GYERMEK ES NOIKAROK"

Z. Kodály

and this beautiful soprano and alto duet from the Cantata #78 by Bach:

J.S. Bach

Kodály composed many two- and three-part works for children. His choral pieces, such as "Ladybird," "The Christmas Dance of the Shepherds," and "Angels and Shepherds," are marvelous works for selected choirs, while his *Bicinia Hungarica, Vols. I* to *IV,* and *15 Two-Part Exercises* offer good part-singing experiences for the classroom. The following is an example from the latter book:

15 TWO-PART EXERCISES

No. 1   Z. Kodály

Whatever choices are made as to music, it is vitally important that at this level children be singing more often in parts than in unison. It was Kodály's belief that no one could learn to sing accurately by singing in unison; that only through polyphonic singing with two, three, or four other parts could true musicianship be developed.[7]

CONCLUSION

Perhaps the most important work of the sixth grade is the singing of the children. Even if none of the other suggested sixth-grade material is covered, the loss will not be great if the time has been spent on singing—not just the folk songs but now also the beautiful art songs and music composed specifically for young voices to sing in two and three parts. The *Bicinia Hungarica* and *Children's Chorus Music* of Kodály offer a wealth of such music. In addition, there are a number of Béla Bartók songs for treble voices and some English-language folk songs in beautiful settings by Aaron Copland, Benjamin Britten, Gustav Holst, Ralph Vaughan Williams, and others. Some of the two-part songs of Bach are within the ability range of youngsters with five years of Kodály Method training, as are songs by Mozart, Haydn, Beethoven, and Schubert.

The artistic performance of such music is the most important work of sixth grade. Children who experience the joy of singing beautiful music in two or three voices will surely develop a love of music which will endure throughout their lives.

[7]For many further suggestions regarding part singing and elementary school choral experience, see Chapter 6 of the author's *The Kodály Context.*

SUGGESTED SONG LIST FOR GRADES FIVE AND SIX
(ARRANGED BY TEACHING PURPOSE)

(Some songs are suggested for more than one teaching purpose. Two asterisks (**) indicate songs which may be sung in canon; three asterisks (***) indicate songs related to music listening.)

Note: There are many North American folk dances suitable for grades five and six. They have not been included in this list, but may be found in: Lois Choksy and David Brummitt, *120 Singing Games and Dances* (Englewood Cliffs, N.J.: Prentice-Hall, 1987).

For rhythmic and metric teaching

♩. ♩ or ♫♩. :

Fire Down Below

*** St. Anthony's Chorale

We're Marching Down the
Levee
Farewell to Nova Scotia

♫♩ or ♩♩♩ :

Handsome Molly
The Devil's Questions

Lonesome Valley

$\frac{9}{8}$ meter:

Down in the Valley

*** Jesu, Joy of Man's Desiring
(Chorale from J. S. Bach's
Cantata #147)

$\frac{12}{8}$ meter:

He Shall Feed His Flock
(G. F. Handel)

$\frac{6}{4}$ meter:

The Banks of the Nile

Mixed meters or asymmetric meters:

The Sailor's Return ($\frac{4}{4}$ $\frac{6}{4}$)
The Dewy Dells of Yarrow ($\frac{5}{4}$ $\frac{4}{4}$)

Shenandoah ($\frac{3}{4}$ $\frac{4}{4}$)

The Ship's Carpenteer ($\frac{5}{4}$)

For melodic and harmonic teaching

In scales smaller than diatonic:

of major character—
My Willie Is Brave
Pauper Sum Ego
Un Canadien errant

of minor character—
** Rise Up, O Flame
*** The Birch Tree
Johnny Has Gone for a Soldier
Brave Wolfe
Bound for the Promised Land
Blue Mountain Lake

in the diatonic major scale:
Blow Ye Winds in the Morning   ** Purcell Canon
The Streets of Laredo
The Merry Golden Tree
Shenandoah

in natural minor:
** *l-t-d-r* Canon   ** Rose Red
The Keys of Canterbury   ** When Jesus Wept
Pat Works on the Railway   O Come, Emmanuel

in harmonic minor:
** Ah, Poor Bird   ** Under This Stone
Mam'zelle Zizi
Farewell to Nova Scotia
(alternating major and minor
phrases with *so* and *si*)

In Mixolydian mode:
My Last Farewell to Sterling   ** Viva La Musica
Poor Sally Sits A-Weeping   ** Non Nobis Domine
The Banks of the Nile

in Dorian mode:
A Kangaroo Sat on an Oak   What Shall We Do with a
Lost Jimmy Whelan   Drunken Sailor?

with chromatic alterations:
** Beethoven Canon   ** By the Waters Babylon

For discovering chords outlined in melodies

I chord *(d-m-s)*:
Blow Ye Winds in the   Rocky Mountain
Morning   Sweet Betsy from Pike
Red River Valley   Vive la Canadienne
The Farmer and the Devil
Mary Ann

I *(d-m-s)* and V *(s,-t,-r)* or V₇
(s,-t,-r-f) chords:
I's the B'y   ** Cherubini Canon
The Kelligrews Soiree

I *(d-m-s)* and IV *(f-l-d')*
chords:
Bonavist' Harbor   ** The Lumberman's Alphabet

Rhythm and Meter Learning in Fifth Grade

MONTH	PREPARE THE NEW LEARNING	MAKE THE CHILDREN CONSCIOUSLY AWARE OF THE NEW LEARNING	REINFORCE THE NEW LEARNING THROUGH PRACTICE
September	Sing & notate songs with easy-to-notate rhythms (that can later be augmented or diminished)		Sing, notate & read songs in $\frac{6}{8}$ meter & review the principles underlying simple & compound meters. Sing, notate & read songs using simple triple meter, $\frac{3}{4}$
October	Sing by rote songs that contain the ♩·♪ rhythmic figure	Augmentation & diminution in rhythm	Sing & notate known folk songs, augmenting & diminishing the rhythms. Find examples of rhythmic augmentation & diminution in listening examples
November	Sing by rote songs that contain the ♩·♪ & ♫♪· rhythmic figures	New rhythmic pattern ♩·♪ tim - ka	Sing, notate & read songs with ♩·♪ Look at the scores of listening examples with ♩·♪ Improvise & compose rhythmic phrases using ♫♪
December	Sing by rote songs in cut time	New rhythmic pattern ♫♪· tik-um	Sing, notate & read songs & phrases from listening examples with ♫♪· . Improvise & compose rhythms using ♩·♪ & ♫♪·
January	Sing songs & listen to music in the less common compound meters	Identify $\frac{2}{2}$ as $\frac{2}{2}$ & as cut time or alla breve: ₵	Sing, notate & read songs in cut time. Conduct cut time. Use the terms "cut time" & "alla breve"
February	As above	Identify $\frac{3}{2}$· as $\frac{9}{2}$ or $\frac{9}{8}$ meter, compound triple, & $\frac{4}{2}$· as $\frac{12}{2}$ or $\frac{12}{8}$ meter, compound quadruple	Sing, notate & read in $\frac{9}{8}$ & $\frac{12}{8}$. Conduct $\frac{9}{8}$ as a triple meter. Conduct $\frac{12}{8}$ as a quadruple meter

MONTH	PREPARE THE NEW LEARNING	MAKE THE CHILDREN CONSCIOUSLY AWARE OF THE NEW LEARNING	REINFORCE THE NEW LEARNING THROUGH PRACTICE
March	As above	Identify $\bullet\cdot$ as $\frac{3}{8}$ meter	Sing, notate & read in $\frac{3}{8}$ meter. Conduct $\frac{3}{8}$ in 1's
April	Prepare for new learnings in grade 6. Sing songs in mixed meters	Identify $\bullet$ as $\frac{6}{4}$ meter	Sing, notate & read in $\frac{6}{4}$ meter
May	Sing songs with asymmetric meters		Identify & compose using compound meters

Melody, Theory and Harmony Learning in Fifth Grade

September	Sing many songs in major which may be harmonized using only I & V	Terms: major second (for "whole step"), minor second (for "half step")	Review scale patterns: major & minor tetrachords, pentachords & hexachords, as they occur in songs. Sing the whole-step patterns of these scales. Identify as "major" & "minor" seconds
October	Accompany songs in major with do (I) & so (V)	Major scale pattern of major & minor seconds. Major & minor thirds in diatonic major	Review thirds; 2 whole steps = major third; 1 half step + 1 whole step = minor third. Find examples of major & minor thirds in songs. Sing thirds in sequence
November	Sing many major mode songs with an implied IV in the harmony. Accompany these with do, fa & so	Major triad as a minor third over a major third. Build major triads over do & so. Find best inversions for voice leading	Find triads I & V outlined in melodies of folk songs & composed music. Use triads I & V to improvise accompaniments to songs. Identify seconds and thirds sung, heard & seen as major or minor
December	Sing many songs in the natural minor scale	Discover the need for the IV chord in some accompaniments. Build major triad on fa. Find best inversions for singing the I-IV-V-I & I-IV-I progressions	Sing sequences of triads in major. Sing, read & notate I & V chords outlined in melodies. Use the symbols "I" & "V" under the melodies to indicate the implied harmonies
January	Accompany songs in natural minor with la (i) & mi (v)	Identify the major & minor seconds pattern of the natural minor scale	Find IV chords outlined in melodies. Sing the I-IV-V-I & I-IV-I progressions to accompany songs. Use the symbol "IV" in indicating song song harmonies

MONTH	PREPARE THE NEW LEARNING	MAKE THE CHILDREN CONSCIOUSLY AWARE OF THE NEW LEARNING	REINFORCE THE NEW LEARNING THROUGH PRACTICE
February	Sing many songs in the harmonic minor scale. Accompany them with *la* & *mi*	Identify, sing & notate the minor triad as a major third over a minor third	Sing & notate the scales of natural minor songs. Sing, read & notate minor triads. Use the triads on *la* & *mi* (i & v) to improvise accompaniments to natural minor songs
March	Sing songs & listen to music in major, natural minor & harmonic minor	Discover the new note *si* needed for harmonic minor	Compare the natural minor scale with the harmonic minor scale. Sing songs in both. Find examples in composed music
April	Prepare for new learnings in grade 6. Sing songs in the Mixolydian mode	Find the i & V chords outlined in harmonic minor melodies. Find the best inversions for singing the minor chord progression i-V-i	Use i (*l-d-m*) & V (*m-si-t*) to improvise accompaniments for harmonic minor melodies. Indicate chord changes in music by writing i or V
May	Sing songs in the Dorian mode	Scale patterns for natural & harmonic minor scales. A second "bigger" than major = augmented second (*fa* to *si* in harmonic minor)	Sing natural & harmonic minor scales from the same starting pitch. Notate both. Analyze the interval structure of each. Find examples of each in music. Use these scales in improvising & composing

Melody, Theory and Harmony Learning in Sixth Grade

September	Sing songs containing the pattern *f-r-t,-s,*, the dominant seventh chord. New intervals: perfect fourths & perfect fifths, through rote songs containing them in obvious places	New chord: the dominant seventh—V_7	Review patterns for diatonic major scale, natural & harmonic minor scales. Sing all with hand signs. Find examples of these scales in songs & listening examples
October	New intervals: major & minor sixths & sevenths through rote	"Perfect" intervals: fourths and fifths. Discover that the inversion of a perfect interval is always perfect: *d-f* is perfect fourth, *f-d'* is perfect fifth	Review major & minor seconds & thirds & major & minor triads. Sing thirds & triad sequences. Find triads outlined in folk songs & listening themes. Harmonize songs & art music themes using I, IV & V_7 chords

MONTH	PREPARE THE NEW LEARNING	MAKE THE CHILDREN CONSCIOUSLY AWARE OF THE NEW LEARNING	REINFORCE THE NEW LEARNING THROUGH PRACTICE
November	Sing themes from art music in which the vi & ii chords are outlined or are implied. Clef reading prepared	Major & minor sixths & sevenths. Discover that the inversion of a major interval is always minor; the inversion of a minor interval is always major. Major third *d-m* inverted becomes minor sixth *m-d'*	Identify by sound & sight all major, minor & perfect intervals; sing them in *solfa* and sing their interval names. Harmonize songs & art music examples using I, IV, V & V$_7$
December	Sing songs or themes from art music in which the ii chord is outlined or is implied	Discover the vi chord *l-d-m* and the deceptive cadence I-V-vi in art music examples. F-clef introduced	Sing & notate chord progressions using I-V$_7$-vi. Identify the vi chord in listening examples. Continue practicing all major, minor & perfect intervals. Reading from F-clef
January	Sing songs in Ionian (major) & Mixolydian modes	Discover the ii chord *r-f-l* in art music examples	Sing chord progressions with the ii chord *r-f-l*. Harmonize folk songs using ii where IV would usually fit. Analyze art music examples containing the ii & vi chords. Read in F-clef
February	Sing songs in modes of major & minor character	New note: ta, the flatted ti The Mixolydian mode. Modes of major character: Ionian, Mixolydian, Lydian	Read & sing folk songs in Mixolydian mode. Sing all modes of major character from the same starting pitch, using *solfa* & hand signs. Notate modal scales. Read in F-clef
March	Sing songs in Dorian mode	The Dorian mode. Modes of minor character: Aeolian, Dorian, Phrygian	Read & sing folk songs in Dorian mode. Sing all modes of minor character from the same starting pitch, using *solfa* & hand signs. Notate modal scales
April	Prepare for grade 7. The VII$^\flat$ chord used to accompany modal songs in place of the V	C-clef introduced	Read & notate in G-, F- & C-clefs. Given specific directions, improvise & compose, using standard compositional techniques

8
Lesson Planning

One of the most important aspects of the Kodály Method as practiced in Hungary is the extensive planning required of teachers. Each teacher must plan in advance a year's work for each grade. There is a general overall plan showing what skills and concepts are to be covered in a given grade, and another highly specific plan of lesson-by-lesson skills and concepts, including the materials and techniques to be used. These specific plans may be kept in detail only a few weeks ahead of the class progress, but the overall plan must be constantly referred to so that no skill is neglected or accidently overlooked.

Both the yearly plan and the detailed lesson-by-lesson program are kept in chart form in notebooks. Each teacher has her own format, but in general, the headings are quite similar, as might be expected. Márta Nemesszeghy, at the Zoltán Kodály School in Kecskemét used the following breakdown in listing the areas to be included in a year's work:

Melodic Elements	Artistic Performance
Rhythm Elements	Form
Tempi	Creative Ability
Dynamics	Song Material Types
Scales	Music Listening and History
Intervals and Chords	Text (words)
Part Singing	Books Used

Using the above list as headings, she listed the work of grade three, for example, as follows:

Melodic Elements: fi, ta, si; the natural; two sharps; two flats.

Rhythm Elements: ♬ , ♩. ♪, ♩♩, ♪♩. , ♩♩ ♩, ♩ o ♩

heterometric rhythms: $\frac{4}{4}+\frac{2}{4}$, $\frac{3}{4}+\frac{2}{4}$, $\frac{3}{4}+\frac{4}{4}$.

Tempi: moderato; andante; allegro.

153

Dynamics: f, ff.

Scales: do and *la* endings; *re* and *so* modes.

Intervals and Chords: major and minor thirds; major and minor seconds; perfect fifth; ascending and descending.

Part Singing: canons; Kodály's "Bicinia"; ostinati (rhythmic and melodic); line interweaving between alto and soprano.

Artistic Performance: clear singing; singing for understanding of words; relation of melody to text; feeling of mood in songs.

Form: Analyze the construction of familiar songs and fifth-jumping tunes; write as well as analyze four-phrase melodies; determine whether phrases are like or unlike, or similar but not identical; individually determine song forms such as A–B–B variant–A.

Creative Ability: Given the scale and the form, compose four-phrase songs (*re* ending, *la* ending, *do* ending, etc.).

Song Material Types: folk songs and composed songs; some two-voiced songs.

Music Listening and History: Differentiate between soprano and alto, high and low voices; identify instruments and chorus types; identify instrument families by name.

Text (words): Correlate with work in other subjects.

Books Used: Ének Zene 3; Kodály's *333 Sight-Singing Exercises; 100 Pentatonic Songs; Let us Sing Correctly;* "Bicinia" *(selected volume).*

Only the new material for the grade is listed in this outline. Thus, under dynamics, f and ff are shown, but the children would also review the mp, p, pp taught in earlier grades.

While it is self-evident that this kind of outline for the work of a grade is of itself helpful, it is not sufficient, since no sequence is given, no specific song materials mentioned, and no teaching procedures suggested. For these, the specifics of teaching, a more detailed type of planning is necessary. An efficient format is the following one, developed by Anna Hamvas at the Alsoerdosor Singing Primary School in Budapest. In tabular form Mrs. Hamvas lists, for each class:

Lesson Number	Inner Hearing
Procedure	Writing
Preparation for New Learning in Rhythm	Position of *do* (key)
Preparation for New Learning in Melody	Reading
Making Conscious New Skill in Rhythm	Ostinato
Making Conscious New Skill in Melody	Part Work

Not all headings have material listed under them for every lesson, but the existence of the headings makes clear to the teacher at a glance whether some important aspect of music learning has been neglected in a given number of lessons.

The column headed "Preparation" is a particularly important one. It is the feeling in Hungary that as a general rule six to eight songs are necessary for teaching one new concept or skill. Taking the note *re* as an example, the children would learn, by rote, four or five songs in which the only unknown note was *re*. Then, from one of these rote-taught songs the *re* would be derived with the class and "made conscious." After the lesson in which *re* was made a conscious learning to the children, all the previously

Three Consecutive Lesson Plans for Grade Two

LESSON NUMBER	PREPARE RHYTHM	PREPARE MELODY	MAKE CONSCIOUS RHYTHM	MAKE CONSCIOUS MELODY	REINFORCE RHYTHM	REINFORCE MELODY	INNER HEARING	WRITING	POSITION OF DO	OSTINATO	PART WORK
10		*re* songs: Closet Key; Hot Cross Buns; Sleep, Baby, Sleep; Hop, Old Squirrel			Patterns of 𝅗𝅥 from familiar songs. Use flash cards.	*m-d* interval. Song: Ding Dong.	Sing: Ding Dong once aloud; then silently, ending together on words "Hot Dog" aloud.	Last phrase of Ding Dong. Ledger lines.	*C-do*	with Hot Cross Buns	
11	𝅗𝅥 Hot Cross Buns; Sleep, Baby, Sleep	*re* songs: as above plus Grandma Grunts	*re* Hot Cross Buns		Familiar patterns of 𝅗𝅥 Listen, clap back, and say.			*re* Hot Cross Buns (whole song)	*F-do*	with Hop, Old Squirrel	
12			𝅗𝅥 Sleep, Baby, Sleep			*re* What'll We Do with the Baby? (*s-mrd*). New rote song. Review of all songs with *re*.		*re* Sleep, Baby, Sleep. First two phrases	*G-do*	with Hop, Old Squirrel	Sleep, Baby, Sleep as a canon

learned *re* songs would be returned to and the place of *re* in each derived. Then in following lessons two or three new songs with *re* would be read, or taught by rote and their notation derived. This last step, although it does not occur on the lesson-plan tables, is consistently observed in Hungarian singing schools and has been referred to in this book as "concept or skill reinforcing."

In order to demonstrate the application of such planning to American school situations, three consecutive lessons for second grade are shown in the table on page 155 using the Hungarian headings but with American materials inserted.

The column labeled "Procedure" stands ahead of all the others on such a planning chart, but it has been omitted here since it is difficult to put one's procedures in so small a space and still have them intelligible to others. As an alternative, a detailed lesson plan is given below, showing one order in which the materials, concepts, and skills listed for Lesson 10 might be given. In presentation there is certainly much room for individual difference among teachers. No one way is right. What follows is merely intended as a guide.

Grade 2. Lesson 10

Purpose.   This is a preliminary lesson on the note *re*. Its purpose is to prepare the children to hear and sing the note correctly in songs; in later lessons they will identify the note by its sound, its name, and its place in the scale of other known notes. All of the songs in the lesson prepare for the intervals of *re*. Even the rhythm work is tied into this purpose through the ostinato with "Hot Cross Buns."

Procedure

1. Review song: "Hot Cross Buns" *(m-r-d)*.
    Sing, tapping beat;
    Sing, clapping rhythm;
    Sing, clapping ostinato | ♩ | ♩

2. Flash card rhythm exercise. Each flash card contains an eight-beat phrase from a familiar duple-meter song, in stem notation, using only ♩, ♫, ♩. Children repeat the rhythms, clapping and saying rhythm duration syllables. Answers are given both by the whole class and by individual children. The last pattern,

    is from the song "Closet Key" and leads into:

3. *Game*—I Have Lost My Closet Key *(m-r-d)*. Children sing the song and play the game. There is individual singing on the last verse by children who "find the key" in the game. After finishing the game, the children sing the song slowly, using *solfa* and hand signs on the known sections and a hum for the unknown note.

4. Songs: "Ding Dong" *(m-d)*. The children

   (a) Sing this rhythmic clapping game and do the game motions;
   (b) Sing the song with *solfa* syllables and hand signs;
   (c) Derive the rhythm of the last phrase with the teacher;
   (d) Place the last phrase of the song in staff notation in C-*do* at their desks (manuscript books or felt staves), being careful to place *do* on the ledger line below the staff;
   (e) Sing the song again, looking and pointing to their written notes of the last phrase as they sing.

5. New song: "Sleep, Baby, Sleep" *(s-mrd)*. Taught by rote by the teacher. The teacher sings the song with attention to artistry and phrasing. The children

   (a) Sing it back, one phrase at a time;
   (b) Sing the entire song, with the teacher's voice helping where necessary.

   Attention is given to the dynamics and to the lullaby quality of the song.
6. Review song with game: "Hop, Old Squirrel" *(m-r-d)*.

This lesson takes about forty minutes with an average second-grade class. If less time is available, some of the material will have to be eliminated. However, it is very important that the children's games not be omitted. They are the joy of the music to young children. It would be better to drop one entire section from the lesson plan than to skip the games and try to cover all the skill material. In the lesson given either #4 or #5 could be postponed until the next lesson without damaging the continuity of the lesson or of the learning.

It sometimes happens that in trying to teach musical skills, teachers become so pressured that they forget the importance of musical enjoyment. The emphasis placed upon rote material in Hungary is due to the realization that if music does not give pleasure to children, the teaching of skills is pointless. There is in any good Hungarian music lesson a balance between singing, clapping, playing, thinking, writing, and creating. It would be well to try to maintain such a balance here.[1]

[1]For a more comprehensive treatment of planning see the author's *The Kodály Context*, Chapters 7 and 8.

9
Introduction to the Songs and the Listening Themes

It has been two decades since the author first encountered the Kodály approach to teaching music. In that time song materials have appeared that make using the Method in North America easier. However, to find the sequence implied by those songs—that is, to analyze them, make counts of the frequency with which specific melodic turns and rhythmic figures occur, and then organize them into a comprehensive framework for teaching, taking into account at the same time what is known about how children learn music, i.e., child developmental characteristics—has been a massive task.

In organizing materials for teaching purposes it is necessary to try to find the best songs for each new note, each new rhythm pattern, and to find songs that in each case contain no unknown elements except the one new note or rhythm. The following songs represent a number of years of research, collection, and testing with children. Each of these songs has been used successfully with children for the teaching purpose suggested.

The songs are not meant to be a total music curriculum. Certainly, in the course of five or six elementary school years, many other songs are taught. These songs have been the core of the curriculum followed by the author. They are arranged according to scale and general melodic teaching order, beginning with the early childhood chanting songs and moving through the various scales of smaller range to the diatonic modes. Composed canons have been included among the folk songs, also placed according to tone set.

All songs listed in the earlier chapters are given here or are to be found in the companion volume by the same author: *The Kodály Context.*

Specific melodic and rhythmic teaching purposes for these songs have been suggested in the chapters outlining the work for each grade. Authentic infant songs, singing games, and folk music comprise the largest part of the collection.

MATERIALS

One might suppose that the differences between Hungarian and North American folk songs could cause problems in applying the Hungarian concept to North American materials, and to the skill sequence implied by those materials. That there are differences between Hungarian and English-language song materials is obvious. Hungarian infant songs are based on three notes, *so-mi-la,* as are the English-language infant songs. However, the common pattern of the Hungarian songs is *so* to *la,* a major second, followed by a minor third, *so-mi,* and such songs always begin on the strong beat:

Children's chants in English consistently contain the rising perfect fourth on an unstressed beat, and often begin with an upbeat:

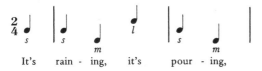

The stress pattern in each example reflects the language, while the notes themselves are the common tones of children's chants in the Western world.

The choice of notes with which to begin teaching in each case is *so-mi-la.* Only the order of interval teaching need be different. In North American schools the *mi* to *la* interval should be taught with the *so* to *la* interval, because of the frequency with which the former occurs in song material and because it exists in the common singing vocabulary of young English-speaking children.

Hungarian early childhood songs are, like North American early childhood songs, frequently pentatonic in character, with the *fa,* if it occurs at all, present only as a passing tone in a descending line at the end of the song. These children's songs in Hungary, as in North America, are generally *do*-centered or major in mode. On the other hand, the folk songs of Hungary, as separate from the infant and early childhood songs, are usually *la*-centered or minor in mode, while minor-mode North American folk songs are less common. Superficially, this might seem to indicate a need for changing the sequence of the method to suit the largely major-mode North American folk song material. However, a closer look[5] at North American folk materials shows that pentatonic, pentachordal, and hexachordal music, although generally major in mode, contains the same basic range as the Hungarian minor modal folk music. That is, most English-language folk music ranges from low *so* and low *la* to high *so* and high *la* rather than, as one might expect, from *do* to *do'.* The principal difference between Hungarian and North American folk music lies in the feeling of the mode and in the final notes: *la* in many Hungarian songs, *do* in most North American ones. Since the Hungarian melodic sequence places *do* immediately after the *so-mi-la* pattern, and the low *la* and low *so* next, it is as well suited to North American folk song as to Hungarian.

The greatest area of difference in rhythm is to be found in $\frac{6}{8}$ meter, common to great amounts of English-language folk material but almost unknown in Hungary. Quite obviously, $\frac{6}{8}$ must be introduced on the conscious level to children in North American schools as soon as they have the necessary competency to handle it. On the subconscious or rote level, English-speaking children should experience $\frac{6}{8}$ meter as early as possible—in kindergarten or first grade, for instance. This meter is the rhythm of the language, as much as the pronounced simple duple is the rhythm of the Hungarian language.[6]

In deciding where to make small shifts in the sequence of skill-teaching to suit differences in American materials, the author consulted with several Hungarian authorities. The consensus was that in the final analysis the sequence *must* come from the materials themselves. This was how the Method evolved in Hungary and this is how it must evolve in North America. The differences in song literature between Hungary and North America present no insoluble problems.

Successful implementation of the Kodály concept in North America is certainly somewhat dependent upon finding sufficient folk songs and good composed songs. Materials exist! There are great numbers of North American pentatonic, pentachordal, hexachordal, and modal folk songs and children's songs, many of them already collected and published by such people as William Wells Newell, John and Alan Lomax, Ruth Crawford Seegar, Richard Chase, Helen Creighton, and Edith Fowke. As for composed music, there are many suitable songs by Mozart, Schubert, Beethoven, et al., available in published collections for children. The Julliard Repertory Library offers perhaps the most comprehensive collection, including art music of every period, selected specifically for school children.

It remains, however, to select, analyze, categorize, and arrange such folk and art material into a teaching sequence. American collections are often annotated with respect to the locale and known history of the song, but are not usually analyzed musically in terms of rhythm, meter, mode, scale, and range, as are the Hungarian collections. Thus, using them demands a high level of musical proficiency on the part of the American teacher, who must know which songs are appropriate for what musical teaching purpose.

Three major collections have appeared in recent years to somewhat alleviate this situation. First and foremost is Richard Johnston's massive work *Folk Songs North America Sings,* (Toronto, E.C. Kirby, 1985) in which the author extensively analyzed for teaching purposes some 450 folk songs. It would be possible to teach for many years from this book alone. Johnston, a composer of some renown in Canada, knew Kodály personally, and is a dedicated supporter of his ideals. He has, in addition, composed several small books of two-part arrangements of folk songs in the style of the *Bicinia Hungarica* for children to sing.

The second resource is equally impressive but, unfortunately, far less accessible. At Holy Names College in California is a collection of more than two thousand North American folk songs all analyzed for teaching purposes—the work of Eleanor G. Locke.[7]

The third resource is far smaller in scope than either of the above, but is deserving of mention simply because so many Kodály teachers have found it to be invaluable: Peter Erdei and Katalin Komlos, *150 American Folk Songs to Sing and Play* (New York: Boosey & Hawkes, 1974). Again, these songs have been analyzed for teaching purposes.

[6]For a more detailed discussion of the $\frac{6}{8}$ meter problem see the author's *The Kodály Context,* pp. 179–185.

[7]A copy of this collection is housed in the Music Department of The University of Calgary—a gift to the present author some years ago.

It should be remembered also that the major song series written for school use contain some folk music and art music of recognized composers and provide a further readily available source of materials. However, these frequently are not organized or arranged for the teaching sequence of Kodály. In every instance the teacher must possess the skill and knowledge to select and organize the music into the concept sequence.

It has been many years since the Kodály approach came to North America, and while in that time a number of school music series publishers have incorporated superficial Kodály techniques into their textbooks, none has yet been willing to publish a wholly Kodály-oriented song series. This is a pity, since the need for a properly printed and produced music book—such as the *Ének Zene* used in Hungarian schools—to place in the hands of North American children in grades two through six is a need felt sorely by Kodály teachers.

THE PEDAGOGICAL USE OF THE SONGS

All the songs to be used in first and second grades are notated in C-, F- and G-*do,* the keys of children's reading and writing. No key signatures are used, since no sharps or flats occur in pentatonic music in these keys.

The *solfa* scale of each song is given, in descending order, on the upper left hand corner. Within each tone set the songs have been arranged from simplest to most complex rhythmically. The tonal center is circled. Key signatures are used after *fa* and *ti* appear in the songs.

At the end of the folk song collection a few themes from composed music have been notated in keys singable by children. These are possible listening examples.

Songs #1 to #14 are all in the *s-m* or *l-s-m* tone set and contain only quarter notes, eighth notes in pairs, and quarter rests. These are the songs through which patterns of "ta," "ti-ti," and *so-mi-la* may be prepared and made conscious knowledge to children.

Songs #15 to #18 may be used to reinforce the *s-m-l* tonal patterns in the context of "skipping music," $\frac{6}{8}$.

Songs #19 and #20 will reinforce the *s-m-l* pattern, but have rhythmic aspects—the upbeat, the triplet—not in the conscious knowledge of the children.

Songs #21 to #23 present the new note *do* in the *s-d* pattern. All are within the rhythmic vocabulary of the children at this stage, except #23.

Songs #24 to #27 present the new note *do* in the *s-m-d* or *d-m-s* pattern. All are within the known rhythmic vocabulary of the children, except #27.

Songs #28 to #31 present the new note *re* in the *m-r-d* trichord.

Songs #32 to #39 present the new note *re* in the *s-m-r-d* tone set. The only unknown in songs #32 to #36 is the half note. They may be used to aurally prepare the children for this. Songs #37 to #39 contain rhythmic complexities, but may be used to reinforce the *s-m-r-d* tonal patterns.

Songs #40 to #45 are in the basic *do*-pentatonic scale. Once the half note has been introduced, songs #40 to #43 are within the known musical vocabulary. Songs #44 and #45 are within the known *solfa* set, but are rhythmically more complex.

Songs #46 and #47 may be used to introduce the new note low *la* in a *do*-pentatonic setting.

Song #48 reinforces the new learning in a rhythmically more complex setting.

Songs #49 to #77 present the *do*-pentatonic scale extended to low *so*. Many of these songs will be used to present the rhythmic figures, in $\frac{2}{4}$ and $\frac{4}{4}$, ♩.♪, ♪♩ ♪, ♪♩., ♫♫, ♫♩, ♩♫, and in $\frac{6}{8}$, ♫♫, ♩., ♩ ♪, and to prepare $\frac{3}{4}$ meter.

Songs #78 to #83 present the *do*-pentatonic scale extended to high *do, re,* and *mi.*

Songs #84 to #92 are in *la*-tetratonic and -pentatonic. These tone sets are of minor character; *la* is the tonal center. They are the songs through which the first identification of major-minor characteristics is introduced.

Song #93 is a pentatonic song ending on *re,* i.e., it has a *re*-pentatonic scale. This mode is uncommon, but interesting and beautiful.[1]

Songs #94 to #98 are *so*-pentatonic. Their tonal center—the final note—is *so.* This mode is more common in English-language folk song.

Songs #99 to #121 introduce the new note *fa.* The earlier ones present the new note in stepwise patterns, while the later ones present it in the context of the broken IV chord, *f-l-d,* or II chord, *r-f-l.* In this group of songs $\frac{6}{8}$ meter is reinforced and $\frac{3}{4}$ and $\frac{6}{4}$ meters are prepared, as are the rhythm patterns ♩. ♩ and ♫. .

Songs #122 to #136 present the new note *ti* in the context of *do*-tonal-center songs with a plagel range, i.e., from low *so* to high *so* or *la.* This is the most common range of English-language folk songs. The earlier songs present *ti* as the leading tone or neighboring tone to *do.* Later songs present it in the context of the broken V or V$_7$ chord $s_,$-$t_,$-r or $s_,$-$t_,$-r-$f.$

Songs #137 to #143 present the new note *ti* in the authentic range from *do* to *do'* with some songs extending above high *do* or below low *do.* Song #139 is based primarily on the upper tetrachord and is a good possibility for first introducing *ti.*

Songs #144 to #155 introduce *ti* as the second degree of the scale in minor modes—modes that are solmized ending on *la.* Special mention must be made of #155, "The Dewy Dells of Yarrow." This is a ballad in the ancient style with literally hundreds of verses.[2]

Songs #156 to #158 are in harmonic minor and introduce the sharped form of *so, si.*

Songs #159 to #165 are in the Mixolydian mode. They may be solmized either as a *do* scale with a flatted *ti, ta,* or with a natural scale from *so* to *so'.* Songs #164 and #165 are ballads from an ancient tradition, with many verses.[3]

Songs #166 to #170 are in the Dorian mode. They may be solmized either as a *la* scale with a sharped *fa, fi,* or with a natural scale from *re* to *re'.*

Songs #171 and #172 employ accidentals. The new note *di,* the sharped *do,* is introduced.

---

[1]Further examples of it may be found in the author's *The Kodály Context.*

[2]A good version of this, with enough verses to tell the story, may be found in: Edith Fowke (Ed.), *The Penguin Book of Canadian Folk Songs* (Harmondsworth, Middlesex: Penguin, 1973), pp. 178–179.

[3]Fowke, *loc. cit.,* pp. 166–167 and 162–164, respectively.

LISTENING THEMES

The themes are given as examples of art music that may be presented to elementary school children through singing. They by no means comprise a total listening program, but they do encompass every period from Baroque to Twentieth Century. Each has been used by the author with children. They are arranged in historical rather than in teaching order. One possible teaching order for a listening program has been suggested in Chapter 9.

A few teaching suggestions for each are offered below.

J. S. Bach:

Chorale from *The St. Matthew Passion;* Chorale "Jesu, Joy of Man's Desiring"; "Little G-minor Fugue."

The melody of the chorale from *The St. Matthew Passion* is an easy reading example for fifth graders. They should read it in *solfa,* memorize it, and harmonize it with *do, fa* and *so* (I, IV and V). The teacher should then play the Bach harmonization, so that they may compare theirs to it. At a later lesson the children may experiment with singing and conducting the chorale in another meter, $\frac{3}{4}$.

The teacher should then play for them "Jesu, Joy of Man's Desiring"—which is the same melody in triple meter. Later still they may focus on the $\frac{9}{8}$ countermelody in this work and learn to sing it in *solfa.* Eventually they should be able to sing it in two parts—the melody and the countermelody.

The "Little G-minor Fugue" may be approached similarly by singing and memorizing before hearing any recording. At repeated hearings children should listen to hear how many times the theme recurs, whether it is in a higher, lower, or middle range at each statement, and what the overall dynamic structure of the piece is.[4]

G. F. Handel:

The Minuet #2 from *The Royal Fireworks.*

This is an excellent study in sequence. The teacher may have the children read the melody from either staff notation or stem and *solfa* notation. They should then find and sing all examples of sequence or altered sequence in the melody. They should then listen to the composition. Later they may use part of the same rhythm and try to compose musical examples using sequence.

F. J. Haydn:

Cello Concerto in D Major, op. 101.

The third movement, allegro, of this concerto begins with an extremely singable melody in $\frac{6}{8}$ meter, which occurs repeatedly. It is an ideal vehicle through which to introduce children to Rondo form.

---

[4]For detailed notes on presenting the "Little G-minor Fugue" see the author's *The Kodály Context,* pp. 95–96.

St. Anthony's Chorale.

This chorale may be read, harmonized with *do, fa* and *so,* and the sequences in it discovered before being listened to. Later Brahms' variations on this theme should also be heard.

W. A. Mozart:

Third movement, Minuet and Trio, from Symphony #40 in G-minor.

The simple singable melodies of the third movement of Symphony #40 may be read, sung in *solfa,* and analyzed before the movement is heard. Attention should be directed to the sequences in the minuet and to the question-answer phrases in the trio. The minuet should be compared to the Handel minuet when the latter is studied.

F. Schubert:

"Landler"; The *Trout* Quintet.

The simple minor melody of the "Landler" may be sung and harmonized before being heard. Later, inner voices also can be read and sung.

The *lied* "The Trout" should be learned simply as a song in its entirety. Later, possible ways of varying the melody should be discussed and experimented with before hearing Schubert's variations on the theme in the last movement of the Quintet.

L. Van Beethoven:

Symphonies #6 and #9.

The last movement of each of these symphonies is extremely vocal in style, with the Ninth, of course, actually employing a choir. They may be taught as melodies by rote, or read or sung as melodic dictation by the teacher. In any case the children should notate them and memorize them before listening to the composer's treatment of these themes.

J. Brahms:

Fourth movement of Symphony #4 in E-minor; Fourth movement of Symphony #1 in C-minor.

The entire last movement of the Fourth Symphony is a passacaglia, i.e., a set of variations, each eight bars in length, on the simple minor scale melody given. The children should sing the theme, discuss possible ways of varying it, and then listen to the Brahms to discover the theme buried in each eight-bar segment.

In the first symphony the finale is built on the extremely singable chorale given here. Children have little difficulty following Brahms' treatment of the theme.

P. I. Tchaikovsky:

Finale from Symphony #4.

This small Russian folk tune is of tripodic phrase structure, i.e., each phrase is three bars long rather than the usual two or four. After learning the melody children should listen to Tchaikovsky's treatment of it to see how he "varied" it. He added measures, making it the more usual four-measure phrase, and he stated it in major and in augmentation, among other devices.

C. Debussy:

"The Girl with the Flaxen Hair."
This small piano piece is a good way to introduce freer forms and less rigid rhythm. The melody is easy to sing and easy to follow throughout the piece.

I. Stravinsky:

Finale from *The Firebird*.
There are numerous singable themes in this monumental early twentieth-century work; the magical creatures in it are all represented by complex chromaticism, but the themes representing mortals are all broadly diatonic. The finale, with its sweeping diatonic melody, interrupted at the very end by the chromatic music of the Firebird, is a good introduction to this piece for children.

CONCLUSION

It is hoped that these examples will serve as a guide to teachers searching for materials with which to use the Kodály Method. Certainly there are other suitable songs and listening themes at every step. As better materials are found they should be added or substituted for those given here. One of the principal purposes of this collection, after all, is to indicate the factors which must be examined in the selection of songs and listening themes.

The Songs

1. THE COUNTING SONG

sm

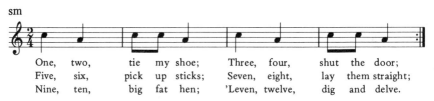

One,   two,   tie my shoe;   Three, four,   shut the door;
Five,   six,   pick up sticks;   Seven, eight,   lay them straight;
Nine,   ten,   big fat hen;   'Leven, twelve,   dig and delve.

2. CUCKOO

sm

Cuck - oo,   where are you?   Cuck - oo,   where are you?

3. ICHA BACKA

lsm

Ich - a back - a   So - da crack - er,   Ich - a back - a   boo,

Ich - a back - a   So - da crack - er,   Out   goes   you!

4. LUCY LOCKET

lsm

Lu - cy Lock-et   lost her pock -et,   Kit - ty Fish - er   found   it,
Not a pen - ny   was there in it,   on - ly rib - bon   round   it.

5. BLUE BELLS

lsm

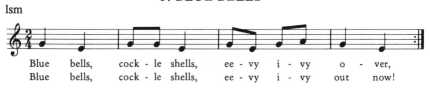

Blue   bells,   cock - le shells,   ee - vy i - vy   o - ver,
Blue   bells,   cock - le shells,   ee - vy i - vy   out   now!

6. THE MILL WHEEL

lsm

Round and round the wheel goes round,   As it turns the   corn is ground.

7. RAIN, RAIN

lsm

Rain, Rain,   go a - way;   Come a - gain some   oth - er   day;
Sun - shine's   here to stay,   Now we can go   out to   play.

8. BYE BABY BUNTING

lsm

Bye   ba - by   bunt - ing   Dad-dy's gone a - hunt - ing to

Catch a lit - tle   rab - bit skin to wrap the ba - by bunt - ing in.

9. SEE SAW

lsm

See   Saw,   up and down,   In the air and   on the ground

10. GOODNIGHT

lsm

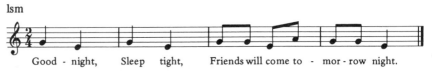

Good - night,   Sleep   tight,   Friends will come to - mor - row night.

11. BYE, LO BABY, O

lsm

Bye,   lo   Ba - by, O,   Off to dream-land   you must   go.

12. THE WISHING SONG

lsm

Star - light   star   bright   First   star   I   see   to - night,

Wish I may,   Wish I might,   Have the wish I   wish to - night.

13. CLAP YOUR HANDS

lsm

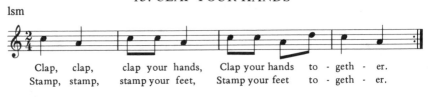

Clap,   clap,   clap your hands,   Clap your hands   to - geth - er.
Stamp, stamp,   stamp your feet,   Stamp your feet   to - geth - er.

14. I'M THE KING OF THE CASTLE

lsm

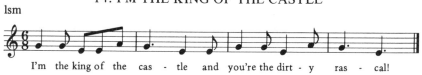

I'm the king of the cas - tle and you're the dirt - y ras - cal!

15. OLIVER TWIST

lsm

O - li - ver Twist, you can't do this, So

what's the use of try - ing; Touch your knees,

touch your toes, Clap your hands and a - round you go!

16. HILL, DILL

lsm

Hill, dill, come o - ver the hill

or else I'll catch you stand - ing still.

17. HICKETY TICKETY

lsm

Hick - e - ty Tick - e - ty Bum - ble Bee,

Can you sing your name to me?

18. A TISKET, A TASKET

lsm

A tisk - et a task - et, a green and yel - low bask - et,

I sent a let - ter to my love and on the way I lost it,

I lost it, I lost it, yes, on the way I lost it.

19. PLAINSES, CLAPSIES

lsm

Plain - ses, clap - sies, Turn a - round to

back - sies, Touch your knee, Touch your toe,

Touch your heel and a - round you go!

20. RING AROUND THE ROSY

lsm ⓓ

Ring a - round the ros - y, Pock - et full of pos - y,

Ash - es, ash - es, All fall down!

21. JOHNNY CAUGHT A FLEA

Tee, hee, hee!   John - ny caught a flea!

Flea died, John - ny cried,   Tee, hee, hee!

22. MOTHER, MOTHER

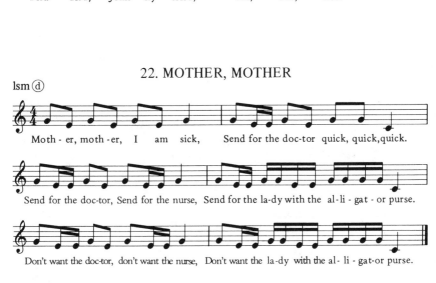

Moth - er, moth - er, I am sick,   Send for the doc-tor quick, quick, quick.

Send for the doc-tor, Send for the nurse, Send for the la-dy with the al - li - gat - or purse.

Don't want the doc-tor, don't want the nurse, Don't want the la-dy with the al - li - gat-or purse.

23. TEDDY BEAR

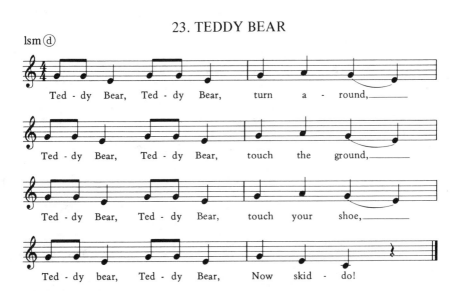

Ted - dy Bear, Ted - dy Bear, turn a - round,_____

Ted - dy Bear, Ted - dy Bear, touch the ground,_____

Ted - dy Bear, Ted - dy Bear, touch your shoe,_____

Ted - dy bear, Ted - dy Bear, Now skid - do!

24. FUZZY WUZZY

sm ⓓ

Fuz - zy Wuz - zy was a bear, Fuz - zy Wuz - zy had no hair.

Fuz - zy Wuz - zy was - n't fuz - zy, was he!

25. I SEE THE MOON

sm ⓓ

I see the moon and the moon sees me,

God bless the sai - lors and God bless me.

26. CURFEW SONG

sm ⓓ

Hear you peo - ple while I tell you,
All the clocks have now struck one.

Keep the fire and keep the light,
Keep our hous - es safe this night.

Love your God to - night.

27. HOT CROSS BUNS

mr ⓓ

Hot   cross   buns!   Hot   cross   buns!

One a pen-ny, two a pen-ny, Hot cross buns!

28. CLOSET KEY

mr ⓓ

I have lost the clos-et key   in   my   la-dy's   gar - den,

I have lost the clos-et key   in   my   la-dy's   gar - den.

2. Help me find the closet key in my lady's garden.

3. I have found the closet key in my lady's garden.

29. HOP, OLD SQUIRREL

mr ⓓ

Hop,   old   squirrel,   ei - dle - dum,   ei - dle - dum,

Hop,   old   squirrel,   ei - dle - dum,   dee!

Hop,   old   squirrel,   ei - dle - dum,   ei - dle - dum,

Hop,   old   squirrel,   ei - dle - dum,   dee!

30. GRANDMA GRUNTS

mr (d)

Grand - ma Grunts said a cu - rious thing,

"Boys can whis - tle but girls must sing,"

That is what I heard her say,

'Twas no lon - ger than yes - ter - day!

Boys can whis - tle, *(whistling . . . .)*

Girls must sing, Tra, la, la, la, la!

31. JIM ALONG JOSIE

smr (d)   Traditional

Hey! Come a - long, Jim, a - long Jo - sie!

Hey! Come a - long, Jim, a - long Joe!

32. SLEEP, BABY, SLEEP

smr ⓓ

Sleep, ba - by, sleep; Fa - ther tends the sheep;

Moth - er shakes the dream-land tree And down come all the

dreams for thee. Sleep, ba - by sleep.

33. SWING A LADY UPTOM

smr ⓓ

Swing a la - dy up - tom, Swing a la - dy down!

Swing a la - dy up - tom, Prom - e - nade a - round!

34. WHO'S THAT?

Virginia

smr ⓓ

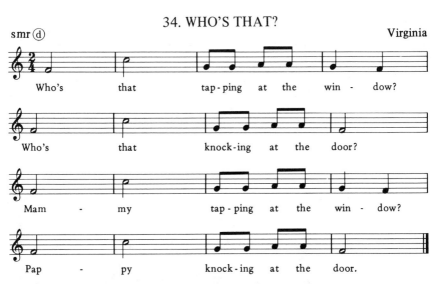

Who's that tap - ping at the win - dow?

Who's that knock-ing at the door?

Mam - my tap - ping at the win - dow?

Pap - py knock-ing at the door.

From *American Folk Songs for Children* by Ruth Crawford Seeger. Reprinted by permission of Curtis Brown, Ltd. Copyright, 1948, by Ruth Crawford Seeger.

35. BYE, BYE, BABY

smr ⓓ

Bye, Bye,— Ba - by,   Ba - by bye,   My lit-tle Ba - by,   Ba - by, bye.

36. OLD BLUE

smr ⓓ

I   had   a   dog   and his   name   was   Blue,———

I   had   a   dog   and his   name   was   Blue.———

I   had   a   dog   and his   name   was   Blue,———

And   I   bet - cha five   dol - lars he's a   good dog   too.

Here———   Blue!   You   good   dog   you.

2. Chased that possum up a hollow tree,
   Best huntin' dog you ever did see.

3. Caught that possum up a hollow tree,
   Best huntin' dog you ever did see.

4. Baked that possum good and brown,
   Laid sweet potaters all around.

5. Old Blue died, he died one day,
   So I dug his grave and I buried him away.

6. I dug his grave with a silver spade,
   Lowered him down with a golden chain.

7. When I get to heaven there's one thing I'll do,
   I'll grab me a horn and blow for Blue!

37. THAT'S A MIGHTY PRETTY MOTION

smr ⓓ

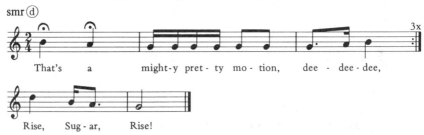

That's   a   might-y pret - ty mo - tion,   dee - dee - dee,

Rise,   Sug - ar,   Rise!

38. MERRILY WE ROLL ALONG

smr ⓓ

Mer - ri - ly we roll a - long, roll a - long, roll a - long,

Mer - ri - ly we roll a - long, o'er the bright blue sea.

39. HERE COMES A BLUEBIRD

lsmr ⓓ   Traditional

Here comes a blue - bird, In through my win - dow

Hey Did - dle - um - a Day - Day - Day.

2. Takes a pretty partner into the garden,
Hey___ Diddle-um-a Day Day Day.

40. KNOCK THE CYMBALS

lsmr ⓓ

Knock the cym-bals, do, oh, do, Knock the cym-bals, do, oh, do,

Knock the cym - bals, do, oh, do, Oh law' Sus - ie gal!

41. WHEN YOU GET A GOOD THING

lsmr ⓓ

When you get a good thing, Save it, save it,

When you get a good thing, Save it if you can.

42. BUTTON

lsmr ⓓ   Traditional

But - ton, you must   wan - der,   wan - der,   wan - der,

But - ton, you must   wan - der   ever - y - where,

Bright eyes will   find   you,   sharp eyes will   find   you,

But - ton, you must   wan - der   ever - y - where.

43. DO, DO PITY MY CASE

lsmr ⓓ

Do,   do   pit - y my case,   In some la - dy's gar - den,

My   clothes to wash when I come home,___ In some la - dy's gar - den.

44. FED MY HORSE IN A POPLAR TROUGH

lsmr ⓓ

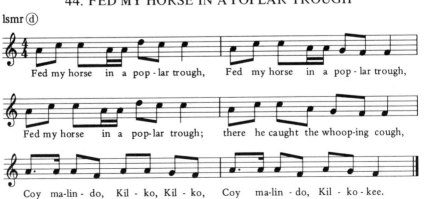

Fed my horse   in a pop - lar trough,   Fed my horse   in a pop - lar trough,

Fed my horse   in a pop-lar trough;   there he caught the whoop-ing cough,

Coy ma-lin - do, Kil - ko, Kil - ko,   Coy   ma-lin - do, Kil - ko - kee.

45. OLD MISTER RABBIT

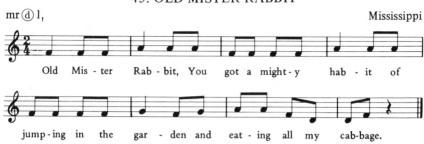

Old Mis - ter Rab - bit, You got a might - y hab - it of

jump - ing in the gar - den and eat - ing all my cab-bage.

46. JIM ALONG JOSIE

Hey, come a - long____ Jim, a - long Jo - sie,

Hey, come a - long____ Jim, a - long Joe.

47. THE BELL COW

Par - tridge in the pea patch, pick - in' up the peas,

Long comes the Bell Cow, kick - in' up her heels,

Oh the Bell Cow, catch her by the tail,

Call the lit - tle gal to milk her in the pail.

48. OLD MACDONALD HAD A FARM

mr ⓓ l, s,

Old Mac - Don - ald had a farm, e - i - e - i - o

And on that farm he had a cow, e - i - e - i - o

With a moo, moo here and a moo, moo there,

Here a moo, there a moo, eve - ry - where a moo, moo,

Old Mac - Don - ald had a farm, e - i - e - i - o.

mr ⓓ l, s,   49. COTTON-EYE JOE   Alabama

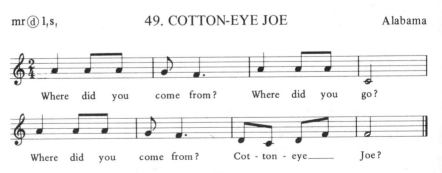

Where did you come from? Where did you go?

Where did you come from? Cot - ton - eye___ Joe?

2. Come for to see you,
   Come for to sing.
   Come for to show you
   My diamond ring.

50. SWAPPING SONG

mr ⓓ l₍s₍

Virginia

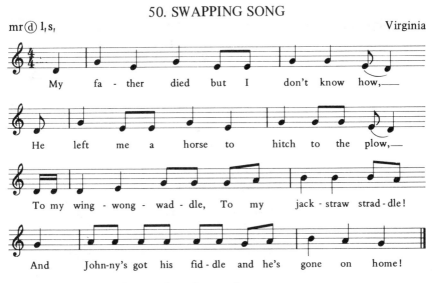

My fa - ther died but I don't know how,——
He left me a horse to hitch to the plow,——
To my wing - wong - wad - dle, To my jack - straw strad - dle!
And John-ny's got his fid - dle and he's gone on home!

2. I swapped my horse and got me a cow,
And in that trade I just learned how.

3. I swapped my cow and got me a calf.
And in that trade I lost just half.

4. I swapped my calf and got me a pig,
The poor little thing it never growed big.

From *American Folk Tales and Songs* by Richard Chase. Dover Publications, Inc., New York, 1956. Reprinted through the permission of the publisher.

51. HERE SHE COMES SO FRESH AND FAIR

smr ⓓ l₍s₍

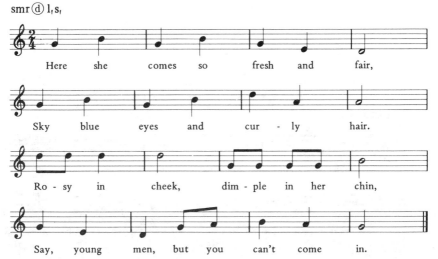

Here she comes so fresh and fair,
Sky blue eyes and cur - ly hair.
Ro - sy in cheek, dim - ple in her chin,
Say, young men, but you can't come in.

52. MY OLD HAMMER

smr ⓓ l, s,   Work Song

My old ham - mer___ shine-a like   sil - ver,___

shine-a like   gold,   boys,___ yes shine - a like   gold.___

2. Ain't no hammer, in-a this mountain,
   Shine-a like mine, boys, yes shine-a like mine.

3. I been working on-a this railroad,
   Four long years, boys, yes four long years.

53. CHICKEN ON A FENCE POST

smr ⓓ l, s,

Chick-en on a fence post, can't dance Jo-sie, Chicken on a fence post, can't dance Jo - sie,

Chick-en on a fence post, can't dance Jo - sie, Hel - lo Su - san Brown!

54. GOLDEN RING AROUND SUSAN

smr ⓓ l, s,

Gold-en ring a-round the   Su-san girl,   Gol-den ring a-round the   Su-san girl,

Gold-en ring a-round the Su - san girl,   All the way a-round our   Su-san girl.

55. OLD ROGER

mr ⓓ l₁ s₁

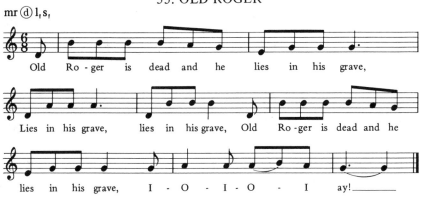

Old Ro - ger is dead and he lies in his grave,

Lies in his grave, lies in his grave, Old Ro -ger is dead and he

lies in his grave, I - O - I - O - I ay!_____

56. THERE'S A HOLE IN MY BUCKET

mr ⓓ l₁ s₁

There's a hole in my buck - et, dear Li - za, dear Li - za,

There's a hole in my buck - et, dear Li - za, a hole.

57. HOLD MY MULE

lsmr ⓓ l₁ s₁

Hold my mule while I dance, Jos - ie, Hold my mule while I dance, Jos - ie,

Hold my mule while I dance, Jos - ie, Hel - lo Sus - an Brown.

58. I'VE BEEN TO HAARLEM

lsmr ⓓ l, s,

Play Party Game

I've been to Haar - lem, I've been to Do - ver,

I've trav - eled this wide world all o - ver,

O - ver, o - ver, three times o - ver, Drink all the bran - dy wine and

turn the glass - es o - ver. Sail - ing east, sail - ing west,

Sail - ing o - ver the o - cean, Bet - ter watch out when the

boat be - gins to rock or you'll lose your girl in the o - cean.

59. MARY HAD A BABY

lsmr ⓓ l, s,

Spiritual

Ma - ry had a ba - by, yes, Lord,

Ma - ry had a ba - by, yes, my Lord,

Ma - ry had a ba - by, yes, Lord, The

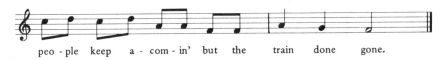

peo - ple   keep   a - com - in'   but   the   train   done   gone.

2. Laid Him in a manger.

3. Shepherds came to see Him.

4. Angels sang His glory.

60. FROG WENT A-COURTIN'

lsmr ⓓ l, s,

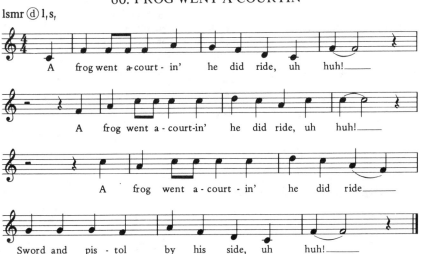

A   frog went a-court - in'   he   did   ride,   uh   huh!____

A   frog went a - court-in'   he   did   ride,   uh   huh!____

A   frog   went a - court - in'   he   did   ride____

Sword and   pis - tol   by   his   side,   uh   huh!____

2. He rode up to Miss Mous-ie's door, uh huh!
   He rode up to Miss Mous-ie's door
   A place he'd never been before, uh huh!

3. He took Miss Mousie on his knee,
   And said, "Miss Mousie will you marry me?"

4. Oh, where will the wedding supper be?
   Way down yonder by the hollow tree.

5. The first to come was Mr. Stick,
   He ate so much it made him sick

6. The next to come was an old brown cow,
   She tried to dance but she didn't know how.

7. The frog and mouse they went to France,
   And that is the end of this romance.

8. Let's put Miss Mousie on the shelf,
   If you want any more you can sing it for yourself.

61. THE SALLY BUCK

lsmr ⓓ l, s,   Appalachian

I start-ed out a hunt - ing one cold and win - ter day. The leaves they were a - grow - ing green, And the flow'rs were fresh and gay, And the flow's were fresh and gay.

2. I tracked the Sally buck all day,
I tracked him through the snow;
I tracked him through the waterside,
And under he did go,
And under he did go.

62. JENNY JENKINS

lsmr ⓓ l, s,   Appalachian

Will you wear white o my dear, o my dear?

Will you wear white, Jen - ny Jen - kins?

I won't wear white, for the col - or's too bright,

I'll buy me a fol - di - rol - di, til - di - tol - di, Seek a dou - ble

Use a cau - sa roll the find me,

Roll, Jen - ny Jen - kins, roll.

63. OLD GRAY GOOSE

lsmr ⓓ l, s,

Southern Folk Song

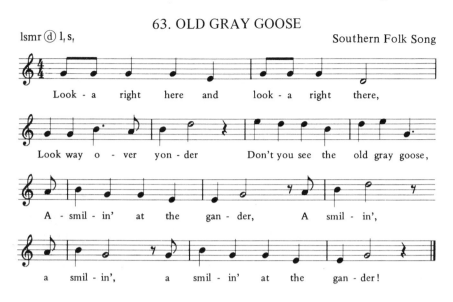

Look - a right here and look - a right there,
Look way o - ver yon - der Don't you see the old gray goose,
A - smil - in' at the gan - der, A smil - in',
a smil - in', a smil - in' at the gan - der!

64. CINDY

lsmr ⓓ l, s,

Southern Folk Song

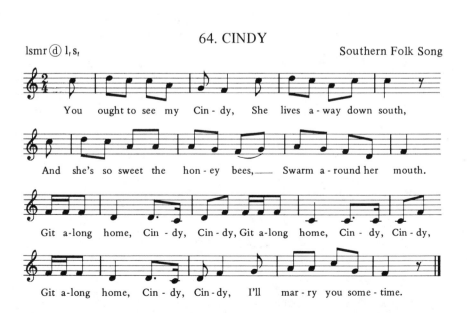

You ought to see my Cin - dy, She lives a - way down south,
And she's so sweet the hon - ey bees,___ Swarm a - round her mouth.
Git a-long home, Cin - dy, Cin - dy, Git a-long home, Cin - dy, Cin - dy,
Git a-long home, Cin - dy, Cin - dy, I'll mar - ry you some - time.

65. YONDER MOUNTAIN

lsmr ⓓ l, s,

Virginia

At the foot of yon-der   moun-tain there   runs   a   clear   stream,

At the foot of yon - der   moun-tain there   lives . a   fair   queen.

She's   hand-some, She's pro - per, and her ways are com - plete,

I_____   ask   no bet-ter pas-time than to   be with my   sweet.

2. But why she won't have me I well understand;
She wants some freeholder and I have no land
I cannot maintain her on silver and gold,
And all other fine things that my love's house should hold.

From *American Folk Tales and Songs* by Richard Chase. Dover Publications, Inc., New York, 1956. Reprinted through the permission of the publisher.

66. COFFEE GROWS ON WHITE OAK TREES

lsmr ⓓ l, s,

Southern

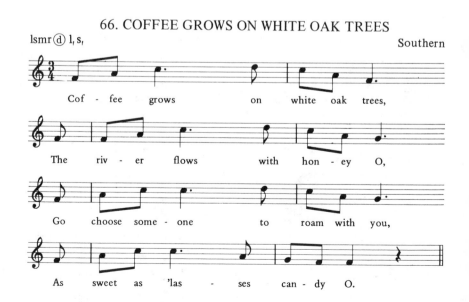

Cof - fee   grows   on   white   oak   trees,

The   riv - er   flows   with   hon - ey   O,

Go   choose   some - one   to   roam   with   you,

As   sweet   as   'las - ses   can - dy   O.

Chorus:

Two in the mid - dle and they can't get o - ver,
Two in the mid-dle and they can't get o - ver, Two in the mid-dle and they
can't get o - ver, Hel - lo, Su - san Brown!

67. LONESOME VALLEY

lsmr ⓓ l, s,

Spiritual

Je - sus walked_____ this lone - some val - ley._____
____ He had to walk_____ it by Him - self.
Oh, no - bod - y else____ could walk it for Him.____
____ He had to walk it for___ Him - self.____

68. THE DEVIL'S QUESTIONS

lsmr ⓓl, s,

Virginia

If you can't an - swer my ques - tions nine,

Sing nine - ty nine and nine - ty!

O you're not God's you're one of mine,

And the crow flies o - ver the white oak tree.

2. O what is higher than the tree? And what is deeper than the sea?

3. O heaven is higher than the tree, And love is deeper than the sea.

4. O what is whiter than the milk? And what is softer than the silk?

5. O snow is whiter than the milk, And down is softer than the silk.

6. O what is louder than the horn? And what is sharper than the thorn?

7. O thunder's louder than the horn, And hunger's sharper than the thorn.

8. What is heavier than the lead? And what is better than the bread?

9. Grief is heavier than the lead, God's blessing's better than the bread.

10. Now you have answered my questions nine, O you are God's you're none of mine.

From *American Folk Tales and Songs* by Richard Chase. Dover Publications, Inc., New York, 1956. Reprinted through the permission of the publisher.

69. PERRY MERRY DICTUM DOMINEE

mrⓓs,

Appalachian

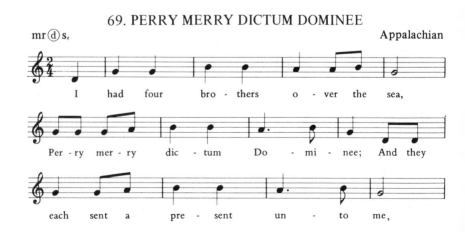

I had four bro - thers o - ver the sea,

Per - ry mer - ry dic - tum Do - mi - nee; And they

each sent a pre - sent un - to me,

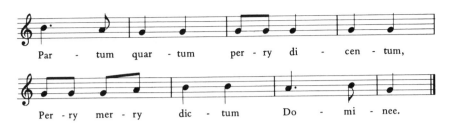

Par - tum quar - tum per - ry di - cen - tum,

Per - ry mer - ry dic - tum Do - mi - nee.

2. The first sent me cherries without any stones. Perry. . . . .
   The second sent a chicken without any bones. Partum Quartum. . . . .

3. The third sent a blanket that had no thread. Perry. . . . .
   The fourth sent a book that could not be read. Partum Quartum. . . . .

4. When the cherries are in bloom they have no stones. Perry. . . . .
   When the chicken's in the egg it has no bone. Partum Quartum. . . . .

5. When the blanket's in the fleece, it has no thread. Perry. . . . .
   When the book's in the press, it cannot be read. Partum Quartum. . . . .

70. THE FARMER IN THE DELL

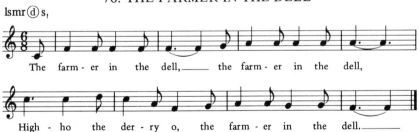

The farm - er in the dell, —— the farm - er in the dell,

High - ho the der - ry o, the farm - er in the dell. ——

71. LADY COME DOWN

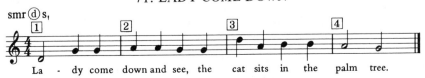

La - dy come down and see, the cat sits in the palm tree.

72. SWEEP AWAY

Louisiana

Sweep, sweep, sweep a - way,

Sweep the road of dreams,

Peo - ple say that in the night,

The tur - tle will talk it seems,

The tur - tle will talk it seems.

73. HUSH LITTLE BABY

Southern

Hush lit - tle ba - by, don't say a word,

Pa - pa's gon - na buy you a mock - ing bird.

2. If that mocking bird won't sing,
   Papa's gonna buy you a diamond ring.

3. If that diamond ring turns brass,
   Papa's gonna buy you a lookin' glass.

4. If that lookin' glass gets broke,
   Papa's gonna buy you a billy goat.

74. SHANGHAI CHICKEN

mr(d)s,

Shang - hai chick-en and he grow so tall, Hoo - day! Hoo - day!

Take that egg a month to fall, Hoo - day! Hoo - day!

2. Shanghai chicken and he grow so tough, Hooday! Hooday!
   Just can't cook him long enough, Hooday! Hooday!

3. Shanghai chicken and he grow so fat, Hooday! Hooday!
   Won a fight with a mean pole cat, Hooday! Hooday!

75. THE FOUNTAIN

smr(d)s,

French Canadian

One night as I lay dream-ing, Lost in a rev - er - ie,

I heard a love - ly foun-tain, Play - ing so close to me;

Some - where that foun-tain is flow-ing, I won-der, where can it be?

76. DERRY DING DONG DASON

smr(d)s,

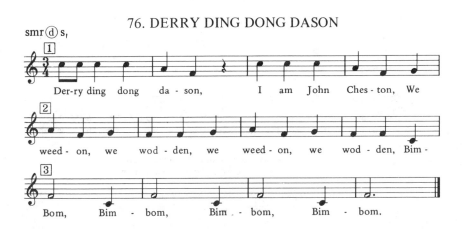

Der-ry ding dong da - son, I am John Ches - ton, We

weed - on, we wod - den, we weed - on, we wod - den, Bim -

Bom, Bim - bom, Bim - bom, Bim - bom.

77. GOODBYE OL' PAINT

lsmr ⓓ s₁   Cowboy Song

Good - bye ol' Paint, I'm a leav - in' Chey - enne,

My foot in the stir - rup, my po - ny won't stand,

I'm a leav - in' Chey - enne and I'm off for Mon - tan'.

2. I'm a ridin' Ol' Paint and a leadin' Ol' Dan,
Goodbye little Annie. I'm off for Montan.

78. BLOOD ON THE SADDLE

d' lsmr ⓓ

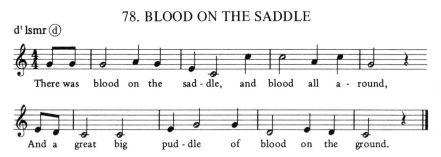

There was blood on the sad - dle, and blood all a - round,

And a great big pud - dle of blood on the ground.

2. The cowboy lay in it all covered with gore,
And he won't go ri-din' no broncos no more.

3. Oh pity the cowboy, all bloody and red,
For his bronco fell on him and mashed in his head.

79. I HAD ME A BIRD

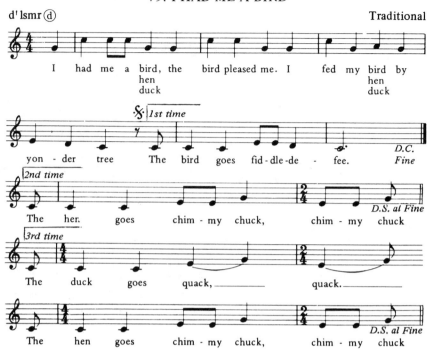

I had me a bird, the bird pleased me. I fed my bird by
  hen   hen
  duck   duck

yon - der tree The bird goes fid - dle -de - fee.   *D.C.*
                                                            Fine

2nd time
The her. goes chim - my chuck, chim - my chuck
                                              D.S. al Fine

3rd time
The duck goes quack, _____ quack. _____

The hen goes chim - my chuck, chim - my chuck
                                              D.S. al Fine

80. BILLY CAME OVER THE MAIN WHITE OCEAN

Bil - ly came o-ver the main white o - cean, Bil - ly came o-ver the sea,

Bil - ly came down to my fa - ther's house, Bil - ly came a court-in' of

me, me, me, Bil - ly came a court - in' of me.

2. Go choose your pot of mother's gold
   And a pot of father's bees
   And to some far country we will go
   And it's married we will be, be, be,
   And it's married we will be.

81. THE GAMBLING SUITOR

d' lsmr ⓓ   Virginia

Sir I see you__ come a-gain; pray tell me what it's for,

When I left you in__ Bar-bour-ville,__ I told you to come no

more.   I   told   you   to   come   no___ more.

2. Miss, I have a very fine house, newly built with pine,
   And you may have it at your command, if you will be my bride.

3. Sir I know it's very fine house, also a very fine yard,
   But who will stay at home with me when you're out playing cards?

From *American Folk Tales and Songs* by Richard Chase. Dover Publications, Inc., New York, 1956. Reprinted through the permission of the publisher.

82. HOP UP, MY LADIES

r' d' lsmr ⓓ   Traditional

Hop   up,   my lad - ies,   three in   a   row,

Hop   up,   my lad - ies,   three   in   a   row,

Hop   up,   my lad - ies,   three   in   a   row,

Don't   mind   the   weath-er if   the   wind   don't   blow.

83. RAIN, COME WET ME

m' r' d' lsmr ⓓ   Texas

Rain, come   wet__ me,   Sun, come   dry__ me,

Keep a - way,   pret - ty girls,   Don't come   nigh__ me!

From *American Folk Songs for Children*. Reprinted by permission of Curtis Brown, Ltd. Copyright. 1948, by Ruth Crawford Seeger.

84. THE MERRY GOLDEN TREE

d' lsmr(d)l, s,   Virginia

There   was   a   lit - tle ship   and she   sailed   on the sea,

And the   name___ of the ship   was the   Mer - ry   Gol - den   Tree,

And she   sailed on   the lone - ly___   lone - some   wat - er,

And   she   sailed on·   the   lone - some___   sea.

2. There was another ship and she sailed on the sea.
   And the name of the ship was The Turkish Robbery:
   And she sailed on the lonely lonesome water,
   And she sailed on the lonesome sea.

3. There was a little sailor boy unto the captain said,
   Oh captain, oh captain, what will you give to me
   If I sink her in the lonely lonesome water,
   If I sink her in the lonesome sea?

4. Two hundred golden dollars I will give unto thee,
   And my youngest pretty daughter for your wedded wife to be,
   If you'll sink her in the lonely lonesome water,
   If you'll sink her in the lonesome sea.

5. Oh it's down into the waves and away swam he;
   He swam until he came to The Turkish Robbery,
   Where she sailed on the lonely lonesome water,
   Where she sailed on the lonesome sea.

6. Then out of his pocket an auger he drew,
   And he bored nine holes for to let the water through,
   And he sunk her in the lonely lonesome water,
   And he sunk her in the lonesome sea.

7. He turned upon his breast and back swam he;
   He swam until he came to The Merry Golden Tree,
   Where she sailed on the lonely lonesome water,
   Where she sailed on the lonesome sea.

8. Oh captain, oh captain, won't you take me on board?
   Oh captain, oh captain, won't you be good as your word?
   For I've sunk her in the lonely lonesome water,
   For I've sunk her in the lonesome sea.

9. Oh I will not take you in, the captain he replied,
   For you shall never have my pretty daughter for your bride,
   And I'm sailing on the lonely lonesome water,
   And I'm sailing on the lonesome sea.

10. If it wasn't for the love I have for your men,
    I would do unto you as I've done unto them,
    I would sink you in the lonely lonesome water.
    I would sink you in the lonesome sea.

11. He turned upon his back and down sank he;
    Fare ye well! Fare ye well to The Merry Golden Tree!
    For I'm sinking in the lonely lonesome water,
    For I'm sinking in the lonesome sea.

From *American Folk Tales and Songs,* by Richard Chase. Dover Publications, Inc., New York, 1956. Reprinted through the permission of the publisher.

85. I GOT A LETTER

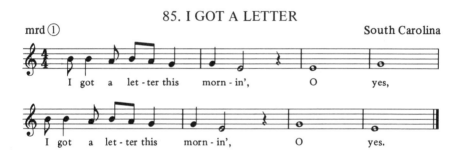

86. CANOE SONG

2. Dip, dip and swing her back,
   Flashing like silver,
   Swift as the wild goose flies,
   Dip, dip and swing.

87. OLD HOUSE

mrd ①

Old house, tear it down! Who's gon - na help me

tear it down? Bring me a ham - mer, tear it down!

Bring me a saw,_____ tear it down! Next thing you bring me,

tear it down! Is a wreck-ing ma - chine, tear it down!

88. BIG-EYED RABBIT

mrd ① s₁

Rab-bit is the kind of thing that trav - els in the dark,

nev - er knows when dan-ger's round till he hears old Ro - ver bark.

Big-eyed rab - bit, Boo! Boo! Big-eyed rab - bit, Boo!

Big-eyed rab - bit, Boo! Boo! Big-eyed rab - bit, Boo!

89. WHO KILLED COCK ROBIN?

1'mrd ①

Appalachian

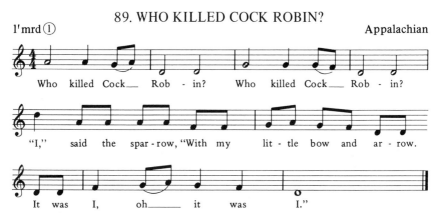

Who killed Cock__ Rob - in? Who killed Cock__ Rob - in?

"I," said the spar - row, "With my lit - tle bow and ar - row.

It was I, oh____ it was I."

From *American Folk Tales and Songs* by Richard Chase, published by Dover Publications, Inc., N.Y. 1956. Reprinted with permission.

90. LAND OF THE SILVER BIRCH

1' smrd ①

Canadian

Boom di - di boom boom, Boom di - di boom boom Ah!

91. WALTER JUMPED A FOX

1' smrd ①

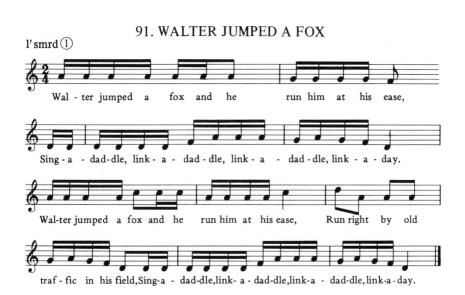

Wal - ter jumped a fox and he run him at his ease,

Sing - a - dad-dle, link - a - dad - dle, link - a - dad - dle, link - a - day.

Wal-ter jumped a fox and he run him at his ease, Run right by old

traf - fic in his field, Sing-a - dad-dle, link- a - dad-dle, link-a - dad-dle, link-a-day.

2. The hounds being poor and the fox being fine,
Sing-a-dad-dle, link-a-dad-dle, link-a-dad-dle, link a day,
That's the reason why he left them far behind,
Sing-a-dad-dle, link-a-dad-dle, link-a-dad-dle, link a day.

92. WAYFARING STRANGER

l′smrd①s₁   Spiritual

I'm just a poor way-far-in' stran-ger, A travel-in' through this world of woe.

And there's no sick-ness, toil, or dan-ger, In that far land to which I go. –

I'm go-in' there to see my Fa-ther, I'm go-in' there no more to roam.

I'm just a - go - in' o-ver Jor-dan, I'm just a - go - in' o-ver home.

93. OLD BETTY LARKIN

dlsm ⓡ

Hop a-round,   Skip a-round,   Old   Bet-ty Lar-kin,

Hop a-round, Skip a-round, Old Bet-ty Lar-kin,   Hop a-round, Skip a-round,

Old   Bet-ty Lar-kin,   Al - so my dear dar - ling.

94. YONDER SHE COMES

s' mrdl⑤　　　　　　　　　　　　Missouri

Yon - der she comes and it's how - dy, how -dy do, Oh,

Where have you been since the last that I met you?

2. Rise you up my lady, present to me your hand,
   I know you are a pretty girl, the prettiest in the land.

From *American Folk Songs for Children*. Reprinted by permission of Curtis Brown, Ltd. Copyright, 1948, by Ruth Crawford Seeger.

95. THE SQUIRREL

mrdl⑤　　　　　　　　　　　　Appalachian

The squir - rel is a pret - ty lit - tle thing; it

car - ries a bush - y tail, It eats up all the

far - mers grain and sits up - on the rail,

From *English Folk Songs from the Southern Appalachians* (Cecil Sharp) by permission of Oxford University Press.

96. I GAVE MY LOVE A CHERRY

mrdl (s)   Appalachian

I gave my love a cher - ry that has no stone,
I gave my love a chick - en that has no bone,
I gave my love a ring____ that has no end,
I gave my love a ba - by that's no cry - in'.

2. How can there be a cherry that has no stone ! . . . (etc.)

3. A cherry when it's bloomin' it has no stone,
   A chicken when it's peepin' it has no bone,
   A ring when it's a - rollin' it has no end,
   A baby when it's sleepin' is no cryin'.

97. JOHNSON BOYS

s' mrdl (s)

The John - son boys they went a court - in',
John - son boys, they did - n't stay, The rea - son why
they did - n't stay, they had no mon - ey for to pay their way.

98. HANDSOME MOLLY

s' mrd1 Ⓢ

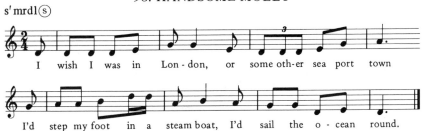

I wish I was in Lon - don, or some oth-er sea port town

I'd step my foot in a steam boat, I'd sail the o - cean round.

2. Don't you remember, Molly, when you gave me your right hand?
   You said that if you married, then I would be the man.

3. Now you've broken your promise, go marry whom you please,
   While my poor heart is aching, you're laughing, at your ease.

99. GO TELL AUNT RHODY

sfmr Ⓓ

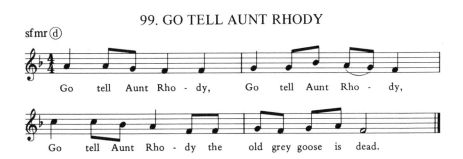

Go tell Aunt Rho - dy, Go tell Aunt Rho - dy,

Go tell Aunt Rho - dy the old grey goose is dead.

100. WHISTLE, DAUGHTER, WHISTLE

sfmr Ⓓ   **Southern Folk Song**

Whis-tle, daugh-ter, whis - tle, and you shall have a cow.
I can't whis - tle, Moth-er, be - cause I don't know how.
Whis-tle, daugh-ter, whis - tle, and you shall have a man.
Whis-tle daugh-ter, whis - tle, I just found out I can.

101. ORANGES, LEMONS

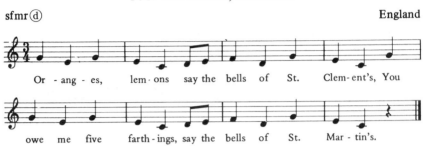

sfmr ⓓ   England

Or - ang - es,   lem · ons   say the bells   of   St.   Clem- ent's, You

owe   me   five   farth - ings, say the bells   of   St.   Mar - tin's.

From *Sally Go Round the Sun* by Edith Fowke. Copyright © 1969 by Mc-Clelland & Stewart, Ltd. Reprinted by permission of Doubleday & Company, Inc. and the Canadian publishers, McClelland and Stewart Limited, Toronto.

102. TIDY-O

lsfmr ⓓ

Skip   one   win - dow,   Ti - dy - o,

Skip   two   win - dows,   Ti - dy - o,

Skip   three   win - dows,   Ti - dy - o,

Jin - gle   at   the   win - dow,   Ti - dy - o.

103. IT RAINED A MIST

lsfmr ⓓ   Virginia

It   rained   a mist,   it   rained   a mist,   It   rained all   o - ver the

town, town, town,   It   rained___ all   o - ver   the   town.___

From *American Folk Songs for Children*. Reprinted by permission of Curtis Brown, Ltd. Copyright, 1948, by Ruth Crawford Seeger.

104. I SAW THREE SHIPS

lsfmr ⓓ   England

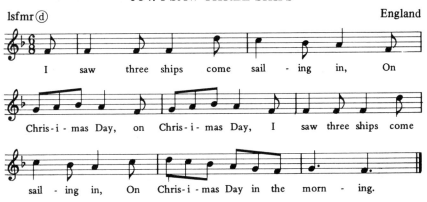

I saw three ships come sail - ing in, On
Chris - i - mas Day, on Chris - i - mas Day, I saw three ships come
sail - ing in, On Chris - i - mas Day in the morn - ing.

105. THE OLD CHISHOLM TRAIL

lsfmr ⓓ   Cowboy Song

Come a - long boys and lis - ten to my tale,
I'll tell you all my troub-les on the old Chis-holm Trail,
Com - a ti - yi yip - py, yip - py yay, yip - py yay,
Com - a ti - yi yip - py, yip - py yay.

106. JOSEPH DEAREST, JOSEPH MILD

lsfmr ⓓ

German

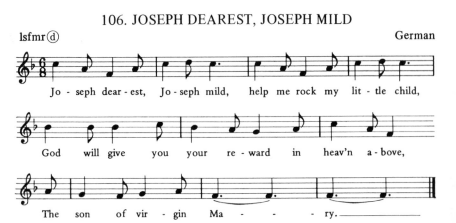

Jo - seph dear - est, Jo - seph mild, help me rock my lit - tle child,

God will give you your re - ward in heav'n a - bove,

The son of vir - gin Ma - - - ry.

107. NEW RIVER TRAIN

lsfmr ⓓ

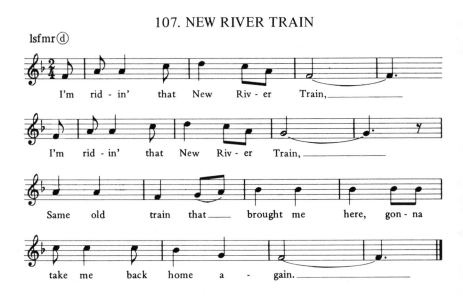

I'm rid - in' that New Riv - er Train,

I'm rid - in' that New Riv - er Train,

Same old train that__ brought me here, gon - na

take me back home a - gain.

108. FIDDLE-DE-DE

lsfmr ⓓ

English Folk Song

Fid - dle - de - de, Fid - dle - de - de, the fly has mar-ried the

bum - ble - bee. Says the fly says he will you mar - ry me, and

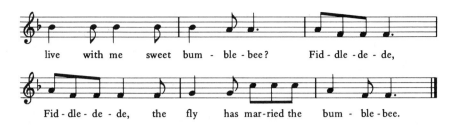

live with me sweet bum - ble - bee? Fid - dle - de - de,

Fid - dle - de - de, the fly has mar-ried the bum - ble - bee.

109. FIRE DOWN BELOW

lsfmr ⓓ

There's fire in the low - er deck, Fire down be - low,

Fire in the main well, The cap - tain did-n't know.

Fire! Fire! Fire down be - low.

It's fetch a pail of wa - ter, girls! There's fire down be - low.

From *American Folk Songs for Children*. Reprinted by permission of Curtis Brown, Ltd. Copyright, 1948, by Ruth Crawford Seeger.

110. LAVENDER'S BLUE

lsfmr ⓓ   England

La - ven - der's blue, dil - ly, dil - ly, La - ven - der's green,

When you are king, dil - ly, dil - ly, I shall be Queen.

2. Call up your men, dilly, dilly, set them to work,
   Some to the plough, dilly, dilly, some to the cart.

3. Some to make hay, dilly, dilly, some to cut corn,
   While you and I, dilly, dilly, keep ourselves warm!

111. O, HOW LOVELY

lsfmr ⓓ   Canon-England

1. O, how love - ly is the eve - ning, is the eve - ning,

2. When the bells are sweet - ly ring - ing, sweet - ly ring - ing,

3. Ding, dong, ding, dong, ding, dong.

112. SAILOR'S RETURN

lsfmr ⓓ

A la - dy walked in yon - der gar - den, A gen - tle - man

chan - ced to pass by. He stepped up to her for to

view her; Says he, "Fair maid, do you fan - cy I?"

From *The Penguin Book of Canadian Folk Songs* by Edith Fowke. Penguin Books Canada Ltd., Markham, Ontario, 1973. Used by permission.

113. STARS SHININ'

d' sfmr ⓓ   Texas

By'n bye, By'n bye. Stars shin-ing

Num - ber, num - ber one, num - ber two, Num - ber three,

Good lawd, by'n bye, by'n bye, Good lawd, By'n bye.

From *American Folk Songs for Children*. Reprinted by permission of Curtis Brown, Ltd. Copyright, 1948, by Ruth Crawford Seeger.

114. OH, DEAR, WHAT CAN THE MATTER BE?

d' sfmr ⓓ

Oh, dear, what can the mat - ter be,
Dear, dear, what can the mat - ter be? Oh, dear,
what can the mat - ter be, John - ny's so late at the fair!

115. VIVE LA CANADIENNE!

d' lsfmr ⓓ

Quebec

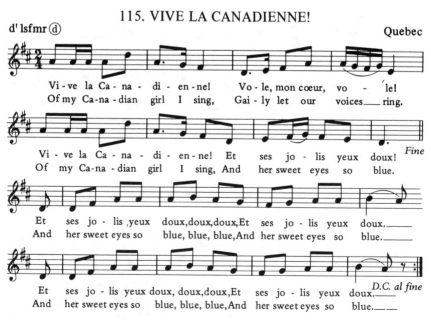

Vi - ve la Ca - na - di - en - ne! Vo - le, mon cœur, vo - le!
Of my Ca - na - dian girl I sing, Gai - ly let our voices ring.

Vi - ve la Ca - na - di - en - ne! Et ses jo - lis yeux doux! *Fine*
Of my Ca - na - dian girl I sing, And her sweet eyes so blue.

Et ses jo - lis ,yeux doux,doux,doux,Et ses jo - lis yeux doux._____
And her sweet eyes so blue, blue, blue,And her sweet eyes so blue._____

Et ses jo - lis yeux doux, doux,doux,Et ses jo - lis yeux doux._____ *D.C. al fine*
And her sweet eyes so blue, blue, blue,And her sweet eyes so blue._____

From *The Penguin Book of Canadian Folk Songs* by Edith Fowke. Penguin Books Canada Ltd., Markham, Ontario, 1973. Used by permission.

116. CHRISTMAS GREETINGS

sfmr ⓓ s,   Traditional Round

God bless all   good friends here,   A mer-ry, mer-ry
Christ-mas and a   Hap-py New   Year!

117. AH! SI MON MOINE VOULAIT DANSER!

sfmr ⓓ s,   Quebec

Ah! Si mon moi-ne vou-lait dan-ser! Ah! Si mon moi-ne vou-lait dan-ser!

Un ca-pu-chon je lui don-ne-rais, Un ca-pu-chon je lui don-ne-rais.

Dan-se, mon moin' dan - se! Tu n'en-tends pas la dan - se,

Tu n'en-tends pas mon mou-lin, lon la, Tu n'en-tends pas mon moulin mar-cher.

118. THE ALBERTA HOMESTEADER

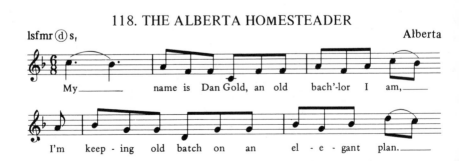

lsfmr ⓓ s,   Alberta

My_____ name is Dan Gold, an old bach'-lor I am,_____
I'm keep-ing old batch on an el - e - gant plan._____

You'll find me out here on Al - ber - ta's bush plain. ___

A - star - vin' to death on a gov - ern - ment claim.

119. UN CANADIEN ERRANT

lsfmr Ⓓ s₁

Quebec

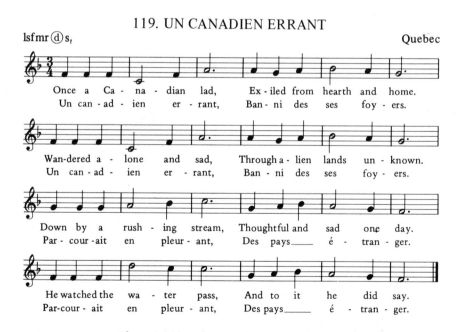

Once a Ca - na - dian lad, Ex - iled from hearth and home.
Un can - ad - ien er - rant, Ban - ni des ses foy - ers.

Wan-dered a - lone and sad, Through a - lien lands un - known.
Un can - ad - ien er - rant, Ban - ni des ses foy - ers.

Down by a rush - ing stream, Thoughtful and sad one day.
Par - cour - ait en pleur - ant, Des pays ___ é - tran - ger.

He watched the wa - ter pass, And to it he did say.
Par-cour - ait en pleur - ant, Des pays ___ é - tran - ger.

2. If you should reach my land, my most unhappy land,
Please speak to all my friends so they will understand.
Tell them how much I wish that I could be once more
In my belovéd land that I will see no more.

From *The Penguin Book of Canadian Folk Songs* by Edith Fowke. Penguin Books Canada
Ltd., Markham, Ontario, 1973. Used by permission.

120. THE LUMBERMAN'S ALPHABET

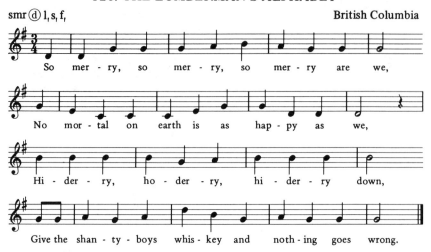

smr ⓓ l, s, f,   British Columbia

So mer - ry, so mer - ry, so mer - ry are we,

No mor - tal on earth is as hap - py as we,

Hi - der - ry, ho - der - ry, hi - der - ry down,

Give the shan - ty - boys whis - key and noth - ing goes wrong.

1. A is for Axes which all of you know,
   And B is for Boys that can use them also;
   C is for Chopping we do first begin,
   And D is for Danger we oft-times are in.

121. MY WILLIE IS BRAVE

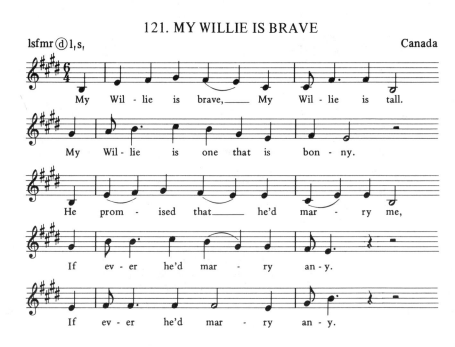

lsfmr ⓓ l, s,   Canada

My Wil - lie is brave,___ My Wil - lie is tall.

My Wil - lie is one that is bon - ny.

He prom - ised that___ he'd mar - ry me,

If ev - er he'd mar - ry an - y.

If ev - er he'd mar - ry an - y.

He prom - ised that___ he'd mar - ry me,

If ev - er he'd mar - ry an - y.

122. HEY, BETTY MARTIN

mr (d) t, l, s,

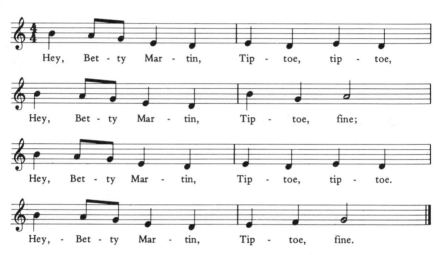

Hey, Bet - ty Mar - tin, Tip - toe, tip - toe,

Hey, Bet - ty Mar - tin, Tip - toe, fine;

Hey, Bet - ty Mar - tin, Tip - toe, tip - toe.

Hey, - Bet - ty Mar - tin, Tip - toe, fine.

123. IN THE BLEAK MIDWINTER

Words: Christina Rossetti (1830 - 1894)
Music: Gustav Holst (1874 - 1934)

lsfmr (d) t,

In the bleak mid - win - ter, fros - ty wind made moan,

Earth stood hard as i - ron, wa - ter like a stone;

Snow had fal - len, snow on snow, snow___ on___ snow,

In the bleak mid - win - ter, long___ a - go.

124. BLOW, YE WINDS IN THE MORNING

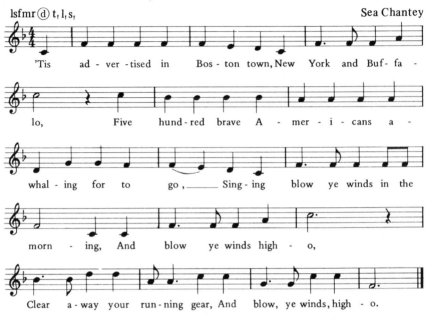

Sea Chantey

'Tis ad-ver-tised in Bos-ton town, New York and Buf-fa-
lo, Five hund-red brave A-mer-i-cans a-
whal-ing for to go, ___ Sing-ing blow ye winds in the
morn-ing, And blow ye winds high-o,
Clear a-way your run-ning gear, And blow, ye winds, high-o.

2. They send you to New Bedford, that famous whaling port,
   They give you to some land sharks to board and fit you out. . .

3. They tell you of the clipper ships a-goin' in and out,
   And say you'll take 500 sperm before you're six months out. . .

4. It's now we're out to sea, my boy, the winds begin to blow,
   One half the watch is sick on deck, the other half below. . .

5. The skipper's on the quarter deck, a-squinting at the sails,
   When up aloft a look-out sights a school of whales. . .

6. Now clear away the boats, my boys, and after him we'll travel,
   But if you get too near his fluke he'll kick you to the devil. . .

7. When we get home our ship made fast, and we get through our sailing,
   A winding glass we'll pass around and damn this blubber whaling!

125. SKIP TO MY LOU

Fly's in the but-ter-milk, Shoo fly shoo, Fly's in the but-ter-milk,
Shoo fly shoo, Fly's in the but-ter-milk, Shoo fly shoo,
Skip to my Lou my dar-ling, Lou, Lou,

Skip to my Lou, Lou, Lou, Skip to my Lou,

Lou, Lou, Skip to my Lou, Skip to my Lou my dar - ling.

126. THE FOX WENT OUT

lsfmr(d)t,

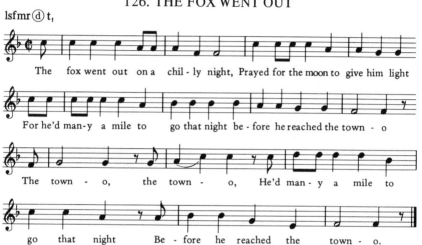

The fox went out on a chil - ly night, Prayed for the moon to give him light

For he'd man - y a mile to go that night be - fore he reached the town - o

The town - o, the town - o, He'd man - y a mile to

go that night Be - fore he reached the town - o.

2. He ran till he came to the farmer's pen
   Where the ducks and the geese were put there in;
   "A couple of you will grease my chin
   Before I leave this town-o. . ."

3. He grabbed the gray goose by the neck,
   Flung a duck across his back,
   He didn't mind their "Quack, Quack, Quack"
   Or the legs all dangling down-o. . .

4. Then old Mother Clipper Clopper jumped out of bed,
   Out of the window she popped her head
   Crying "John, John, the gray goose is gone
   And the fox is on the town-o. . ."

5. Then John he ran to the top of the hill,
   Blew his horn both loud and shrill,
   The fox he said, "I'd better flee with my kill
   Or they'll soon be on my trail-o. . ."

6. He ran till he came to his cozy den,
   There were the little ones, eight, nine, ten.
   They said, "Daddy, better go back again
   For it must be a mighty fine town-o. . ."

7. The fox and his wife without any strife,
   Cut up the goose with a fork and knife,
   They never had such a supper in their life
   And the little ones chewed on the bones-o. . .

127. THE STREETS OF LAREDO

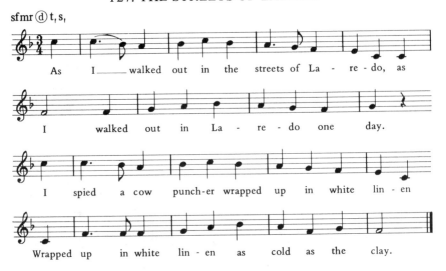

sfmr ⓓ t₁ s₁

As I ____ walked out in the streets of La - re - do, as
I walked out in La - re - do one day.
I spied a cow punch-er wrapped up in white lin - en
Wrapped up in white lin - en as cold as the clay.

2. "I see by your outfit that you are a cowboy,"
   These words he did say as I boldly stepped by;
   "Come sit down beside me and hear my sad story,
   I was shot in the breast and I know I must die.

3. "It was once in the saddle I used to go dashing,
   It was once in the saddle I used to go gay;
   First to the dram house and then to the card house,
   Got shot in the breast and I'm dying today.

4. "Get six jolly cowboys to carry my coffin,
   Get six pretty maidens to carry my pall,
   Put bunches of roses all over my coffin,
   Roses to deaden the clods as they fall.

5. "Oh, beat the drum slowly, and play the fife lowly,
   Play the dead march as you carry me along;
   Take me to the green valley, there lay the sod o'er me,
   For I'm a young cowboy and I know I've done wrong."

128. I'S THE B'Y

sfmr ⓓ t, s,   Newfoundland

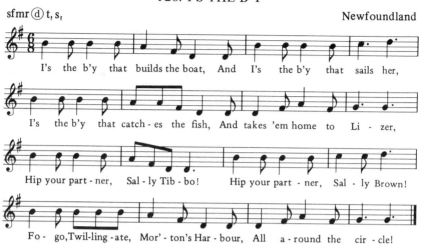

I's the b'y that builds the boat, And I's the b'y that sails her,

I's the b'y that catch - es the fish, And takes 'em home to Li - zer,

Hip your part - ner, Sal - ly Tib - bo! Hip your part - ner, Sal - ly Brown!

Fo - go, Twil-ling - ate, Mor' - ton's Har - bour, All a - round the cir - cle!

2. Sods and rinds to cover yer flake,
   Cake and tea for supper,
   Codfish in the spring o' the year
   Fried in maggoty butter.

3. I don't want your maggoty fish,
   That's no good for winter;
   I could buy as good as that
   Down in Bonavister.

129. LOVE SOMEBODY

sfmr ⓓ t, s,

Love some-bod - y, yes I do Love some - bod - y, yes I do

Love some - bod - y, yes I do Love some-bod-y, but I won't say who.

130. SIMPLE GIFTS

sfmr (d) t, s,   Shaker Hymn

'Tis the gift to be sim - ple, 'tis the gift to be free

Tis the gift to come down where we ought to be

and when we find our - selves in the place just right,

'Twill be in the val - ley of love and de - light.

When true sim - plic - i - ty is gained,

to bow and to bend we shan't be a - shamed, To turn, turn,

will be our de - light, till by turn - ing, turn - ing we come 'round right.

131. THE KELLIGREWS SOIREE

fmr (d) t, s,   Newfoundland

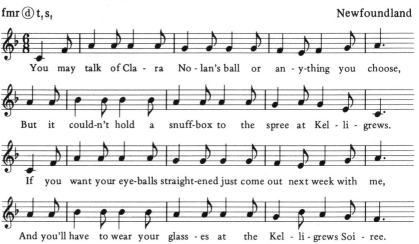

You may talk of Cla - ra No - lan's ball or an - y-thing you choose,

But it could-n't hold a snuff-box to the spree at Kel - li - grews.

If you want your eye-balls straight-ened just come out next week with me,

And you'll have to wear your glass - es at the Kel - li - grews Soi - ree.

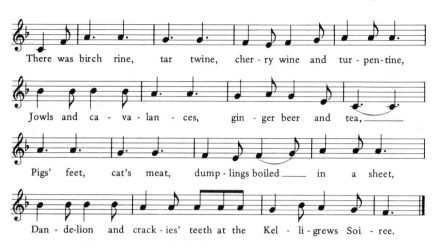

There was birch rine, tar twine, cher - ry wine and tur - pen-tine,

Jowls and ca - va - lan - ces, gin - ger beer and tea,____

Pigs' feet, cat's meat, dump - lings boiled____ in a sheet,

Dan - de-lion and crack - ies' teeth at the Kel - li - grews Soi - ree.

From *Old Time Songs and Poetry of Newfoundland* by Gerald S. Doyle. Reprinted by permission of Gerald S. Doyle Ltd.

132. MARCHING DOWN THE LEVEE

lsmr ⓓ t₁,l₁,s₁   Southern

We're march - ing down the lev - ee, We're march - ing down the lev - ee,

We're march - ing down the lev - ee, To old Shi - loh.

Swing 'em on the cor - ner, too - dle - la, Too - dle - la, too - dle - la,

Swing 'em on the cor - ner, too - dle - la, Too - dle - la - da - ay.

133. MUSIC ALONE SHALL LIVE

All things shall per - ish un - der the sky,

Mu - sic a - lone shall live, Mu - sic a - lone shall live,

Mu - sic a - lone shall live, Nev - er to die.

134. RED RIVER VALLEY

From this val - ley they say you are go - ing. I shall

miss your bright eyes and sweet smile, For a - las you have tak - en the

sun - shine, That has bright - ened my path - way a - while.

Come and sit by my side if you love me, Do not

hast - en to bid me a - dieu, But re - mem - ber the Red Riv - er

Val - ley, And the cow - boy who loved you so true.

135. THE RYANS AND THE PITTMANS

sfmr ⓓ t, l, s,

Newfoundland

We'll rant and we'll roar____ like true New - found - land - ers,

We'll rant and we'll roar____ on deck and be - low,

Un - til we see bot - tom in - side the two sunk - ers,

When__ straight thru the chan - nel to Tos - low we'll go!

2. My name it is Robert, they call me Bob Pittman,
   I sail in the "Ino" with Skipper Tim Brown,
   I'm bound to have Dolly, or Biddy, or Molly
   As soon as I'm able to plank the cash down.

3. If the voyage is good, then this fall I will do it;
   I wants two pound ten for a ring and the priest,
   A couple o'dollars for clane shirt and collars,
   And a handful o'coppers to make up a feast.

136. DOWN IN THE VALLEY

sfmr ⓓ t, s,

Down in the val - ley, the val - ley so low,____

Hang your head o - ver, hear the wind blow.____

Hear the wind blow, dear, hear the wind blow,____

Hang your head o - ver, hear the wind blow.____

137. BILLY BARLOW

tlsfmr ⓓ t₁1₁   Texas

"Let's   go   hunt - ing," says   Risk - y   Rob,

"Let's   go   hunt - ing," says   Ro - bin   to   Bob,

"Let's   go   hunt - ing," says   Da - n'l   to   Joe,

"Let's___   go   hunt - ing," says   Bil - ly   Bar - low.

138. HAUL ON THE BOWLINE

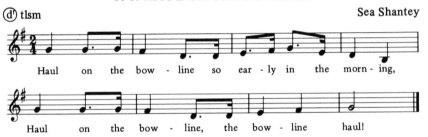

ⓓ¹ tlsm   Sea Shantey

Haul   on   the   bow - line   so   ear - ly   in   the   morn - ing,

Haul   on   the   bow - line,   the   bow - line   haul!

139. BONAVIST' HARBOUR

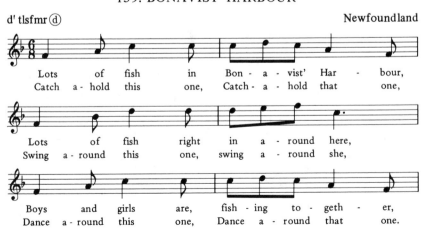

d¹ tlsfmr ⓓ   Newfoundland

Lots   of   fish   in   Bon - a - vist' Har - bour,
Catch a - hold   this   one,   Catch - a - hold   that   one,

Lots   of   fish   right   in   a - round   here,
Swing a - round   this   one,   swing   a - round   she,

Boys   and   girls   are,   fish - ing   to - geth - er,
Dance a - round   this   one,   Dance a - round   that   one.

For - ty five from Car - bon - near!
Did - dle - dum this one, Did - dle - dum - dee!

2. Oh, Sally goes to church every Sunday
Not for to sing or for to hear,
But to see the feller from Fortune
That's been down here fishin' the year.

140. SWEET BETSY FROM PIKE

d' tlsfmr ⓓ

O, have you heard tell of sweet Bet - sy from Pike?

She crossed the wide prai - rie with her hus - band, Ike;

With two head of ox - en and a brown spot - ted cow,

An __ old Shang - hai roos - ter and a good i - ron plow.

Sing - ing to - ra - lay to - ra - lay to - ra - lay - ay.

141. SHENANDOAH

d' tlsfmr ⓓ s,   Virginia

Oh, Shen-an-doah, I long to hear you, A - way you roll-ing

riv - er, Oh, Shen-an-doah, I long to hear you.

A - way, I'm bound to go, 'Cross the wide Mis - sour - i.

142. MARY ANN

From *Come Singing* by Marius Barbeau, Arthur Lismer, and Arthur Bourinot. Published by National Museums of Canada, Ottawa, 1947. Used with permission.

143. PAUPER SUM EGO

144. RISE UP, O FLAME

145. THE KEYS OF CANTERBURY

mrdt ①

O   Ma-dam I   will   give   to you   the   keys   of Can - ter - bu-ry,
And   all   the bells   of   Lon - don   will   ring   to make   us   mer-ry,

If   you will be   my   joy___   my   sweet and on - ly   dear___

And   walk   a - long   with   me   an - y - where.___

2. I shall not, Sir, accept of you the keys of Canterbury,
   Nor all the bells of London shall ring to make us merry.
   I will not be your joy, your sweet and only dear,
   Nor walk along with you anywhere.

146. HUSH MY BABE

smrdt ① s, m,   Appalachian

Hush   my   babe,   lie   still   and   slum - ber

Ho - ly   an - gels   guard thy   bed.   Heav'n-ly   bless - ings

with - out __ num - ber   gent - ly   fall - ing   on   thy   head.

147. ROSE RED

mrdt ① s, m,   English

[1]   [2]

Rose, Rose,   Rose   Red,   Shall I   ev - er   see   thee __ wed?

[3]   [4]

I   shall mar - ry   at   my __ will, sir!   At   my ___   will!

148. PAT WORKS ON THE RAILWAY

rdt ① s₁, f₁, m₁

In eight - een hund-red and for - ty one I put me cor - du - roy
britch - es on, I put me cor - du - roy britch - es on to
work up - on the rail - way. Fill - a - mi - oo - re -
oo - re - ay, Fill - a - mi - oo - re - oo - re - ay,
Fill - a - mi - oo - re - oo - re - ay, To work up - on the rail - way.

2. In eighteen hundred and forty-two I left the Old World for the new,
   I left the Old World for the new to work upon the railway.

3. In eighteen hundred and forty-three, 'twas then I met sweet Biddy McGee,
   An elegant wife she's been to me while working on the railway.

149. JOHNNY HAS GONE FOR A SOLDIER

dt ① s₁, m₁, r₁, d₁   Revolutionary War Song

Here I sit on But - ter - milk Hill,
who could blame me cry my fill? And ev - 'ry tear would

turn a mill, John-ny has gone for a sol - dier.

2. He, Oh my, I loved him so, Broke my heart to see him go;
  And only time can heal my woe. Johnny has gone for a soldier.

3. I'll sell my flax, I'll sell my wheel and buy my love a sword of steel;
  That it in battle he may wield. Johnny has gone for a soldier.

150. O COME, EMMANUEL

From an 18th Century
French Mass Book

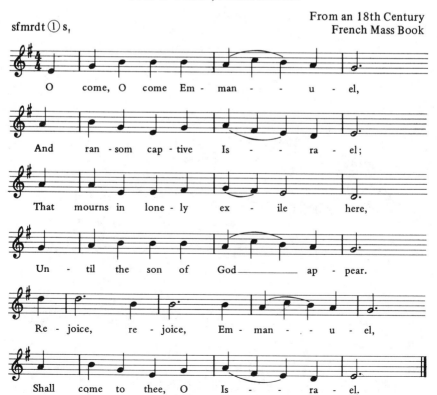

151. BLUE MOUNTAIN LAKE

l'sfmrdt ①   New York

Come all you good fel - lows, where - e - ver you be,

Come set down a while____ and lis - ten to me,

The truth I will tell you with - out a mis - take,

A-bout the rack - ets we had a - round Blue Moun - tain Lake,

Der - ry down, down, down, der - ry down.

152. BOUND FOR THE PROMISED LAND

l' mrdt ① s,   Spiritual

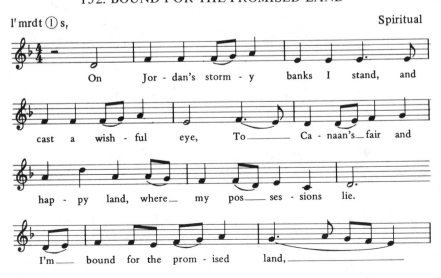

On Jor - dan's storm - y banks I stand, and

cast a wish - ful eye, To____ Ca - naan's__fair and

hap - py land, where__ my pos__ ses - sions lie.

I'm__ bound for the prom - ised land,____

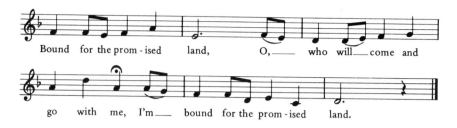

Bound for the prom-ised land, O,—— who will—come and
go with me, I'm—— bound for the prom-ised land.

153. FAREWELL TO NOVA SCOTIA

mrdt ① s₁ f₁ m₁

The sun was set - ting—— in the—— west
The— birds were sing - ing on ev - 'ry—— tree,
All— na - ture seemed in—— clined for—— rest,
But— still— there— was— no— rest for me.

Chorus:

Fare - well to No - va Sco - tia, the sea bound— coast,
Let your moun - tains dark and drea - ry—— be.
For when I am far a - way on the brin - y o - cean tossed,
Will you ev - er heave a sigh—— and a wish for me?

2. I grieve to leave my native land,
   I grieve to leave my comrades all,
   And my agéd parents whom I always held so dear,
   And the bonny, bonny lass that I do adore.

154. WHEN JESUS WEPT

Canon

William Billings (1746–1800)

l'sfmrdt ① s₁m₁

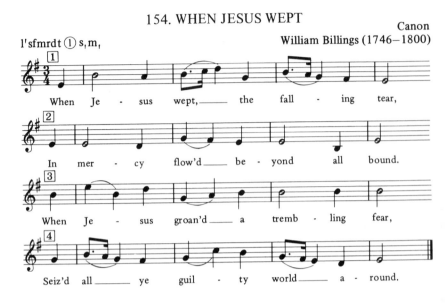

When Je - sus wept,___ the fall - ing tear,

In mer - cy flow'd___ be - yond all bound.

When Je - sus groan'd___ a tremb - ling fear,

Seiz'd all___ ye guil - ty world___ a - round.

155. DEWY DELLS OF YARROW

smrdt ① s₁m₁

There lived a la - dy in the north;

You could scarce - ly find her mar - row.

She was court - ed by nine nob - le - men

On the dew - y dells of Yar - row

From *The Penguin Book of Canadian Folk Songs* by Edith Fowke. Penguin Books Canada
Ltd., Markham, Ontario, 1973. Used by permission.

156. AH POOR BIRD

l'*si*mrdt ①

English Canon

Ah poor bird, take your flight,

Far a - bove the sor - rows of this sad night.

2. Ah poor bird, as you fly,
   Can you see the dawn of tomorrow's sky?

157. MAM'ZELLE ZIZI

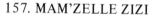

smrdt ① *si,*

Creole

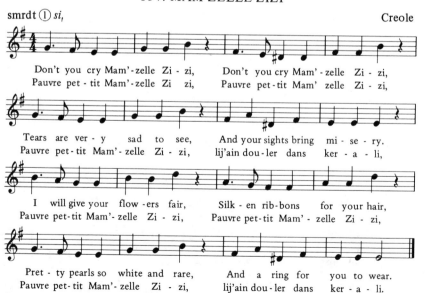

Don't you cry Mam'-zelle Zi - zi,
Pauvre pet - tit Mam'-zelle Zi zi,

Don't you cry Mam' - zelle Zi - zi,
Pauvre pet - tit Mam' zelle Zi - zi,

Tears are ver - y sad to see,
Pauvre pet - tit Mam' - zelle Zi - zi,

And your sights bring mi - se - ry.
lij'ain dou - ler dans ker - a - li,

I will give your flow - ers fair,
Pauvre pet - tit Mam' - zelle Zi - zi,

Silk - en rib - bons for your hair,
Pauvre pet - tit Mam' - zelle Zi - zi,

Pret - ty pearls so white and rare,
Pauvre pet - tit Mam' - zelle Zi - zi,

And a ring for you to wear.
lij'ain dou - ler dans ker - a - li.

The music and the French words, spelled exactly as shown here, were found in an old out-of-print Creole cookbook.

158. UNDER THIS STONE

sfmrdt① *si, f, m, r,*   Henry Purcell (1658–1695)

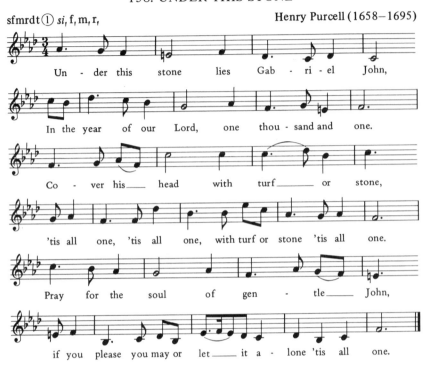

Un - der this stone lies Gab - ri - el John,

In the year of our Lord, one thou - sand and one.

Co - ver his___ head with turf___ or stone,

'tis all one, 'tis all one, with turf or stone 'tis all one.

Pray for the soul of gen - tle___ John,

if you please you may or let___ it a - lone 'tis all one.

159. OLD JOE CLARK

Mixolydian   Tennessee
ta lsfmr ⓓ

Round and round, Old Joe Clark, round and round I say,

Round and round, Old Joe Clark, I aint got long to stay.

Old Joe clark, he had a dog, Blind as he could be,

Chased a red - bug round a stump and a coon up a hol - low tree.

160. VIVA LA MUSICA

Mixolydian
s'fmrdtl Ⓢ f,

Canon
Michael Praetorius (1571–1621)

Vi - va, Vi - va la mu - si - ca, Vi - va, Vi - va la

mu - si - ca, Vi - va la mu - si - ca.

161. THE JAM ON GERRY'S ROCKS

Mixolydian
d' *ta*lsfmr ⓓ

American Logging Song

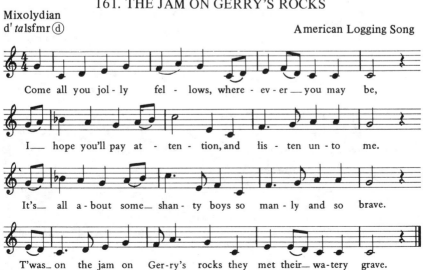

Come all you jol - ly fel - lows, where - ev - er __ you may be,

I __ hope you'll pay at - ten - tion, and lis - ten un - to me.

It's __ all a - bout some __ shan - ty boys so man - ly and so brave.

T'was __ on the jam on Ger-ry's rocks they met their __ wa-tery grave.

162. POOR SALLY SITS A-WEEPING

Mixolydian
r' d' *ta*lsfmr ⓓ

Poor__ Sal - ly__ sits a weep-ing__ down by__ the sea__ side,__

Poor__ Sal - ly__ sits a weep-ing__ down by__ the sea__ side,

What ails my pret-ty jew - el? What__ heart's pain so__ cru - el?

What ails my pret-ty jew - el __ that do cause her__ for to cry?

2. Oh I am uneasy and troubled in mind,
   Oh I am uneasy and troubled in mind.
   Here's no joy nor pleasure, here's sorrow none can measure,
   Here's no joy no pleasure, in this world I can find.

From *Eighty English Folk Songs from the Southern Applachians* by Cecil Sharp and Maud
Karpeles. Published by Faber and Faber Ltd., London, 1968. Used by permission.

163. MY LAST FAREWELL TO STIRLING

Mixolydian
d' tlsfmr ⓓ *ta,*   Australian Folk Song

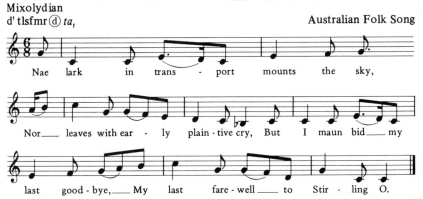

Nae lark in trans - port mounts the sky,

Nor__ leaves with ear - ly plain - tive cry, But I maun bid__ my

last good - bye,__ My last fare - well __ to Stir - ling O.

From *The Penguin Book of Australian Folk Songs* by John Manifold, The Dominion Press,
North Blackburn, Victoria, Australia, 19

2. Nae mair I'll wander through the glen
   To rob the roost of the pheasant hen,
   Nor chase the rabbits to their den
   When I am far frae Stirling O.

3. Now fare ye weel, my dearest dear,
   For you I'll shed a bitter tear,
   But may you find some other dear
   When I am far frae Stirling O.

4. Now fare ye weel, for I am bound
   For twenty years to Van Diemen's Land,*
   But speak of me and of what I've done
   When I am far frae Stirling O.

*Van Diemen's Land is Tasmania, off the southern coast of Australia.

164. THE BANKS OF THE NILE

Mixolydian
d' ta lsf mr (d) t,   Canadian

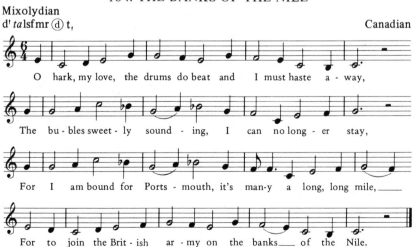

O hark, my love, the drums do beat and I must haste a - way,
The bu - bles sweet - ly sound - ing, I can no long - er stay,
For I am bound for Ports - mouth, it's man - y a long, long mile,___
For to join the Brit - ish ar - my on the banks___ of the Nile.

From *The Penguin Book of Canadian Folk Songs,* by Edith Fowke. Penguin Books Canada, Ltd., Markham, Ontario. Used by permission.

165. THE SHIP'S CARPENTEER

Mixolydian
d' *ta* lsfmr (d) *ta*₁

'Twas in Lis - burgh of late a__fair dam - sel did dwell;

Her wit and her beau - ty__ no one could e'er tell.

She__was loved by a fair one__who called her his dear,

And he by his trade was__ a ship's car - pen - teer.

166. SCARBOROUGH FAIR

Dorian
ls*f*imrdt (l) s₁

English

Are you go - ing to Scar - bor - ough Fair?

Par - sley, sage, rose - mar - y and thyme,

Re - mem - ber me to one who is there,___

She was once a true love of mine.

167. A KANGAROO SAT ON AN OAK

Dorian
l'sfimrdt①s₁

Canadian

A Kan-ga - roo sat on an oak, to my in-kum, Kid-dy-kum - ki - mo.

Watching a tail - or mend his coat, to my in-kum, Kid-dy-kum - ki - mo.

Ki - mi - ne - ro, Kid-dy-kum kee ro, Ki - mi - ne - ro ki - mo,

Ba - ba Ba - ba Bil - ly Bil - ly in - kum, in - kum,Kid-dy-kum - ki - mo.

From *Traditional Folk Songs from Nova Scotia,* by Helen Creighton and Doreen Senior. McGraw-Hill Ryerson, Toronto, Canada. (Out of print)

168. AS I ROVED OUT

Dorian
sfimrdt①

Newfoundland

As I roved out one fine sum - mer's eve - ning,

To view the flowers and to take the ___ air,

'Twas there I spied a ten - der___ moth - er,

Talk - in' to her___ daught - er___ fair.

2. A sailor boy thinks all for to wander,
And he will prove your overthrow.
O daughter, you're better to wed with a farmer,
For to sea he'll never go.

169. HAUL AWAY, JOE

Dorian
l'sfimr ①

American
Sea Chantey

When I was just a ti-ny lad my dear old moth-er told___ me,

Way - haul a - way we'll haul a - way, Joe,

That if I nev-er kissed a girl my lips would go all mould-y.

Way, haul a - way, we'll haul a - way, Joe.

170. LOST JIMMY WHELAN

Dorian
t'l'sfimrdt ① s,

Lone - ly I strayed by the banks___ of a riv - er

Watch - ing the sun - beams as eve - ning drew nigh.

As on - ward I ramb - led I spied a fair dam - sel,

She was weep - ing and wail - ing with man - y a sigh.

From *The Penguin Book of Canadian Folk Songs,* by Edith Fowke. Penguin Books Canada, Ltd., Markham, Ontario. Used by permission.

171. CANON

f' m' r' *di'*d' tlsfmr ⓓ   Ludwig van Beethoven (1770–1827)

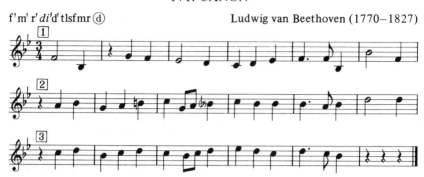

172. BY THE WATERS BABYLON

d' t' *ta'* l' *si*sfmrd ①   Anon. Canon

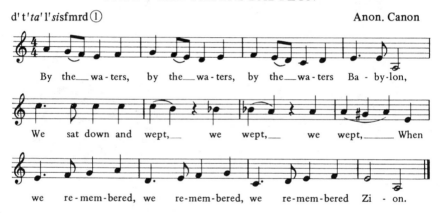

By the___wa-ters, by the___wa-ters, by the___wa-ters Ba - by-lon,

We sat down and wept,___ we wept,___ we wept,___ When

we re-mem-bered, we re-mem-bered, we re-mem-bered Zi - on.

THE LISTENING THEMES

173. CHORALE from *THE ST. MATTHEW PASSION*

J. S. Bach (1685–1750)

174. JESU, JOY OF MAN'S DESIRING
from Cantata No. 147

J. S. Bach (1685–1750)

Je - su, joy of man's de - sir - ing,
Drawn by Thee our souls as - pir - ing,

Ho - ly wis - dom love_____ most bright.
Soar to un - cre - at_____ ed height.

Word of God our flesh_____ that fash - ioned,

With the fire of life_____ im - pas - sioned.

Lead - ing still to truth un - known.

Soar - ing, sigh - ing round___ Thy throne.

Counter-Melody:

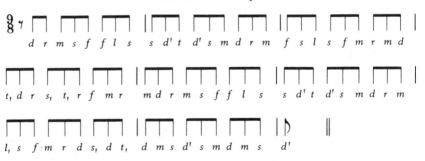

d r m s f f l s   s d' t d' s m d r m   f s l s f m r m d

t₁ d r s₁ t₁ r f m r   m d r m s f f l s   s d' t d' s m d r m

l₁ s f m r d s₁ d t₁   d m s d' s m d m s   d'

175. LITTLE FUGUE IN G-MINOR

J. S. Bach (1685–1750)

176. MINUET #2
from *The Royal Fireworks* music

G. F. Handel (1685–1759)

177. CELLO CONCERTO IN D MAJOR

F. J. Haydn (1732–1809)

178. ST. ANTHONY'S CHORALE

formerly attributed to F. J. Haydn (1732–1809)

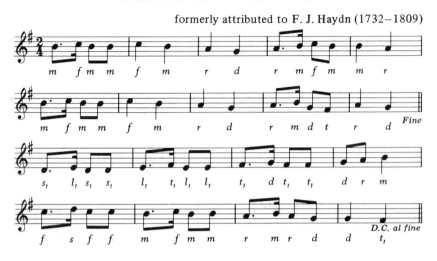

179. MINUET AND TRIO

from the Third Movement of Symphony #40 in G minor

W. A. Mozart (1756–1791)

180. THE *TROUT* QUINTET
Last Movement

F. Schubert (1797–1828)

181. SYMPHONY ♯6 (*The Pastoral*)
Fifth Movement

L. van Beethoven (1770–1827)

182. SYMPHONY #9
Chorale from the Fourth Movement

L. van Beethoven (1770–1827)

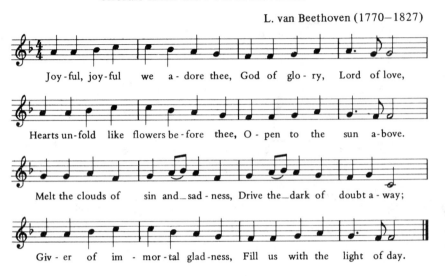

Joy - ful, joy - ful   we   a - dore thee, God of glo - ry,   Lord   of love,

Hearts un-fold   like   flowers be - fore   thee, O - pen   to   the   sun   a-bove.

Melt the clouds of   sin and_ sad - ness, Drive the_ dark of   doubt a - way;

Giv - er   of   im - mor -tal glad -ness, Fill   us   with the   light of day.

183. SYMPHONY #4 IN E MINOR
Fourth Movement

J. Brahms (1833–1897)

l   t   d   r   ri   m   m₁   l

184. SYMPHONY #1 IN C MINOR
Fourth Movement

J. Brahms (1833–1897)

s₁   d   t₁   d   l₁   s₁   d   r   m r m   d   r

s₁   d   t₁   d   l₁   s₁   d   r   m f m   d   r   d

185. SYMPHONY #4, Finale
(Uses a Russian folk melody)

P. I. Tchaikovsky (1840–1893)

186. THE GIRL WITH THE FLAXEN HAIR

C. Debussy (1862–1918)

187. THE FIREBIRD, Finale

I. Stravinsky (1882–1971)

Alphabetical Index of Songs

Index of Listening Themes Alphabetized by Composer

Appendix

I. Chromatic solfa Alterations:

SOLFA	♯ (AN "EE" SOUND)	♭ (AN "AH" SOUND)
ti	none	ta (as in "Tom")
la	li (as in "leek")	lo (as in "low")*
so	si (as in "see")	sa (as in "sah")
fa	fi (as in "feet")	none
mi	none	ma (as in "mama")
re	ri (as in "reed")	ra (as in "Ravel")
do	di (as in "deed")	none

*lo is necessary because the normal *solfa* syllable *la* already has the "ah" sound.

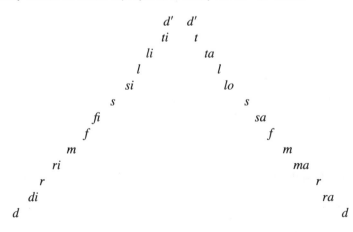

1. *Solfa* names are shown with *lower case* letters: e.g., *d r m f s*. Absolute note names are shown with *CAPITAL* letters: e.g., C D E F G.
2. Notes below the *tonic* are shown by a subscript prime on the syllable: e.g., *s f m r d t*, l, s, or *m r d t l s*, f, m,.

254

The octave above the *tonic* and notes above the octave are shown by a superscript prime on the syllable: e.g.,

m′ r′ d′ t l s f m r d or *d′ t′ l′ s f m r d t l.*

The *tonic* is the tonal center, the final pitch.

II. Absolute Note Names:

Note names altered by a ♯ are pronounced with an *eese* sound, as in "geese":

C♯—cease
D♯—dease
E♯—eas(t)
F♯—feas(t)
G♯—jeese
A♯—ace
B♯—beas(t)

Note names altered by a ♭ are pronounced with an *es* sound, as in "bes(t)":

C♭—cess
D♭—des(k)
E♭—es(t)
F♭—fes(t)
G♭—jes(t)
A♭—us
B♭—Bess

Note: A♯ and A♭ are exceptions.

III. Rhythm Syllables:

The syllables currently in use by the author are: